U2

AN IRISH PHENOMENON

U2

AN IRISH PHENOMENON

Višnja Cogan

U2

AN IRISH PHENOMENON

Published in 2006 by
The Collins Press
West Link Park
Doughcloyne
Wilton
Cork

The author has attempted to contact the copyright holders of the lyric extracts reproduced. At the time of going to press, some permissions were outstanding. If the copyright holders would contact the publishers, they will be acknowledged in any further edition.

British Library Cataloguing in Publication Data

Cogan , Višnja

U2 : an Irish phenomenon
1. U2 (Musical group) 2. Rock musicians - Ireland -
Biography
I. Title
782.4'2166'0922

ISBN-10: 1905172222
ISBN-13: 978-1905172221

Typesetting: The Collins Press

Font: Goudy, 11 point

Printed in Germany

I wish to dedicate this book to Paul Brennan who made the writing of it possible. He passed away suddenly on 10 November 2003. He was a well-known and respected academic who dedicated his professional life to the development of Irish Studies in France. I met him in about 1986 and he supervised my Master's degree research in 1988. When, a few years later, we talked about my possible PhD research in Irish Studies, he encouraged me. He suggested U2 as a topic. I doubt that many others would have agreed to it. He saw the importance of the band to Irish musical life and culture. I met him many times to discuss the progress of my work. He was unfailingly courteous, calm and humorous. He was ambitious for other people and encouraged me early on to try to have my work published.

I am sorry that he is not around to see this book come to fruition, as he could be seen as its instigator.

I will always remember him fondly.

Višnja Cogan 2006

CONTENTS

FOREWORD

Constant reinvention – maybe that's the key (or just one of the keys) to the success of the biggest band on the planet. At the end of 1989 U2 played four gigs at home in Dublin to finish off their Lovetown tour. As the biggest band of the decade, they'd been criticised for playing stadiums; now both media and fans complained because the venue was too small for everyone who wanted to see them. It was one of those lose-lose things.

At one of the gigs Bono alluded to a possible break-up or at least a long lay-off during which the band would have to 'go away and dream it all up again' for a new decade. If it had ended there and then, history would still have placed them at the top of the pile. They'd done it all and they'd done it their way.

When they got back together in Berlin (that's the Berlin of Bowie's *Low*, *Heroes* and *Lodger*) things were messy and, to say the least, difficult. But the result of their snowy sojourn, *Acthung Baby*, was one of the great albums of the '90's – and the subsequent Zoo TV tour, one of the biggest, boldest and best. It was a million miles from that long journey through the roots of the rattle and hum of the blues and gospel music that had first inspired them.

By mid-decade, as Britpop stole headlines in this part of the world, they were off on an Eno trip, getting all weird and experimental with *Passengers*. Popmart put the whole thing on a different planet and they returned to Earth with the multimillion-selling *All That You Can't Leave Behind*. So the '90's turned out to be even bigger than the '80's. Who'd a thunk it? More than a quarter of a century later, with yet another double-figure-million-selling album under their belts and with a Vertigo tour which has played to over three million people, U2 have torn up the rule book. They're still the biggest band around.

And just when you thought you knew it all, along comes a book like this to bring you on a wild, erratic and fascinating all-new journey into the very heart of what makes U2 so special.

Here's your chance to delve into U2's genome (!), unravel the secret of the band's remarkable longevity and examine their Irishness, social consciousness and heightened sense of community. And, now that you ask, yeah, there is fun along the way.

No matter how many detailed detours the story takes – from quotes from psychologists and cultural critics to fascinating minutiae (bet you thought the *All That You Can't Leave Behind* album sleeve was just that – an album sleeve with the band pictured in a French airport? Think again.) – the one constant which pops up so charmingly every-so-often is that Visnja is an unapologetic U2 uberfan. Right in the middle of some seriously deep shit she just comes right out and says stuff like, 'I must admit I love the way Bono uses words'. Same story with Visnja.

DAVE FANNING
January 2006

ACKNOWLEDGEMENTS

How could I thank all the people who have been part of this adventure, who have allowed this book to happen, who have shared with me this passion for U2, who have borne patiently my constant babbling about the band, pretending to be interested, or who simply supported me out of love and friendship?

First of all, a huge thank you to my parents Ernestina and Vinko, for their love, support and dedication. They know all about U2 at this stage! Thanks to my brother Damir for his advice on many things, and for his help on the charts and other little difficulties (his scientific mind and experience were so helpful! *Merci* Dada!). Thanks to my nephew Thomas. We'll make a U2 fan of him yet! Hopefully his brother Nathan will follow! Thanks to my husband Bernard for believing in this more than myself and for reading some of the chapters. I love you all.

Thanks to Dave Fanning who was the first person I met in connection with U2 years ago and who photocopied early articles about the band in the days when the Internet was but a distant dream. I still appreciate that gesture to this day.

Thanks to all the friends who have seen me struggle over the years with my PhD and who have always believed in me, even when I didn't believe in myself. This book is the culmination of those years.

Thanks to all the people I met while a PhD student or with whom I was in touch from the music business, including Keith Donald, Christy Dignam from Aslan, Seamus MacMathuna, Angela Dorgan, Eamon Shackleton, Greg MacAteer, Maura Eaton, and Susan Hunter of Principle Management.

I'm indebted to all the fans of U2 who took part in this book by lending me their thoughts, insights, stories, their U2 experience and sometimes encounters with the band, as well as photographs. I wouldn't have done this without them. Thanks to u2achtung.com in France, to u2interference.com in the USA, and to hanoverquay.info in Ireland. Thanks especially to Anna, Laurent, Stéphanie, Cyril, Flavia, Liesbeth, Valentina, Jessica, Tina and all the others for their undying passion and commitment. They have been truly inspirational, and have come from all over the world. Some have become good friends.

And finally, thanks to Larry, Bono, Adam and The Edge for their beautiful music. May the inspiration and melodies still flow for a long time to come!

INTRODUCTION

This book is the result of a musical passion that has endured for 23 years. I remember very well the first time I heard U2 on the radio. It was early 1983. That year was important for me as I was preparing for my *baccalauréat* (secondary school final year exams). I was sitting in my teenage bedroom in Paris and heard the single 'New Year's Day'. Just like many young Europeans, it was the first time I'd heard a U2 song and the band were put forward as potentially huge. I actually stopped what I was doing to listen. The melodic qualities, the spontaneous way of singing, the sheer strength that came from the song gave me a sense of listening to a very special moment.

U2's music is uplifting in a way music is when it becomes important in someone's life and holds a special meaning for the person listening. It is also uplifting because of its musical qualities. The English sociologist Simon Frith says that 'music offers the immediate experience of collective identity'.[1] He also puts forward that: 'to grasp the meaning of a piece of music is to hear something not simply present to the ear. It is to understand a musical culture, to have a "scheme of interpretation" ... The "meaning" of music describes not just an interpretive but a social process.'[2]

Music is an object that is socially relevant to many and that forms part of a cultural identity. Music in Ireland is in no way different. U2's music, as a matter of fact, is also in no way different. It defines a rock culture. It also defines what music can become. But where the difference lies is that it is still relevant, it fits into this era as much as it did twenty years ago. In that way, it is socially relevant.

U2's music is not only uplifting and carries meaning to Irish fans but also to

1

foreign fans, who seem to understand it sometimes even better than the Irish themselves. It seems that the band appeals to many around the world because they haven't closed themselves to foreign influences but on the contrary have embraced those influences without ever losing sight of what it means to be Irish. That unique mixture makes them recognisable yet unusual, original, almost exotic. That's why they can be at ease with the two labels attached to them. They are an Irish band, first and foremost and no one could ever deny that fact. But they are also an international band because the medium they use to express their artistic endeavours is originally American but has become international. And also their artistic inspiration is as much foreign as it is Irish. This unique combination gives them a truly wide appeal.

There is The Edge's guitar, taking the listener to joyful and sometimes sorrowful places, a sound that defines U2. Bono describes him as the scientist of the band, trying out new things, experimenting. I am not surprised at that definition. If The Edge had gone to college instead of joining U2, he would have become a scientist. Contrary to popular belief, scientists have an incredible artistic sense. They need a lot of imagination to reach their goals, whatever they are. I know about that from first-hand experience, as my brother is a physicist and he draws really well without ever having learned. Many doctors have artistic talents, of one kind or another. The Edge just did the reverse. He became a musician and puts his intellectual talent to the service of music. In my opinion, that talent could only enrich U2's music.

There is Adam Clayton, the true U2 rock star, the only rock star in the band. A man of ambition and talent, a charmer, the man who rescued U2 from its downfall in the early days, the man who was rescued by U2's three other members before his own downfall, a talented and ingenious musician who has worked hard at becoming one of the best.

There is Larry Mullen Junior, of course, the founder and father of the band, the only real musician when the members of U2 met. He is again an extremely talented artist, whose true desire from the beginning was to be part of a rock band. He set up his own and appears as intelligent as he is ambitious in his vision of the band.

Then, there is Bono and his voice. On 'New Year's Day' as on many other songs, he sings 'with his guts'. Years after hearing the song for the first time, when I came across an article by the French cultural critic, Roland Barthes, I immediately thought about why I felt what I felt that day and the way I feel when I hear Bono's voice. French social critic Roland Barthes talks about 'the grain of the voice'.[3]

In his article, he explains the reasons why some singers appeal to us more than others, and the effect they create. Barthes argues that to interpret music with words is a very difficult task indeed. The adjective is the only word which is used to convey musical meaning. He believes that it is a very poor substitute for what music really means and for how it sounds. Music has more to do with feeling and the sense of pleasure that it creates than any adjective could ever convey. He also talks about all the things 'in the performance which are in the service of communication, representation, expression', (what he calls the pheno-song) and about 'the diction of the language' (what he called the geno-song). He compares two opera singers, the way they sing, pronounce the words, and convey emotion and meaning to them. The first, a famous baritone, Fiescher-Dieskau, doesn't touch Barthes, leaves him cold. The second, a less famous baritone, Charles Panzera, touches Barthes at a much deeper level, in something quite inexplicable that his voice conveys, the way he pronounces the words, the syllables, even some letters. Although Barthes talks mostly about classical music, he doesn't dismiss popular music, and says that this 'grain of the voice' can be found in any genre of vocal music.[4] The first time I read the article, I thought that I had a explanation as to why I love the way Bono sings. It has nothing to do with technique or perfection. Pop music allows for those flaws in a way that opera doesn't. How many pop or rock singers have actually learned to sing properly? I can think of a few but there are not many. The members of the Doors learned classical music, for example. The American singer Pat Benatar actually learned opera before moving on to rock 'n' roll. And, how many of them can actually read notes? Listening to someone singing and enjoying it is connected to the pleasure of hearing a sound that is unique, that goes beyond perfection. It is an uplifting experience. Everybody can actually think of other singers who have that effect on them. I can think of a few myself, people as different as Bruce Springsteen, Bob Seeger, Billy Idol, Carol King, Karen Carpenter, Jimi Hendrix, and more recently Adam Gurvitz of Counting Crows. However, here I am talking about a man whose voice touched me at a very deep level, a voice I could recognise anywhere and whose Irish accent comes through when he sings. That's what gives Bono's voice that uniqueness, I believe. I have to stress that most of the time, when we like a piece of music, it is because it has touched us deeply at an emotional level that is quite inexplicable. Only after we have understood and accepted that can we move on to more scientific explanations about why and how a phenomenon like U2 was created, has lasted through two and half decades and is still one of the biggest players on the music world scene. I am taking the word phenomenon in its current meaning, that is to say an event that can be observed but also an event whose exceptional character has to be pointed out.

Finally, there is Paul McGuinness, probably the best manager U2 could have found. He is widely considered the fifth member of the band. He works most of the time in the shadows, yet is well-known inside and outside the restricted frame of rock. He has had the same ambition, the same drive as Larry, Bono, The Edge and Adam. He learned the business at the same time as them. And he has learned it well. Why does it work so well between them all? Looking towards the same goal, no big ego problems, a lot of respect and a lot of fights! That is a healthy way of dealing with things, don't you think?

Since that day in early 1983 when I heard 'New Year's Day' for the first time, U2 have gone on to become one of the biggest bands, if not *the* biggest band in the world. In 25 years, they have sold over 100 million albums, have played 1,185 concerts (up to December 2005) in 31 countries around the world, have seen nine out of their eleven studio albums reach number one in the world charts and have become multi-millionaires. This trend seems set to continue. 'U2 is classic', an American guy told me on one of my trips back from Dublin to Paris in 2004. I thought how right he was. They are classic yet they are new because young people discover them every day. Their songs are witnesses to the present. They may look on the past sometimes but they are relevant.

U2 did not make it to the top with talent only though. They undeniably have it but it is not enough. You can squander it if you don't have a framework to work in, if you don't put in the hours, if you don't perspire, even when you're inspired. One great song is not enough to make an album. One great album is not enough to make a career. On the other hand, what U2 have achieved is longevity without repeating themselves, originality even when the U2 sound was recognisable a mile away.

There are not many U2 albums. Eleven studio albums in 25 years is not a lot. But it isn't quantity that has been driving them; it's quality and also the fact that the genesis of each album is pretty long and difficult. Bono explains: 'We're not, or have never been, confident players, we struggle with some of the basics. It doesn't come easy. We don't write fifteen songs in three weeks. We find it difficult.'[5] Did you know that modern psychologists such as Graham Wallace in 1926 have put forward the different stages of creation and have come up with four categories: preparation, incubation, illumination and verification? There are a lot of comings and goings between those categories and according to research by a French Canadian author, Gérard Côté, the musicians that he interviewed on that point fit into those categories.[6] Indeed, hard work is an essential part of the process and U2 are nothing but hard workers. Another myth that must be dispelled is that creation comes just like that, and that it is easy. Rarely is it like that though. It takes a long gestation period and a lot of the time before things come together. And then, there are limitations. There are stumbling blocks. Inspiration doesn't always come at the right time. It is also, despite what many think, an intellectual process. That's why a U2 album takes time. That's why they are all great in their own right, because U2's members take the time to work on them. Hard work does pay eventually. Talent is just part of that process. It cannot be the whole thing.

The first question I have asked myself in the course of my research is why no book has ever attempted to find an explanation for the phenomenon, why no one has dared touch on the phenomenon. Is is because if they did it, they would completely blow up the myth, the legend? I don't believe that by explaining why the phenomenon exists and by studying it in its entirety will it change the way U2 are seen. If many aspects are very logical and have a rational explanation, some of the other aspects are quite intangible and, if anything, add to the legend. On the tangible side, U2 set out with a very clear strategy of conquest. They tried to make it on the world stage, while remaining fiercely independent. On the intangible side, their fate was to meet at the right place at the right time. They also became known at a time when a new generation was looking for a voice and was in search of meaning.

Is it still necessary to point out that the Irish foursome are the only Irish rock band to have achieved that level of success and longevity? Some of the questions that I ask in this book are rather simple but require complex answers. Why has an Irish rock band become the biggest band in the world? What is the secret of their longevity? What are the factors that have helped their rise to fame? Despite the Irish music industry's apparent healthy state, no Irish band can compare itself to U2, let alone compete with them. What are the reasons for the lack of competition in Ireland? What can we say about Ireland itself through U2? What kind of influence have they had on the Irish music industry? Has their spirituality sheltered them from the demons of rock 'n' roll? U2 have also struggled with their image over the years. That particular aspect has partly created the myth of the 1980s. U2 have tried to deconstruct it at the beginning of the 1990s. What about their image nowadays? And is the myth still alive?

No other band epitomises better than U2 the saying: the journey is more important than the destination. Bono revealed: 'Chris Blackwell (founder of Island Records) used to say: "That's the thing about U2. The band always feels like it's coming, never that it's arrived".' And it's true. Their search for the right sound, for the right word, the search for inspiration, so that the end result is great is what sets U2 apart from many other bands. U2 have always worked harder than other bands, according to Bono. But they also had the spark.[7] And in the end, combined with blind faith, that spark was able to ignite the world.

Bono also said that U2 was an 'organism',[8] an interesting way of putting it, but one that I totally agree with, as I have always thought of U2 as an entity, a living, breathing thing, four individuals who make up an organism indeed, with a genetic code that had to be deciphered. And that's what I did in this book: I went in search of what I would call U2's 'genome', in other words what makes the band what it is, its intrinsic elements. What I discovered is a real entity, much closer to life than one could imagine: a colourful map of beautiful places, of small and big ideas, of human tragedies and great joys. The whole thing bears an uncanny resemblance to life – that's what it feels like. Larry, Bono, The Edge and Adam gave life to what was originally an idea. And they did it really well. They are not superheroes. They are four human beings who were very lucky to meet when they did and to have the lucidity to discover that they could do something with that little spark.

When people talk about U2, when they try to analyse what makes them who they are, they generally focus on one aspect: their faith. Doing that is simplistic. Nobody is one-dimensional and certainly not U2.

During the course of a very long journey that brought me from a course in Irish Studies to a very concrete Ireland, where I learned more than I ever thought I would, I have myself discovered that what makes U2's 'genetic code' unique is a combination of eight permanent features that have been present throughout the band's career (community, 'Irishness', independence, spirituality, creative drive, ambition, social conscience, the fans). 2005 has seen the band's twenty-fifth anniversary. It is therefore possible, considering that the band has lasted that long without changing its line-up, to point to the features that have accompanied the band since their beginnings, hence the way the book is divided.

The first permanent feature I identified is U2's heightened sense of community. U2 is unique in that no other rock band has lasted this long without changing at least one of its members. Bitter feuds and constant rows have accompanied the most successful of them. American music journalist, Bill Flanagan says about the Irish band: 'It is by far the most considerate operation of its size I have ever seen in the rock world. The sort of backstabbing and dirty fighting that is routine in most comparable outfits is almost absent (…) Even the tensions and fights tend to be like arguments in a family.'[9]

The second permanent feature is U2's Irishness, which is linked to the band's strong sense of independence. Irishness runs through their music, veiled yet so powerful. U2's originality undoubtedly stems from their Irish identity, but also from the fact that they have always put forward the fact that they are Irish. Their fierce independence is also due to their origins, the refusal to be part of a scene, a testament to their freewill and desire to make it as an Irish rock band living and working in Ireland.

The creative process is the third permanent feature. From U2's modus operandi, to the people collaborating with them, to the various musical influences, to the analysis of the main themes found in the songs, a picture emerges of a group of people whose main concern is to be true to themselves. They write songs which reflect the times they live in and their current state of mind, an ever-evolving way of seeing things.

Spirituality is another permanent aspect. Present at every turn, sometimes even overwhelming, it finds its way in everything that U2 do, from the words of the songs, to the music, to the concerts, to the interviews of the band. There is a clear consensus among the fans, who are very tolerant of that aspect of U2, who respect their choice and who even think that it adds another dimension to the band.

The fifth permanent feature is ambition. The members of U2 have been ambitious from the start and have created strategies to get to the top. The band has also been a tremendous catalyst for the Irish music industry. Through the different strategies employed, and the results they have yielded, a link between U2 and the development of the Irish music industry becomes obvious.

U2's social consciousness is the sixth permanent feature. Charting its birth and evolution, the influence the Irish band and the mega-events of the 1980s they took part in have had on those interested in rock is brought to light. It is also possible to point to the the influence U2's image overhaul in the 1990s has had on the image of a band with a social consciousness. The reasons for the conscious shift that U2 operated and the way it is linked to their political side become apparent. Subsequently, Bono has created a new kind of political and social struggle, through his involvement with DATA and Africa, which could well be another way for rock stars to act socially.

The seventh permanent feature is U2's image and the consequences it has had on the myth that emerged in the 1980s. The reasons why U2's myth came to life, bolstered by the band's image, are rooted in that decade, although the members of U2 have always had a hard time with the very idea of image. The question of 'the next U2' can also be answered through the notion of myth.

The final permanent feature is the fans. To understand why U2 became the voice of a generation in the 1980s, and why the band is still important to later generations is essential to understand the U2 phenomenon. The fans' identities have been shaped to a certain extent by U2. The social, political and philosophical context has also shaped U2's view of the world and its own identity. The epilogue completes this picture, by allowing fans to talk about their favourite band. I couldn't imagine writing a book about U2 without including the people who support the band through thick and thin.

Some of the important episodes in U2's career are found in more than one chapter. This is inevitable as some of them can be put in different categories. I try to deal with them from another angle each time.

You might also wonder why I don't talk specifically about the live aspect of U2 or why I haven't chosen to devote one whole chapter to it. Firstly, this particular aspect has been talked about at length and I don't think that I could add to it. Secondly, it runs through the whole of the phenomenon and defines what U2 is. Therefore, I talk about it within the relevant chapters, as it is one of the main threads of U2's career.

This book was born out of passion. I hope that whoever reads it will agree passionately or will disagree passionately. I also hope that it will be an enjoyable experience and that a corner of the veil on the U2 phenomenon will at least have been lifted.

1

COMMUNITY

U2's sense of being a community is one of the foundations of the band and also one of its permanent features. It is difficult to imagine U2 without each of its four members because the idea of community is anchored in the four members. Even though Bono, as the singer and the member who is interviewed most often, is the best known in the band, the other three are an integral part of U2. When Bono talks about their music, he talks about it as a collective, not an individual endeavour. The unique chemistry that exists within the group is actually rare in the rock 'n' roll world. It seems that U2 could not exist without Adam, The Edge, Larry or Bono. And if you added an element, the chemistry could well be put off balance also. Furthermore, most bands will have one or two members who write the music and the lyrics, where the others are just there to play. In U2, the four members each have an input in their sound, and if Bono writes most of the lyrics, the music is composed by all of them.

Let's take two examples of bands who became very famous, whose line-up has been changed and whose singer and guitarist, it turned out, were the driving and creative forces behind them.

The Rolling Stones have sold millions of records and have played hundreds of concerts. One central figure emerged very quickly: Brian Jones, followed by Mick Jagger and Keith Richards. Brian Jones had founded the Rolling Stones but problems arose between the members of the band due to his drug and drink habit. He left the band in 1969 and died that same year, leaving Keith and Mick as the main representatives and creative force in the band. Another example is Simple Minds. Contemporaries of U2 and successful in their own right, especially in the 1980s, they have also had their line-up changed, but the singer Jim Kerr and the guitarist Charlie Burchill still remain as the two creators of the songs and the band's sound.

U2 can be termed an oddity. Indeed, it is very difficult to think of another band with the same success who hasn't had its line-up changed at least once. The Irish band's sense of being a community is one of its permanent features but it also partly holds the explanation for its longevity and for its keeping the same band members.

The first step towards understanding the concept of community and see how it applies to U2 is to give a definition of it. A community is a group of people sharing ideas and ideals who are working towards the same goal. It may seem quite obvious to most that music has the power of bringing people together. Ireland is no stranger to that notion. Traditional music is indeed a vector of community. Young and old in Ireland share a passion for it. It is also true of other people in other countries, but music belongs to Irish history and art in a very special sense, and it probably holds as high a place in the country as literature, for instance. It is an intangible force that seems to unite every Irishman and woman. It has become an essential element of the life of the community. As Professor Micheal Ó Suilleabhain puts it: 'Music, with its twin tradition of dance, runs like an underground river along the bedrock of our cultural thought.'[1] For example, a 1994 survey by Bord Fáilte (the Irish tourist board) showed that a third of the Irish population attended one musical session in a pub every month. The figure for the twenty to 24-year age group reached two-thirds. And that notion has spread beyond the borders of Ireland. Professor Ó Suilleabhain continues:

> This extraordinary island, so much alive and vibrant with the arts, so local in its groundedness, and so international in its search, continues to increasingly astound those who view us from without, even as more and more of us who are players on the ground grow into a realisation of the artistic riches which surround us.[2]

Of the 3.6 million tourists who visited Ireland in 1994, half attended a traditional music session in a pub and 1.1 million attended a popular music concert in a pub.[3] Also, in 2001, Bord Fáilte conducted another survey, asking tourists what were the main factors that had brought them to Ireland. A huge 48 per cent rated music as one of the main factors that made them choose Ireland as a holiday destination.[4] The perceived notion that Ireland is a musical nation is not the point here. These surveys merely show that the country has that reputation and that U2 have undoubtedly contributed to that through their success.

One can immediately point to the Irish rock band as sharing the same collective vision, the same ambition, having the same ideals and the same communal goals within the band. They resemble their fellow countrymen in their love of music and in the sharing of it. They would not have achieved worldwide success without a common ground and a collective vision. Larry Mullen says:

> We don't fight, but we all have very strong personalities. But in the end we want the same thing. You know, we're very competitive: we want to be on the radio, have big singles. We don't want to be thought of as a veteran band. We like the fact that people mention Coldplay as our contemporaries.[5]

However, U2 work within a medium that is quite unique in its nature. Bertrand Ricard, a French sociologist, talks of rock 'n' roll in the lives of young people as being an instrument capable of playing the role of a social link. He takes the example of amateur rock groups and shows how those young people create a real 'community way of life',[6] allowing them to create a new and diverse social link which encompasses notions such as ethics, affect and aesthetics.

When the members of U2 met, there is no doubt that they wanted to take part in something that would create social meaning but they also wanted to belong to a special community of their own. Bono says:

> My father had lived through the 50s depression ... and as a result he taught us not to expect too much in case we might feel let down. His attitude was: don't do anything that seems like you're aiming higher than your allotted station. All my mates were intent on going to college and on doing things. I'd always been bright at school and the last thing I wanted was to stay stuck in any kind of rut. Joining the band was my emancipation from all this. It was my ticket to freedom. It was my way of attempting to change the circumstances of the world I was living in.[7]

This view is rather common with people who have set up rock bands; a sense of boredom, of not belonging, of not knowing what to do with their lives has pushed many people to play music and dream of making it big one day. However, there is only a handful of those groups that has achieved worldwide success. Bono and his friends in U2 had something going for them though. They shared the same values and the same goals, and they still do. They built their own community on principles, on ethics. One of those principles is aesthetic and will be examined later, but it is important to note that the vision they share within their community is also artistic and therefore aesthetic. One cannot go without the other. In other words, U2 have an aesthetic ideal, as far as their songs are concerned and it must be followed, so that the songs reflect that ideal. That is what makes U2 a community of artists, of musicians, as well as friends. And I will go further and say that U2 have retained some of the ideals that amateur bands have, and maybe that is one of the reasons why they still appeal to people. U2 are still in some ways a garage band. At the Grammy Awards ceremony in February 2002, Bono said of U2: 'This is a punk-rock band hearing mad tunes in their head.' The quote is a reminder of what U2 really are: a rock band who still believes in the same values it always has. The identity U2 created for themselves hasn't changed since the band was set up. They have built ethical codes that they follow to accomplish the band's ideals: respect for each other, a work ethic, and aesthetic codes.

The views expressed by members of the band are also proof of their common ideal. Bono keeps repeating that the influence of the band is itself. The Edge says that U2 is based on friendship. Larry Mullen claims that it is a democracy. Twenty-one years after the release of the band's first album, *Boy*, during the concert that was filmed in Boston in June 2001, Bono talked about U2 as a 'family business'. The notion of community, it seems, has endured, even 26 years after the band's first release.

Let's now take a look at the band members' origins. We can subsequently discover how and why the U2 community was created, and unravel one of the secrets of its longevity.

Larry Mullen's Origins

Larry (Laurence) Mullen Junior is the founder and drummer of U2. Born on 31 October 1961, in Dublin, the only son of the family, he has one older sister, Cecilia, born in 1957. A younger sister, Mary, died as a child. They all lived in Artane. His mother Maureen Gaffney raised the children, while his father, Laurence Mullen Senior, worked as a civil servant in the Department of Health and the Environment. Larry first attended Scoil Colmcille, in Marlborough Street in Dublin city centre, where all the teaching was done through Irish. When he was due to attend secondary school, his parents decided that he would go to Mount Temple Comprehensive, the first ever non-denominational school in Ireland, which opened in 1972. Both boys and girls mixed in class which, at the time, was almost unheard of, and social and religious differences were forgotten. The case of Mount Temple is interesting because it had a very different approach to schooling to other institutions. As a non-denominational institution, it was not tied to the teaching of the Roman Catholic church or to the Protestant church and had a clearly different approach to discipline, centring its teaching on the individual development rather than on purely academic achievement.

At the age of eight, Larry had attempted to take piano lessons, but that did not work out and after a year, he started taking drumming classes in a music school in Chatham Row. His teacher, Joe Bonnie, had a solid reputation and was well known all over Ireland. Larry became a member of the famous Irish brass band, The Artane Boys Band in 1974. However, he left shortly afterwards over a disagreement about the length of his hair! He then joined another brass band, the Post Office Workers Union Band. Music was already a passion for Larry and his only hobby outside of school. Cecilia had bought him a drum kit in 1973 and he spent his time watching Top of the Pops on television and imitating the drummers of the rock 'n' roll bands who appeared on the programme.

The Edge's Origins

The Edge (born David Howell Evans) is U2's guitar player and was born in London on 8 August 1960, the second son of Garvin and Gwenda. His brother Dick was two years older. Where Larry Mullen comes from a Catholic background, The Edge comes from a Protestant family whose origins can be found in Llanelli, in Wales. His father and mother decided to move to Dublin when Garvin's employer, Plessey Engineering, offered him a post in Ireland. Having spent two years in Northern Ireland completing his military duty in the Royal Air Force, Garvin liked the idea of going back to Ireland to raise his children. The whole family moved to Saint Mary Park Road in Malahide in 1962 and a couple of years later, a sister, Jill, was born in Dublin. As a child, The Edge attended Saint Andrew's Church of Ireland School in Malahide, where he briefly came across Adam Clayton. He then was sent to Mount Temple. He was always a very good student, rather shy and very diligent. He worked hard and his ambition was to go to university and study science. Gwenda, in the meantime, had become a member of the Malahide Musical Society and Garvin was one of the founders of the Dublin Male Welsh Voice Choir. Music was an integral part of the Evans family but in the 1970s, The Edge was not certain that he wanted to pursue a musical career. His school results were good and he could go on to higher education.

Bono's Origins

Bono (born Paul David Hewson) is U2's singer and writes 95 per cent of their lyrics. Born in Dublin, on 10 May 1960, he is the youngest son of Iris Rankin and Robert (Bobby) Hewson. His brother Norman is eight years older. Bono and Norman are products of a Catholic/Protestant union, Iris being the latter while Bobby the former. They contracted what was termed at the time a 'mixed marriage'. This religious background already singled Bono out. The boys were raised in the Protestant faith, however, Bobby considering that a child spends more time with its mother and should therefore be raised in her religion. Iris was a housewife while Bobby worked at the Post Office. When houses were built in Ballymun and there were still green fields around, Iris and Bobby bought a home there. Bono was still a baby and he was raised in the warmth of a loving family. In 1972, he was sent to Mount Temple Comprehensive. His father thought that attendance there would ease Bono's growing pains as well as the tensions that may arise from his religious background. However, tragedy struck in 1974 when Iris suffered a brain haemorrhage, the day after her own father's funeral, and died in hospital a few days later. The impact of this event on Bono, the teenager, and later on Bono, the man, would have lasting consequences and would be inevitably reflected in some songs, years after the tragedy. However, the future singer's loss was somehow smoothed by a very important social environment. Bono had a lot of friends, who would later form the cult band, the Virgin Prunes. In the mid-1970s, they founded a community called the Lypton Village. It was a way for the teenagers to escape an adult world that they rejected, and to remain as close to childhood as possible. 'We got into this *Lord of the Flies* idea of not growing up ...' Bono recounts. 'We said, "We won't grow up. We'll stay as we are ... nine!" It was a little bit gauche and a little bit all over the place but that's where it was coming from.'[8]

But Lypton Village was also invented as an intellectual and philosophical response to the youth gangs hanging around in the area. It was more than just a simple gathering of teenagers looking for kicks. It was a hidden form of rebellion against the adult world, against conventions and against the loss of illusions. The Lypton Village members had their own language, which symbolised the rejection of the adult world, a form of sanctuary in which to hide, where innocence and honesty were preserved and compromise was non-existent. John Waters believes that:

> Lypton Village was an extreme case, a revolt against banality. It was not a petulant, ideological revolt, but a weary, existentialist one against both the tackiness and emptiness of the lower middle-class culture around them, the

way in which their immediate environment seemed to embody the isolation and alienation they felt from the society as a whole, and also against the fatalistic jocularity, the Cheer Up It Might Never Happen syndrome, that lay like a damp sheet under everything.[9]

We can see the complex nature of this community, a precursor of the approach that would be taken by its members in the founding of U2 but also of its brother-band, the Virgin Prunes. Lypton Village also rebelled, and that was in line with its ethos, against the drink and television culture that was developing around Ireland at the time. Indeed, none of the members drank, smoked or took drugs. They were already on the side of the uncool.

The members of the Village gave each other nicknames. There was Derek and Trevor Rowen, Fionan Hanvey, Dick Evans (brother of The Edge), David Watson and Anthony Murphy. To follow the rules adopted by the Village, each individual would christen another according to a specific trait of his personality. Derek became Guggi, Trevor became Strongman, Fionan became Gavin Friday, Dick became Dik, David became Dave-id and Anthony became Pod. Paul Hewson became Bono Vox from the name of a hearing aid shop in Earl Street North, off O'Connell Street, called Bonavox, which means 'good voice' in latin, a rather good omen. It was Bono himself who christened Dave Evans The Edge. The story goes that it was because of the shape of his head but also because he was always on the outside, looking in and analysing things.

Adam Clayton's Origins

Adam Clayton is the bass player of U2. Born in Chinnor, Oxfordshire, on 13 March 1960, he also comes from a Protestant family. His father, Brian, a former pilot with the RAF, got a post with the Irish airline company, Aer Lingus. His mother, Jo, is a former air hostess. He has one younger sister, Sarah Jane, and a younger brother, Sebastian, born in Dublin. Adam had a pretty chaotic schooling and arrived in Mount Temple in 1976. Before that, he had spent time in two boarding schools, Castle Park, Dalkey (between 1968 and 1973) and Saint Columba's, Rathfarnham (between 1973 and 1976). According to biographies, he hated going to boarding school but his father did not know how long he would be posted in Ireland and did not want his son to fall behind on his schooling if the family had to return to England. Adam was not fond of school, had a rebellious nature and would not study in class. However, he had a positive music experience in Saint Columba's when his mother bought him a bass guitar and he tried to learn how to play by tentatively founding a band with his friend, John

Lesley. In Mount Temple, he was rather different from the other pupils and stood out. When he first saw Adam, Larry describes him as having 'bushy blond hair, tinted glasses and a long afghan coat, and all the beads and all the gear and he just looked so cool'.[10] Not only was he cool but he was also unfailingly polite to the teachers and obviously full of charm.

The Founding of U2

The U2 community started to form when Larry Mullen put a note on the notice board of Mount Temple school looking for musicians, encouraged by his music teacher, Albert Bradshaw, who was also instrumental in talking to The Edge about the band. The future U2 guitarist made his way to Larry's house in Artane along with his brother Dick and met up with Adam Clayton, Bono, Peter Martin and Ivan McCormick. Peter and Ivan were quickly ousted and, interestingly enough, U2 as it is today was formed, though Dick Evans would stay for a little while before joining the Virgin Prunes. Firstly, they had to decide who would play which instrument. Larry would logically be the drummer because he had a drum kit and was able to play. Adam Clayton had a bass guitar and even though it was not certain if he could play or not, he owned the guitar! The Edge had built a guitar with his brother and had a musical background. So Bono would have to be the singer, whether he liked it or not! He even confessed years later that he nearly did not make it as the singer. They now had to decide on a name and chose Feedback. They were very lucky in that they were allowed to rehearse in Larry's shed but also in the school, with the help of Albert Bradshaw and another teacher, David Moxham.

The U2 community was slowly taking shape, firstly by nurturing the burgeoning friendship between the members. Bono especially seems to have found in U2 what was missing in his teenage life: the warmth of a family. And that is how the members of U2 describe themselves to this day. In 2004, Larry confessed: 'What kind of band goes on holiday to the same place? What kind of families just mix? … We are a tight family, with all the pulses and disadvantages of that. But we don't have an ego problem in the band. We all are involved in the process. We all struggle together.'[11]

It is undeniable that one of the band's many strengths comes from their friendship and the idea they have of U2. It seems that building U2 was like building a relationship, giving it every chance to survive.

When the band played 'Show Me the Way' by Peter Frampton during a music competition in Mount Temple, their enthusiasm was evident. A few months later, on 11 April 1977, during a concert in Saint Fintan's school in

Sutton, they changed their name to The Hype, a more grabbing name in the context of the punk era that saw their birth. They played a few concerts under that name and started building a small fan base. However, on 20 March 1978, there were new changes. The Hype played the first part of their concert in the Howth Community Centre with five members. After the break, they came back on stage with a new name, U2, and minus one: Dick Evans had left the band during the interval!

It was Steve Averill[12], U2's future designer and member of the band The Radiators From Space, who suggested the name U2 to the young band. The spy plane was obviously not the idea. Is it 'you too' or even 'you two'? It is definitely difficult to give an answer as U2 themselves don't seem to know precisely what it is or what it means. But the sound of the name makes it easy to remember and it would not be very surprising if the sound of the U and of the 2 put together was more important than anything else. However, according to Mark Chatterton, author of U2, *The Ultimate Encyclopedia*, if Adam Clayton agreed to the name almost straightaway, it took some persuading for the others to accept it.[13]

As for the manager of the band, Adam was de facto in charge of the band's business in the absence of another competent person. Playing both roles of bass player and manager was a situation that Adam was not willing to face for too long. It was indeed very difficult to survive in the music business anyway. But when one had to play several roles, it was even more problematic. It has to be pointed out, however, that U2 won the Harp Lager/*Evening Press* young bands contest of 17 March 1978 without a manager. The first prize was a recording session in April of that same year, offered by Jackie Hayden, the then marketing director of CBS Ireland. U2 were also offered a contract with the same company, having been rejected by the London office. They declined the offer and were still actively looking for a manager.

Paul McGuinness and U2

U2 met Paul McGuinness in 1978. He was older than them. Born in 1951, of English descent, he was well educated. He had been sent by his parents to boarding school (Clongowes College, in County Kildare), then had attended Trinity College but had decided to work in the entertainment industry. Paul had a dream of finding a rock band that he could manage and take to the top. He was introduced to U2 by the rock journalist Bill Graham, who was, at the time, championing their cause after seeing them on stage and who remained a mentor until his death in May 1996. U2 seemed to be that band from the way they performed on stage and interacted with the audience.

The idea of community in U2 not only encompasses the band members and their personnel but also their audience. U2 fans always feel that they belong to the U2 community. The ease with which the members of U2 communicate with their audience, even through their albums, is an essential ingredient in their sense of community. The 'family' is much larger than one actually thinks. When Bono, in a gesture that has become an immutable ritual, invites a female, or sometimes a male fan, and more recently a child on stage to dance with him or play the guitar, he welcomes every other fan on stage and makes them part of the U2 family.

Paul McGuinness must have felt that when he first saw the band on stage. It is this capability to communicate at a level that every fan can understand that is unique to a band like U2. It is music as communication. Simon Frith says that '... rock is a crucial contemporary form of mass communication.'[14] The members of U2 seem to have understood that notion, the fact that rock could be used as an extremely powerful communication tool, playing on the emotions of the audience, fulfilling an obvious need for something closer to the famous collective unconsciousness than most believe. The affective power that a band like U2 can generate has to be looked at in the light of the need to belong to a community. A community, as I said before, is a group who gather together because they have the same values, share the same dreams and like the same things. The members share the same values and the same dreams. Larry, The Edge, Bono and Adam had the same ambition and the same drive to get to the top. But they were not prepared to do it at any cost. Paul McGuinness shared that philosophy and that is the reason why, when he officially became the band's manager,[15] he named his company Principle Management, because his idea of managing a band is based on principles that others don't necessarily have.

Meeting Paul could be seen as a miracle encounter in the history of U2. They came to trust him completely with their affairs and he trusted them with the creative side, never interfering and knowing that they would produce the work on time, and that the goal would be achieved. He is responsible for their signing the contract with Island Records in 1980 and also for securing further deals down the road.

U2 and The Virgin Prunes

Other people that are part of the U2 community are the members of the now defunct Virgin Prunes. The members of U2 and The Virgin Prunes have a very long history. The latter founded their band shortly after U2 was created and were inspired by their (very small) success. But the Prunes were very different. Their music was theatrical (they often used props), they wore dresses and make-up.

Could they be termed a rock band in that case? A performance art/avant-garde musical group would be more appropriate. Gavin Friday and Guggi were the singers, as well as Dave-id. Strongman played bass, while Dik played the guitar, and Pod played the drums. Instead of simply playing music, they confronted the audience with what they called 'Art-Fuck' and, more often than not, they created outrage and shock among those who came to see them. They would, for instance, simulate the sexual act on stage. They also opened several U2 shows in the early days as support act.

They were inspired by dadaism and the Cabaret Voltaire. The latter originated in Zurich and was founded on 5 February 1916 by several artists, who were exiles there. Amongst the founders were Hugo Ball, a playwright and poet, and Emmy Hennings, a German singer. The group gathered in a cabaret called the Holländische Meierei and staged their own characters, made noise with musical instruments and provoked and shocked the audience. The aim was to try and destroy traditional arts, and beyond that, the traditional concepts of culture and social ideas. It is this Voltaire Orchestra, whose shows often ended in brawls, which is behind dadaism. Interestingly enough, the word Dada was actually chosen at random in the dictionary during the first show. Five months later, the Cabaret Voltaire was defunct but Dada, a subversive and anarchical movement, spread from Berlin to Paris, while a parallel movement was born in New York. Dadaism advocated nonconformism, the freeing of instinct and the rejection of all preconceived ideas through literature, music or painting. A desire for renewal appeared: the idea that everything should be wiped out and started all over again.[16] We can see here the parallels between Dada and the Virgin Prunes; the will to reject conformism, to shock the audience, to use theatre and music as instruments for a different kind of art, but also the will to communicate with the audience, with whatever means were available. They definitely shared the idea that communication was essential between artist and audience to put one's point across.

U2 also had an interest in theatre and their early shows were about music but also about performance. They drew their inspiration from everywhere, but mostly comedy and literature. The Irish rock writer Bill Graham pointed out that this literary link to Irish rock 'n' roll is actually very unusual as the antecedents of Irish rock are more likely to be rooted in a literary than in a musical tradition. Elsewhere in the western world, no band would say that they were inspired by literature, as a rock tradition already existed. In Ireland, however, that tradition was non-existent and therefore, rock artists relied on different influences than those of a rock 'n' roll tradition which did not belong to them:

You'll see Van Morrison relating himself to Yeats, you see it in Shane MacGowan also. You'll see a lot of people identifying with Flann O'Brien. You'll see it in the Radiators. Philip Chevron has all sorts of references to Joyce and O'Casey and Behan and so forth. There is that sense: if you are Irish you measure yourself a little bit against those people. You will never see an English musician taking anything from T.S. Eliot or Auden.[17]

Playing music, playing a character, performing in the widest meaning of the word, were features that U2 and The Virgin Prunes shared, and through those performances they were able to communicate with each other and their audience. Both bands came to rock and art from opposing directions and John Waters suggests that:

If the U2 and Virgin Prunes' stories are taken separately, the friendship of the two bands makes very little sense. Taken together, they suggest the twin guiding principles of Dada, destruction followed by creation – the overlooked second plank of the Dada agenda, stillborn as Hugo Ball's disillusionment bore witness, in the first flush of Dada in the century's teenage years.[18]

The Virgin Prunes imploded and disintegrated while U2 exploded on the world stage and became a powerful force within the rock music world, both at home and abroad.

Pressure within the Community

The story of U2 is undoubtedly a story of dedication, hard work, friendship and success, all qualities that many other bands in the rock world must envy. The U2 community has, however, been put to the test several times, but it seems to have come out at the other end stronger than ever. For example, during the War Tour, Bono's reputation for climbing to the top of the stage scaffolding was the stuff of legend. In an interview for Hot Press in 1983, he related an incident that made him stop and think:

At the US festival, I climbed to the top of the stage to get to the people at the back – there were 300,000 there – and I put a white flag at the top and it counted as a symbol, a broadstroke to that mass of people. But another time I went into the audience in LA at a big sports complex – there were about 120,000 people there – with a big white flag, and the flag was torn to shreds and I was nearly torn to shreds. I got onto the balcony and I found myself looking down and then I found myself jumping about 20 feet into this sea of people, and they caught me and passed me along from the back until eventually I got up onto the stage nearly naked, wondering 'What have I done, what's happened?' Because although the people caught me, some other people jumped off the balcony after and there was, but there may not have been, people to catch them. And it was at that stage I had to think – responsibility. I mean, the place had gone berserk – what if somebody had died? Also, punks in LA are into slamdancing which is quite aggressive and as they were tearing the flag to shreds I found myself getting this guy and slamming him against the wall – I was really going for him. I thought: 'What's happening to me?'[19]

That same evening, Bono was asked by the other members of the group to stop that nonsense, that the music should speak for itself and that they refused to be dragged along. In the end, this was a minor incident compared to others that almost disintegrated U2.

Two major incidents have been crucial to the band's artistic survival. The first involved the charismatic Christian group Shalom, and the second involved the recording of *Achtung Baby* and subsequent Zoo TV tour. They show the struggles that the members of U2 had to face, in the creation of their music as well as in their relationship with each other and others. They also show the type of relationship that the members of the band have, and that the community that is the basis of the band could only have survived because of the friendship that binds them together.

U2 and Shalom

Boy, U2's first album, was released in 1980. It was a success in Ireland; the sound of the band was fresh and original, and their Irish fan base was getting bigger as time went by. The band toured incessantly. They enjoyed the stage and their frontman had the gift of entertainment. He also came across as sincere and giving in his stage performance.

But for reasons that still remain opaque, three of the band members joined the Charismatic Christian group Shalom shortly after the release of *Boy*. Some of the former members of the Lypton Village and members of The Virgin Prunes would play a significant part in this 'enrolment.'

Pod and Guggi met Dennis Sheedy in Grafton Street after an altercation between the latter and a member of the Hare Krishna sect. He invited them to come along to a Shalom prayer meeting in a house on the North Circular Road, on Dublin's northside. Bono remembers:

We were doing street theatre in Dublin, and we met some people who were madder than us. They were a kind of inner-city group living life like it was the first century AD. They were expectant of signs and wonders; lived a kind of early-church religion. It was a commune. People who had cash shared it. They were passionate, and they were funny, and they seemed to have no material desires.[20]

They were later joined by Larry Mullen, The Edge, his girlfriend Aishling, Bono, his girlfriend, Ali, as well as Virgin Prune Gavin Friday and an old school friend, Maeve O'Regan. Following this meeting, the Shalom group became the centre of their lives for a while. Adam Clayton was the only band member who declined the invitation to join. He did not feel comfortable with belonging to a religious group.

Shalom was part of the charismatic movement that was flourishing at the time. One is tempted to question why the members of U2 joined the group. Did their religious community of origin not fulfil the spiritual needs they obviously had? Was it not enough? Why had they joined a group that could be regarded as a sect? Although there was never talk of money being given to Shalom, when the members of U2 recounted what eventually pushed them out of the group, the reasons seemed to be of a psychological nature.

Larry, The Edge and Bono continued to go to the prayer meetings after that first time. The group moved to a house in Templeogue. Some meetings lasted up to three hours. The intensive study of The Bible would later serve Bono greatly in writing lyrics. The group also owned a caravan in Portrane, north County Dublin, that stood in the middle of a field, and shortly before the recording of *October*, some of the members of Shalom (including Larry, Bono and The Edge) moved there to pray and fast. The film-maker and writer, Peter Sheridan, whose family owned a house nearby, recalls hearing them chant.

In the meantime, on both a personal and business front, Adam Clayton and Paul McGuinness were worried about the future of the band. Contracts had to be honoured. The band had tour and other commitments. Paul sympathised with Adam, who was left alone when the others gathered to pray before concerts, for instance. Although a Christian, Adam could be termed an agnostic and didn't share the others' commitment to the Shalom group. There is no doubt that he must have felt rejected and Paul's support must have been precious.

The problem was deeper than anyone realised though. The three Christian members of U2 were torn between staying in the band and leaving it. How could they reconcile the rock 'n' roll lifestyle with the life of a Charismatic Christian, whose duties went beyond Sunday mass? However, the decision they made to stay in U2 and to leave Shalom was triggered by the growing demands put on them by the religious group. Great pressure was exerted on them to conform to certain Christian ideas and practices, which the members of U2 were not ready to accept. Therefore they left Shalom, Larry being the first one. However, it is not known how difficult it was for them to leave or what the exact reasons were. Were pressures exerted? Did Shalom ask for money? Were there psychological reasons? Bono says that U2 went on tour and basically didn't go back, although they would visit.[21]

What can be said of that period of fervent belief was that firstly, it produced a very beautiful second album, *October*, full of the doubts that any believer feels at times. Neil McCormick even said at the time of its release that it was 'a Christian LP that avoids all the pedantic puritanism associated with most Christian rock, avoids the old world emotional fascism of organised religion ...'[20] Indeed U2 were never part of the Christian rock scene, which emerged in the USA in the 1970s as a response to the more secular, mainstream rock music that was around, and which talked about God and Christianity with the same musical instruments as traditional rock. If they were seen by some as proselytisers, it was not the way the album was received.

Secondly, the U2 community was reinforced. Bono asked Adam to be his best man when he married Alison Stewart in August 1982. It was a gesture of reconciliation and the whole band was reunited from a career point of view but also as regards their friendship.

The Recording of Achtung Baby

Nearly ten years after the Shalom incident, U2 were recording their first album of the 1990s, *Achtung Baby*. On New Year's Eve 1989, the band performed their last concert of the decade and Bono declared: 'We have to go away and dream it all up again.' For some, that remark spelt the end of U2. For most fans though, it probably only meant a renewal, a reinvention. U2 had reached a dead end, had become too big, a sort of a dinosaur before its time, and they had the difficult task of reinventing what it was to be U2. I believe they knew they could not talk to the 1990s generation in the same way that they had reached the 1980s one. The band members were barely 30 and had been in U2 for fourteen years already. They belonged to the community of the band, they loved it and wanted it to go on. It was a collective decision. But the problems that arose from this reinvention were probably unexpected.

Bono, Larry, the Edge and Adam went to Berlin to record in the legendary Hansa Ton studios. What came out of those sessions was both beautiful and heartbreaking. One of U2's most moving and most popular songs 'One', was recorded there. At the same time though, some deep problems appeared. The band was obviously encountering problems during the recording of the album. Two incidents related in Niall Stokes' book, *Into the Heart: The Story Behind Every U2 Song*, are good examples of the tension that the members of U2 had to deal with at the time. Larry Mullen had to wait in Berlin for hours one day not knowing where the others were. He ended up phoning the studio and made a scene, feeling legitimately betrayed.[22] Adam concludes about the Berlin sessions: 'All one's relationships, with your family, with your friends, with the members of the band – everything started to disintegrate with that record.'[23] When they did not produce the expected material, the band returned to Dublin to record some more songs in a house in Dalkey. As 'Mysterious Ways', which was to become the second single from the album, was being created, there was a deep disagreement over the song between Bono and, producer and friend, Daniel Lanois. According to those present during the heated argument, the row nearly turned to blows. All the same, *Achtung Baby* was released to unanimous critical acclaim; the first single 'The Fly' and the album itself went to number one in many countries and the band started what was to become their most talked-about tour of the 1990s.

However, the deep-rooted problems that had arisen during the recording sessions were not completely sorted out. Adam Clayton became romantically involved with a supermodel. His relationship with Naomi Campbell was reported in the papers and the couple became engaged, Naomi flashing her engagement ring at the cameras of the Pat Kenny Show on Irish television. The relationship was, however, shortlived. Adam descended into alcohol dependency. It came to a head at a concert U2 were to play on 26 November 1993. The bass player had to be replaced by his guitar technician, Stuart Morgan. The official reason was that he had a virus. The real reason, however, was that Adam Clayton had a bad hangover, and he could not attend the concert. The other band members were concerned about his health but also about him playing the next day, as the concert was being beamed live to America, and would also be used for the commercial video, Zoo TV Live From Sydney. U2's bass player considered his commitment to the band, to the fans and to the community, and made it on stage on 27 November 1993. The previous day's concert was the only one that a member of U2 had ever missed in a thirteen-year career and it has never happened again.

Bono was also concerned that Adam was unhappy in the band. Adam himself knew he had to cure his alcohol addiction if he wanted to remain in U2. But the others obviously helped him because of the friendship that binds them. According to music journalist, Bill Flanagan, U2 and Paul McGuinness were actually relieved that Adam's addiction happened in such a dramatic way.[24] But Bono also confessed to Niall Stokes: 'We thought it was going to be the end, to be honest with you. We didn't know if we wanted to go on if somebody was that unhappy and not enjoying himself.'[25]

And if friendship is essential, trust is too: trust between the members of the band, and between Paul McGuinness and the members of the band. The Edge told Bill Flanagan at the end of the Zoo TV Tour:

> We're still friends. This is not a band like most bands. We're still very close. We still care a lot about each other. There is a lot of support for each other and a lot of leeway and a lot of understanding. I like to think it would be difficult for one of us to really get off the wall and really go out there without the others realising it and being there to do something about it.[26]

In 2004, just before the release of *How to Dismantle an Atomic Bomb*, Adam Clayton also confessed:

> We are not hugely intimate with each other, yet there is tremendous tolerance, room and understanding and love. There is intimacy, but a lot of the time it is a work situation and then everyone goes back to their families. It's more adult ... We are our own survival mechanism.[27]

It may, in fact, seem really odd that a band like U2 exists in the rock world. They are an oddity, almost an aberration, the exception that proves the rule. The rule seems to be that the musicians in a rock band must change at least once and that the band cannot claim longevity without some line-up change. The case of U2 is probably unique in the world to which they belong. Not only is the line-up the same but their manager has been the same since their beginning. This is where the sense of community is the most obvious, almost palpable.

The Community in Video Clips
There are other places where we can see the community of the band in action. This is mainly visually, in video clips and during concerts. U2's image is complex and what they wanted the world to see in the 1980s was very different from what they showed in the 1990s. However, what can be seen and sensed when one watches the videos of the band, or the concerts, is a closeness that is obvious in the gestures but also in the discourse. English sociologist, Andrew Goodwin says of video clips and of U2: 'Music video clips (including performance clips) often seem to be concerned

with establishing a sense of community within a group of musicians (...) or between the musicians and their fans. U2's videos work in this way.'[28]

He goes on by taking the example of the video for 'Where the Streets Have No Name', shot on the rooftop of a liquor store in Los Angeles, and referencing the Beatles' song 'Get Back', for the movie *Let It Be*, shot on a rooftop in 1969, that of their record label, Apple. He suggests that this type of music video works like a pseudodocumentary, produced by advertising agencies 'in which televisual and cinematic discourses associated with factual appeals (*cinema vérité*, the TV interview) are used to promote idealised fantasies about the music industry itself'.[29] Rock musicians are indeed often portrayed as having fun, getting along well with each other whilst working together. Much of the time, however, it is quite the reverse. Life as a working musician can be difficult, and sometimes even unbearable, as many interviews testify. But the most important feature of the videos of that time is that the musicians are shown as a group of friends rather than workers. In the case of U2's videos, many highlight that aspect of the band. Amongst the most famous are those for 'Sunday Bloody Sunday', 'A Sort of Homecoming', 'I Still Haven't Found What I'm Looking For', 'Where the Streets Have No Name', 'One' (version 1) and 'Beautiful Day'. The sense of community is very present with the band interacting with one another and with fans.

On what has become a legendary clip, taken from *Under a Blood Red Sky* – U2 at Red Rocks (a natural amphitheatre in Denver, Colorado) filmed in June 1983 – the performance of 'Sunday Bloody Sunday' is particularly interesting because it is live and shows the band interacting with the audience. This is one of the features of U2 that remains a characteristic to this day. When Bono is given a white flag, he goes to the audience and urges them to 'hold it and let it fly'. When he asks the crowd to sing 'No more!', they reply with the same passion.

The song 'A Sort of Homecoming' was also filmed in concert, during *The Unforgettable Fire* tour. The band is travelling on a tour bus, interacting with one another and with the audience. It shows U2 at work, and it looks as though they are having fun. It doesn't show the hard work involved in putting on a stage performance. However, what this video wants to show is U2 at their most authentic, reaching out to each other and to the fans.

The video for 'I Still Haven't Found What I'm Looking For' was filmed in Las Vegas and shows the band walking down the street meeting fans and enjoying the moment. They are singing together in an apparently relaxed and enjoyable atmosphere. Bono behaves in his usual manner, hugging and kissing female fans, shaking hands with male fans, laughing and dancing.

The video for 'Where the Streets Have No Name' shows a band that has achieved worldwide success and that is at the top. They are drawing a large crowd for the shooting of the video, which was part of a documentary called *Outside It's America*, filmed by Irish director Meiert Avis. The video not only shows the band but also Paul McGuinness, U2's sound engineer Joe O'Herlihy, their photographer Anton Corbijn, the producer Michael Hamlyn, and the video director. Incidentally, most of those people still work with U2. So, the community is enlarged and the video shows people with the same goals and interests. But the community also includes the fans. According to Mark Chatterton, this clip remains a favourite with the fans.

All the video clips mentioned are from the 1980s, a decade where U2 were known for their sincerity and integrity. The 1990s are different on the surface. U2 are then superstars. However, one can see through some of the 1990s' videos, notably that for the single 'One', that U2 have still kept the tradition of perform-ance video that they started with as shown in videos for 'The Fly', 'Mysterious Ways', 'Even Better Than the Real Thing', 'Discothèque', or 'Staring at the Sun'.

The single 'One' has three videos, the first of which shows the band dressed as women. Apart from its rather surprising visual content the video is of interest in that it looks at the band's relationship. It is indeed one of the undercurrents that permeates the song. Although 'One' is about crises in relationships, Bono confesses that it is also about the band.[30] The video deals with the theme of an HIV positive son talking to his father also, possibly the reason why Bono's own father appears in the video. The proceeds of the single were going to Aids char-ities but the video was quickly pulled out because the band were afraid that the clip itself could be misinterpreted. The Edge explains:

> We didn't want to be involved in putting back the Aids issue into the realm of sexuality. Thank God it seems to have gone beyond that. It wasn't worth the risk of people imagining we were saying something about the Aids issue through the drag footage, which was totally not what we were trying to say. So, unfortunately we had to stop it.[31]

The video for the single 'Discothèque' is original, showing the band suppos-edly in a disco: dancing, posing, adjusting their clothes and hair. But it also shows a more fun aspect of U2, with them even showing that they can laugh at themselves as the 1970s disco band The Village People.

The video of 'Beautiful Day' shows U2's rebirth for the year 2000 and beyond. Filmed at Roissy-Charles de Gaulle airport, near Paris, it shows the band depart-ing (or returning?). The scenes of the band leaving or arriving together illustrate the idea of renewal; people kissing, collecting luggage, talking, all the band dressed in black, Bono grabbing someone's luggage, eating an apple out of a girl's hand (even if it is all or partly staged), all show that U2 still belong to a community.

Finally two more recent videos are symbolic of the idea of U2 going back to their roots. 'All Because of You' goes back to U2's roots, with the band perched on the top of a vehicle going through the streets of New York. The band is playing while fans are running after them, screaming. The more symbolic 'City of Blinding Lights' was filmed live and the live recording is used on the video, with all its imperfections and emotion.

The Community Live

The idea of community is also apparent during live concerts. There are two forms of community shown here: U2 the band as a community, and U2 plus the fans as a community. In the latter category, there is a difference between foreign fans and Irish fans.

The band as a community works on the same level as in the video clips. This is the U2 camp in action. The community is larger than the band because it includes all the people working for the band. Unlike the video clips, you can actually see the staff working during a live concert. They are everywhere: light and sound engineers, roadies and the people involved in the process of putting together a concert. Some of them are long-time collaborators of U2. On stage, the members of the band have to literally listen to each other to make it work.

The fans are included as part of the community when the members of U2 interact with them, most notably Bono. As the singer, he is more free from some of the constraints that the others have, so he can run around the stage, touch hands, look people in the eyes and make a connection with them.

U2 have always been a band keen on making contact with the audience when on stage. Despite the fact that their songs were only starting to take shape in the late 1970s it was apparent that the Irish band was there to connect with the audience. They were born in the middle of the punk movement and channelled that energy, while rejecting its most violent and visual aspects.

> Their sound was a mess, their stage act all over the place and their songs inaudible. Yet it was clear that they did not indulge the chaotic devices of punk or its accompanying visual shocks (...) U2, unlike a lot of other bands, played an emotionally connecting music, one that made an effort to reach its public (...).[32]

And that was the main concern of the band: that the audience would enjoy the music and understand it, that they would connect with the musicians, in a very simple way. Beyond all the technology and the search for perfection in the shows, I believe this is still a priority for U2.

Nowhere is that more visible than when the band play in Ireland and especially in Dublin. During the Elevation Tour in September 2001, when U2 played their second concert in Slane Castle, County Meath, the band performed their very first single, 'Out of Control', and Bono's speech during the song reminded everyone where U2 came from, what their goal was, and that they still believed that they belonged to that place:

> Father, I need a lend of 500 pounds, cos we're gonna go over to London and we're gonna score ourselves a record deal and when we get our record deal, we're not gonna stay in London, we're not gonna go to New York City. We're gonna stay and base our crew in Dublin. Cos these people, this is our tribe.[33]

Bono went on to thank all the U2 parents for lending them money for the band. What is, however, more interesting is the fact that Bono includes all the Irish fans in the family, in the community. He calls them his 'tribe' and that is a revealing choice of words. He is thanking them in that way for being part of the U2 adventure, knowing that without those fans, the U2 dream would possibly not have come true. Basing the band and its business in Dublin must have been a difficult but very bold decision at the time. The music industry in Ireland was still in its infancy and no Irish rock band had ever made it to the world stage without first basing its operation in London. We can say that U2 was instrumental in creating a fertile ground where other bands could flourish.

U2 and the Irish Music Industry

The Irish music industry is indebted to U2, for the band was a powerful catalyst for its development. Indeed, U2's decision to base their operation in Ireland, when so many others had gone to London to pursue an international career, was a courageous move. Thus they became pioneers. They did not see Ireland as being without infrastructure, for instance, but rather they were ready to invest artistically and otherwise in the country, undoubtedly seeing Ireland as a source of inspiration. But what did U2 give the community of Irish rock musicians? How did they help the industry to grow and allow more musicians to stay at home and pursue a career?

In 2002, the *Hot Press Yearbook* and *Irish Music Directory* pays homage to U2 and underlines the importance of the band and of that initial decision to stay in Ireland:

The band's pioneering decision to base their operation in Ireland gave an enormous shot of confidence to the Irish music industry and set a precedent that many were to follow. The reverberations of that decision are still being enjoyed today, as the Irish music infrastructure developed and grew in response to, and inspired by U2's success.[34]

Three broad strategies can be outlined that allowed U2 to become what they are and the U2 community is linked to them.

The first strategy was their remaining in Ireland and working from there. In 1980, Bono said: 'We had the chance to leave the country when we signed the recording deal with Island Records but we are still here because basically the roots of the group are in Dublin (...) U2 is an Irish expression.'[35] Setting up Principle Management in Dublin meant employing Irish people in all the sectors that had a link with the music industry.

U2 also wanted to record in Ireland, which they then did. They recorded all their albums in part or in full in Dublin, using Windmill Lane Studios, or Hanover Quay Studios, for instance. Even though the band decided to work mainly with English or Canadian producers (Steve Lillywhite, Brian Eno and Daniel Lanois), the rest of the team is Irish, which follows the philosophy set by the band and their manager, who said in 1986: 'We saw ourselves as Irish and saw absolutely no reason to employ American or English people to tell us how to do the rock 'n' roll business.'[36] Not only is the team Irish but most of its members have been working with U2 for years. Two examples will suffice. Joe O'Herlihy has been U2's chief sound engineer since the first album and Steve Averill has become U2's designer and 'keeper of their image', after he was asked to become the band's manager in the late 1970s, a position he refused.

The second strategy lies in the nature of the contracts that U2 signed. The very first one dates from 1980 and was signed with Island Records. Despite being bought by Polygram in 1989 (Polygram itself merged with Universal Music – part of the Vivendi-Universal group – in 1999 when their parent company Seagram bought them out) the name of the original label has appeared on every U2 record to date.

Why was the signing of that contract so important? According to the band members, no other company wanted U2 on their catalogue. But it seems that Island Records offered the young band the opportunity to stay in Dublin and to grow at their own pace, without the pressure that is too common in the business to produce three hit singles in a row within a very short space of time. So that first contract allowed U2 to stay on their home turf, while growing artistically.

As Bono put it in 1980: 'Living in London, it is possible to get blown up too quickly and finally blown out. You can get swallowed up and it becomes difficult to see yourself objectively.'[37] Island Records had clout despite not being a major. It was one of the biggest independent labels in the world, having on its roster the legendary reggae singer Bob Marley and his group The Wailers, amongst others. U2 had a five-year contract and had to deliver four albums. The initial amount paid to them was £100,000 sterling, with £50,000 for recording and the same amount for touring. As for the publishing rights, they belonged to Blue Mountain Publishing, also owned by Island Records founder, Chris Blackwell. The contract was renegotiated in 1984 with U2 in a much stronger position to make demands. The album *War* had reached the number one position in the British charts and U2 were nominated for band of the year in 1983 by the readers of the American magazine *Rolling Stone*. The deal, negotiated by Paul McGuinness and U2's accountants, Ossie Kilkenny and Owen Epstein, gave the band a $2 million advance on the recording of the next four albums and doubled their royalties. They also had total freedom in selecting the producer of the albums, and the record company had to accept the finished product as it was. More crucially, they became financially secure for the rest of their lives as they now owned the publishing rights to their songs. Between 1989 and 1998, three more contracts were negotiated, giving them, for example, in 1993, $60 million for six albums, plus a 25 per cent royalty rate, which is more than generous and rarely seen.

The freedom of the first contract followed by the financial security of the others gave U2 the means to stay in Ireland. It is very possible that they would have had to emigrate had they not secured such good deals.

The third main strategy lies in the type of audience the band were looking for. They literally went on a trail of conquest that would prove inspired and that would yield results.

Of course, they first built an Irish audience which is faithful and dedicated to this day. They focused on the gigs as these would strengthen their reputation as a live act and eventually constitute part of the myth, as they became legendary. We must understand the era in which U2 was founded to explain this particular strategy. The year they met (1976) was also the year of the birth of punk. The members of U2 were inevitably inspired by its energy, its vitality, its power. However, they refused the notions of violence and nihilism associated with it.

Bono, Larry, The Edge and Adam wanted to have an international career. They wanted to conquer the world. They therefore needed an international audience. Early on they started playing gigs in England, in small clubs. But their main objective was America. Inspired by the British bands of the 1960s who saw the

USA as an essential part of their career, U2 decided to play live in America and to build an American audience. Bill Graham wrote in a *Hot Press* article in 1989:

> U2 never saw America as their antagonist. Similarly with the earlier generation of the Stones. From '77 on, most new English bands outside the heavy metal camp would distance themselves from those earlier examplars. In contrast, U2 would pick up those classic role models without ever feeling guiltily out of sync.[38]

Thus, out of the 248 concerts that the band played during their *Boy* and *October* tours, half took place in Europe (with 80 in England), the other half taking place in America. Another very important feature of those gigs is that U2 always headlined, therefore controlling their own songs and not running the risk of playing in front of the wrong audience. Finally, the fact U2 played live meant they were following in the footsteps of the greatest rock 'n' roll artists and building a new tradition. Focusing on live performance gave them a head start and an experience that others did not necessarily have. Building a community by playing gigs was an essential part of the relationship the band had with each other, with their employees and most of all, with the audience. U2 went on a completely different course to their contemporaries, who played new-wave, appeared reluctantly on stage and finally could not last because the appeal of that music was not strong enough for people to really stop and listen. Most of the bands of that era were like shooting stars and their music, while fun and sometimes uplifting, was ephemeral and lacked the sincerity that U2's music possessed, as well as U2's sense of commitment towards one another. In fact, at the end of the 1980s, Bill Graham's analysis of British rock music was deeply pessimistic:

> All the visionaries had fled to their desert hermitages. Somehow England had lost the will, imagination and ability to shape any positivist rock populism. Cynicism, self-consciousness and the pop cultural defeats of the early 1980s had poisoned the wells of hope and pushed any rebel rock tradition into parody or off the pike.[39]

At the end of the 1980s, U2 were given the title of band of the decade by several music magazines in Europe (*Hot Press* in Ireland, *Melody Maker* in Britain, *Best* in France, to name a few). The interesting point is that they had all reached a consensus about the place of the Irish band within the world of rock music. U2 were one of the rare bands (if not the only one) to have survived the decade and to have created music that spoke to a generation. That in itself was an achievement. They could not be compared to their contemporaries. They were definitely on their own when it came to longevity and quality. Most of the bands of the 1980s had not survived the era because most did not have the communication skills U2 had. And that is the way we see U2. The community rests on friendship, hard work, a common goal but it also rests on communication.

Communication Skills

The members of U2 developed their communication skills early in their career but they also seemed to possess them naturally.

The theatrical aspect of the early U2 shows isn't mentioned often in the various biographies but appears to be very important and resurfaced years later, during the Zoo TV tour. It is significant in that it tells what U2 is about. It portrays a lot about the band's artistic skills and about the fact that they want to communicate that to the audience, that they want to make them see beyond the mere façade of a rock show, and want to communicate something at a deeper level of music and art.

Towards the end of the 1970s, Bono had already created two characters that had stepped out of his very fertile imagination, the Boy and the Fool.

> Bono was exciting in those early days, always trying out new routines, such as his boy in a box act, where he would mime opening a box, to find himself in another, then another, then another ... talking agitatedly about this predicament. Bono grabbed the audience constantly, over and between songs, never knowing when to shut up.[40]

The singer used those characters to try and communicate as much as possible with his audience. If he could not stay quiet and just sing the songs, it is probably because of this desire to communicate. However, if, to some, it was and is an endearing trait, to others, it was and is difficult to bear and many people in Ireland have often felt embarrassed at Bono's constant talking. I heard many people over the years complain about this and they would often say: 'He'd better just sing and shut up for a while.' However, verbal communication is the medium of rock 'n' roll, as the vast majority of songs have words. And most people want to know what the songs mean. The audience at a rock show needs at least a little verbal communication. Andrew Goodwin actually gives a very interesting example of how that need arises. He talks about the English pop band, the Pet Shop Boys, and about their 1991 world tour where the band, instead of simply singing the songs, decided to act them out, to portray the songs in character and never to talk to the audience. Neil Tennant and Chris Lowe acted out scenarios around the songs, performing around vocalists and dancers. However, despite the effort to almost shut off the audience from the show and 'to close off the usual channels of communication, the Pet Shop Boys found that their fans expected them to step out of the diegesis of the song and address them directly'.[41] In other words, people wanted to be pointed at, sung at, touched. They wanted to be recognised. Theatre in its purest sense within rock 'n' roll doesn't work. Theatre, where a play is performed, a story told, and where people don't expect to be looked at and talked to is exactly that, theatre. They come, they watch the story unfold in front of their eyes, they applaud and the actors only interact with them during the applause. A rock 'n' roll audience needs to be interacted with throughout the show. They literally want to be part of it. And that is what U2, like most bands, give their audience.

Zoo TV

During the Zoo TV tour, the band achieved a balance between the music and the more theatrical aspect of the show. Bono created two alter egos. One was The Fly, inspired by the song. He appears first in the video. Bono said about the song and the character that it was 'like Jerry Lee Lewis and Jimmy Swaggart, in my mind, are the same guy. The song was written like a phone call from hell but the guy liked it there. It was this guy running away – "Hi, honey, it's hot, but I like it here." The character is just on the edge of lunacy. It's megalomania and paranoia.'[42] In fact, the whole concept of the Zoo TV tour is contained in that clip: the interactive TV (Bono sitting in front of Bobsboxes and using the remote control to swap channels), the slogans used during the show (for instance, 'Everything you know is wrong', or 'Watch more TV', appearing in the background), the Zoo TV logo itself, and of course, The Fly.

During the tour, The Fly was present at the very beginning of the show, wearing his famous 'Fly shades' and singing 'Zoo Station'. During the American shows dubbed 'Outside Broadcast', the second alter ego appears, this time especially created for the show. The Mirrorball Man was a strange character because he was trying to be so many people at once: he was a car salesman who was like a gameshow host who was trying to act like a preacher, trying to convert his audience to the god of money, in his gold lamé suit and his stetson hat. At the end of the song 'Desire', he would throw dollar bills into the audience. He acted as if he was performing in a show in Las Vegas.

The third and most interesting alter ego, the most flamboyant, the funniest and also the saddest in some ways is Mr MacPhisto. Bono describes him as The Fly down the years. He first appeared during the Zooropa leg of the tour and reflected the European state of confusion in 1993. He is the last of the rock stars but resembles an old music-hall actor. He tries to recreate the golden era of rock 'n' roll. But he is also the devil as the last rock star, the Fallen Angel, Satan as a mixture of Elvis Presley, Frank Sinatra and a 1930s Berlin cabaret singer. Elements of each appear in the character. He is also Goethe's Mephistopheles in *Faust*. He is all of those things and more. He is also Bono, which is something that should not be forgotten. Each time he appeared on stage, he recited a long monologue about whatever he was thinking at that moment. He also made a phone call at the end of each of his speeches. In fact, the phone calls had become famous at that stage. In America, Bono was trying to ring the White House nightly to talk to George Bush, or phone a pizza place to order 1,000 pizzas (100 ended up being delivered!). In Dublin, he phoned his house and his young daughter's voice was recorded on the answering machine, literally ordering him to take his horns off before he could go back home!

In Sydney, Australia, he threw himself into another long monologue:

Look what you've done to me. You've made me very famous and I thank you. I know you like your popstars to be exciting so I bought these. Now my time among you is almost at an end. The glory of Zoo TV must descend and take its place with all the other satellites. Don't fear. I'll be watching you. I leave behind video cameras for interview. So many people are listening tonight. I have a list. People of America, I gave you Bill Clinton. I put him on CNN, NBC, C- SPAN ... Too tall to be a despot. But watch him slowly. People of Asia, your time is coming. Without your tiny transistors, none of this would be possible. People of Europe, when I came among you, you were squabbling like children. Now you're all hooked up to one cable, as close together as stations on a dial. People of the former Soviet Union, I've given you capitalism. So now you can all dream of being as wealthy and glamorous as me. People of Sarajevo, count your blessings. There are those all over the world who have food, heat and security but they're not on TV like you are. Frank Sinatra, I give you MTV, demographics, you're welcome! Salman Rushdie, I give you decibels! Goodbye, Squidgy! I hope they give you Wales! Goodbye, Michael! I hope you get your new penis. Goodbye, neo-Nazis! I hope they give you Auschwitz! Around about this time I often make a phone call, sometimes to the president of the United-States. But not tonight. Tonight I'm going to call a taxi.[43]

This was one of the last concerts of the tour and he seems to have wrapped the whole of Zoo TV in that last speech. From Zoo TV, to Bill Clinton, to Sarajevo, to Salman Rushdie (the writer came on stage at one of the London shows), to Princess Diana, to all the changes that took place in the world in a very short space of time. Elements of postmodernism are clearly marked here: the will to bring down barriers between genres, for instance, to blur the barrier between the aesthetic and the commercial, between art and commerce, between high and low culture, all of it being the symbol of a new phase of capitalism, characterised by the new technologies, globalisation, new social classes. The use of television during the shows, the mere fact that the tour was called Zoo TV points towards that idea of postmodernism, television being one of its most important symbols.

Bono made the obvious connection between Zoo TV and the early U2 shows:

> Those early Dandelion Market concerts, those McGonagles concerts were actually quite similar to where we are now (...) Surrealism – Irish surrealism, those ideas that Zoo TV plays with, we were playing with them back then, but we never knew what we were doing ...[44]

There is again a connection between U2 and dadaism. It lies at the inter-section of the punk movement, U2's early shows and The Virgin Prunes. Where U2 quickly embraced the mainstream, the Prunes were provocative in their stage performances and directly inspired by the dada movement. Both bands were also inspired by punk and punk was inspired by dada. Greil Marcus, in a very origi-nal and unique work, talks of that connection. He says: 'In the early days of London punk, one could hardly find an article on the topic without the word 'dada' in it: punk was "like dada", everybody said, though nobody said why, let alone what it was supposed to mean.'[45] One can indeed find in the punk move-ment founding elements of dadaism: the rejection of high culture, of the domi-nant culture, visual and verbal provocation, subversion, the idea of anarchy. In fact, the Sex Pistols' 'Anarchy in the UK' could have been its anthem. Despite the fact that U2 were more or less always part of the mainstream, they also had a more intellectual approach to their music than most bands.

> This thing with dada and surrealism is very interesting ... But that's not rock 'n' roll. That's very different. Rock 'n' roll is about being cool. Dada is shav-ing one side of your moustache off. That's where we're coming at rock 'n' roll. That was the birth of the uncool, as far as we were concerned.[46]

U2 never wanted to be cool, as is most often the case with rock 'n' roll bands. They feel rock 'n' roll in their own way without ever conforming to a specific way of being or thinking but they also have an intellectual approach to it. They try to analyse it and it was at its most obvious during the Zoo TV tour. They went back to dada for those shows. But they added the technology. They mentioned the Cabaret Voltaire, they took inspiration from other shows, and they tried to communicate this intellectual search to their audience.

However, the songs were still the essence of the show, as they are supposed to be, and Bono became one or the other of his alter egos only at certain times during the concerts. He still talked to the audience, either as himself, or, more interestingly as Mr MacPhisto, for instance. He played a very theatrical role, yet engaged the audience, almost as a comedian does. He was MacPhisto but he was also Bono. At times, you even wondered who was who amid all the madness of a rock 'n' roll show.

The show worked really well because of the type of communication it tried to establish and despite the obvious connection to postmodernism. Bono knew early on that rock was more than just music: 'Rock 'n' roll is always married into theatre, poetry, lots of other mediums',[47] even if the music is its most important feature.

Art as a Means to Communicate Ideas

Rock 'n' roll, as perceived by U2, is art on a massive scale. It is popular art. It is art that touches people. It is universal and it continues to touch new generations. However, I would stress that a lot people who were young in the 1960s and who got to love rock 'n' roll still feel a connection to that music. Of course, a majority of rock records are bought by younger generations but it is certain that some people who are over 35 still like to listen to rock 'n' roll songs. Rock is reaching more and more people but has also kept an older fan base. It is bridging the generation gap. U2's fan base is getting older as well but I have met people who are fifteen or twenty years younger than me and who have fallen in love with U2's music the way I did in the early 1980s. A rock 'n' roll band can bridge the generation gap by communicating through their music. And what better tool to communicate their ideas, ideals and therefore to communicate their music could U2 have used? Rock 'n' roll is communication at its most simple and its most complex. It is the art of communication at its most extreme because it plays directly to and at the audience. A rock show is playing on a massive scale a music that touches each person in a different way. That is why it is so complex and yet, U2 have been able to recognise the fact that they could play to 50,000 people but that they were also capable of reaching each person in that audience on a personal level. It is a complete contradiction in itself but it works.

The Seduction Game

There is one last element that was mentioned many times but rarely in the terms I am going to use now. And it applies not only to *Achtung Baby* and the Zoo TV tour but also to U2 in the 1990s.

That element is seduction in its purest sense but also seduction as a means of communication. Let's go back to U2 in the 1980s. Their music talks to a generation, they are socially conscious, their clothes are dark, their image is one of seriousness and lack of humour. And one thing that most rock musicians use as a tool to conquer their audience is seduction. However, the members of U2 seem to have deliberately forgotten about that aspect of rock. They turn to the music, play it with all they have and they actually don't need to excite their audience visually, they don't need to seduce them in a sensual sense. The music seems to be enough.

Come the end of the 1980s and U2 have become megastars. They are on the cover of *Time* magazine and have become monstrously big with *Rattle and Hum*; so much so that they don't know how to handle the phenomenon they have helped create; so they reinvent themselves. And they do it by seducing the next generation the way a young band would to conquer their first fans. They use the image they have created to talk in a different way to the 1990s generation. If the generation of the 1980s can easily see through all the hype, (after all they grew up with U2), the 1990s generation is still naive. And as a matter of course, Bono is voted the sexiest male artist of 1992 by the readers of *Rolling Stone* magazine. It is that confusion and that change in U2's method of communication that is interesting. U2 used seduction retrospectively, when they were already as famous as they could have been. Bono especially changed his image dramatically. The singer, as the frontman of the band, was supposed to be the most interesting character in the band. And he played that role really well, becoming what a lot of people thought he was, a megalomaniac who did not accept that fact. But by becoming that, he also had to change his image. He had to change his haircut, his clothes. He even started smoking. He wore his fly shades everywhere he went. And he went all the way to seduce his audience. He did things on stage that he had not done before. The use of the camcorder, for instance, was very suggestive. He was like a voyeur, catching everything on film. The sexual element was very present, whereas it had not been seen before at a U2 concert (in the 1980s, even the girls he pulled out of the audience were rather well-behaved). On some of the footage of the Zoo TV tour, he played with the camera that was filming him, bringing it down to his crotch and making suggestive movements. Some of the girls that he pulled up from the crowd to dance with him during the gigs were very daring, and were (I would almost say finally) behaving like groupies. We can relate one incident at a London concert during Zooropa where a girl climbed on to the stage during the song 'Baby Face'. Bono lay down, she climbed on top of him and there was a simulation of sex. That type of incident, whatever people's beliefs, is almost inevitable, considering the circumstances. All of a sudden, the members of U2 were seen as sexual beings, and not simply socially conscious superheroes, whose love songs are rare and obscure. The level of communication is therefore different. Here the senses are much more involved and people react on a more instinctive level. This seduction game worked well for a while, but U2 went back to a more simple and authentic approach with their album *All That You Can't Leave Behind*.

However, the 1990s approach has left traces and U2 could never be seen again as a one-dimensional band. The history that they carry with them has shaped the community and has given it a new lease of life.

U2 are great communicators and that is one of the reasons why they are successful. They seem to know exactly how to turn on an audience, and how to instil a sense of belonging to a very special community and sharing special moments.

However, there is one question that is nagging at Bono and he came back to it in an interview with the American talk show host Oprah Winfrey in 2004. He observes:

It's much easier to be successful than it is to be relevant. The tricks won't keep you relevant. Tricks might keep you popular for a while, but in all honesty, I don't know how U2 will stay relevant. I know we've got a future. I know we can fill stadiums. And yet, with every record, I think, is this it? Are we still relevant?

It's a very important and fundamental question that Bono asks, which is how to survive the present in the midst of new generations, new ways of thinking, new ideas. How to be a witness of your time without sounding old-fashioned, without showing that you are trying too hard? The question is also how to keep on communicating with the audience on the same level? So far, U2 have succeeded in that challenge through their communication skills and through their understanding of the times they live in. Their sense of independence and their 'Irishness' have no doubt helped them in that endeavour.

2

'IRISHNESS' AND INDEPENDENCE

In the late 1980s, in his book *Across the Frontiers: Ireland in the 1990s*, the Irish philosopher Richard Kearney interviewed some famous artists about what it meant to be Irish. Amongst them was Bono. The singer explained what it means for him to be Irish and how it relates to U2's music:

> When I was growing up I didn't know where I came from ... I didn't know if I was middle class, working class, Catholic, Protestant ... I knew I was from Ballymun but I didn't know what that meant. I didn't know I was Irish until I went to America. I never actually thought about it (...) It is curious that U2 are seen as this 'Irish' thing. So much emphasis is placed on it. And we ourselves emphasise it. But if you look at the surface level of music – its obvious content – there's maybe nothing very Irish about it. It comes from a suburban blank generation which I grew up in, watching cartoons on TV (...) That was the real world, concrete, grey, kicking footballs and admiring English football stars. That's the culture I came from, and that's what our music reflects, on the surface at least (...) However, I now realise that beneath the surface there are certain Irish characteristics to the music ... even the choice of words. Our producer, Brian Eno, said that he thought that I was a better poet than a songwriter ... What I think he meant by that was the sound, rhythm and colours of the words seem at times as important as the meaning. The love of language for its own sake and not just as a vehicle

to comment on or describe events, seems to me to be very Irish – you grow up reading Joyce for God's sake or Beckett, and they seem to abuse and therefore use the English language in new and interesting ways (…) To me the sound and colour of the language in a song like 'A Sort of Homecoming' is more Irish [than 'Sunday Bloody Sunday']: 'The wind will crack in wintertime / A bomb-blast lightning waltz / No spoken words … just a scream … / See the sky the burning rain, she will die and live again / Tonight, we'll build a bridge across the sea and land.' This is not American folk or blues. The words are much more influenced by poets like Heaney or Kavanagh … than say Woody Guthrie.[1]

Bono wasn't as aware of being Irish when he was younger, in the early days of U2. As John Waters points out, early U2 interviews don't mention Ireland 'other than as an incidental backdrop',[2] and he suggests that the place and era that the members of U2 grew up in had little to do with the construction of their identity. He says that he himself grew up and didn't fit in an Ireland that was ideologically constructed of 'a landscape comprising the Lemass Era, the Catholic Church and The Late Late Show'.[3] He was aware of what was happening around him but his worries were more down to earth (school, home, having fun with friends, listening to Radio Luxemburg and John Peel.) Where I wouldn't agree with John Waters is where he says: 'U2 grew up in a context that was not merely external to the cultural entity that was Ireland, but external to the Dublin of the time as well. You might say that they developed as a reaction to both.'[4] U2 didn't grow up in a cocoon, and if Bono says that what he remembers most is violence, that was part of the Dublin they grew up in, another facet, the lower middle-class side of things. That is not to say that they came from nowhere. They may have had that feeling but they unconsciously soaked up the atmosphere around, the 'Irishness' that existed despite what they thought. The most concrete example is the Dublin accent that both Bono and Larry have. They didn't get it 'from nowhere'. One's environment is essential to the construction of one's identity and is very powerful.

Sometimes, it takes someone a long journey to become aware of their identity though, and it may be that U2 were simply too young to have been really conscious of who they were when it came to their roots. We often take for granted where we come from. And it may have been even more difficult for them, considering the context. But they were all if not born, then bred in Ireland and their identity as Irishmen would inevitably surface sooner or later.

For Bono, America seems to have been a powerful catalyst of that recognition.

'Irishness' could be rediscovered and redeveloped from there. It could be indeed reinvented. He says:

> [America] is the land of reinvention. It was never about where you come from, it's always about where you're going. And people accept that beginning again is at the heart of the American dream. The Irish came over from a death culture, of famine and of colonisation, which of course was emasculation. They found a new virility in America. They began a new life in America.[5]

However, up until then, 'Irishness' was dormant in him and only needed a trigger to come out. Richard Kearney himself observes:

> The Irish thing surfaces, almost in spite of oneself, when the obsession with a unique identity is abandoned. The reason we could not find it was perhaps that we were looking too hard, too self-consciously, too fanatically. Now, as we are rediscovering ourselves through our encounter with others, reclaiming our voice in our migrations through other cultures and continents – Europe, Britain, North America – we are beginning to realise that the Irish thing was always there. (...) It takes the migrant mind to know that the island is without frontiers, that the seas are waterways connecting us with others, that the journey to the other place harbours the truth of homecoming to our own place.[6]

It seems that U2 needed to go away and to play music that had on the surface no connection with Ireland to go back to their roots. There was an obvious need in the band to find their roots so as to continue on their musical journey. U2's music is rock music but is also in spirit Celtic, therefore doesn't have a unique identity but several layers that needed to be rediscovered.

This question of identity is a very difficult one for U2, as it is for anyone else. It may be even more difficult because of the origins of the different members. This mixture is quite strange, almost uncanny, for a band who at every turn will put forward the fact that they are Irish. Despite Adam Clayton's and The Edge's English and Welsh origins, despite the fact the majority are Protestant, they all consider themselves Irish. It isn't surprising, is it? Adam and The Edge were raised in Ireland and are part of it. The place you are raised in is as important, if not more so, than the place you were born. By all accounts, their parents integrated into the Irish community and grew very fond of the place. Do they not all still live in Ireland after all?

One sentence stands out in John Waters' book, *Race of Angels*. He says, running the risk of being too obvious: 'U2 are Irish.' Reading further, I understood why he was so insistent. He points that out not as a self-evident fact but as a stress on their origin, which may sometimes be forgotten, if one considers the type of music the band plays. The fact also that the origins of two of the members of U2 lie elsewhere and that there is, in fact, a Catholic minority in the band, as opposed to the majority in the country. This is only surface. The Edge and Adam Clayton feel as much part of Ireland as Bono and Larry Mullen. All of them insist that they are Irish and proud of it. But this mixture is interesting because it has allowed for a unique influence in the band. John Waters might have been afraid that people would forget that U2 are Irish because of the music they play and their international success.

The fundamental question that needs to be asked here is if one of the reasons U2 are as successful as they are is because of their 'Irishness', and if it is also the reason for their sense of independence.

I believe there is a connection between the fact that they are Irish and their sense of independence, which they have displayed throughout their career.

From the beginning, U2 were atypical. They did not want to be part of the London or New York rock scene. They did not want overnight success. They wanted to be Irishmen playing rock 'n' roll in Ireland and later, all over the world. And they wanted to do it well, to do it at their own pace. It looks as if they wanted to create a new tradition that did not yet exist in the form we know today.

A New Rock Culture?

Bands like Thin Lizzy or Taste were, despite themselves, swallowed up in the British music industry. Outside the English-speaking world, everybody thought they were English. They played rock 'n' roll after all. On the other hand, everyone interested in rock music around the world knows that U2 are Irish. The members of the band work and live in Ireland and when they started, it was the first time[7] an Irish rock band could say: not only are we Irish and we come from Dublin, but we also live and work here and we can make it from here. That period is when a real Irish rock culture and tradition started emerging. That particular Irish rock culture had to emerge so that Irish rock could become independent from its British counterpart. But it took time to build what is now beginning to become a tradition, in the good sense of the word. An interesting example of this process is the Irish Music Rights Organisation (IMRO), an official organisation which administers copyrighted music in Ireland and has over 60 affiliated foreign members.

This is just one example, but there are others: the number of recording studios, the number of artists, the number of records sold. The Irish music industry has come a long way since U2 decided to make Dublin their base. It still needs to develop but it is already successful considering the size of the country. And U2 were instrumental in allowing that development to take place. There is no doubt that the spirit of independence that is characteristic of the band has a lot to do with that.

Independence

The idea of independence as seen by U2 was strongly shaped by their origins. It falls within the scope of a wider independence ideal, historically speaking. Ireland fought British rule for centuries and only became independent in 1921. But that influence (amongst others) could never be forgotten and shaped what the Irish are today. That cannot be denied. Even the former president of Ireland, Mary Robinson, stated in her 1995 address to the Houses of the Oireachtas that:

> This island has been inhabited for more than 5,000 years. It has been shaped by pre-Celtic wanderers, by Celts, Vikings, Normans, Huguenots, Scottish and English settlers. Whatever the rights or wrongs of history, all those people marked this island: down to the small detail of the distinctive shipbuilding of the Vikings, the linen making of the Huguenots, the words of Planter balladeers. How could we remove any one of these things from what we call our 'Irishness'? Far from wanting to do so, we need to recover them so as to deepen our understanding.[8]

Ireland could not but have been enriched by all those external influences, and rock music is but a very vibrant and modern example of that influence. It has undoubtedly shaped U2, what they were then and what they are now. But U2 have also shaped Irish rock music.

U2 were definitely influenced by everything American and British in rock music but they never wanted to be part of the British music industry solely because they wanted to be self-sufficient first and had their eyes on the world.

> We accepted the UK – they never accepted us (…) I love the English reserve, I love the rigour, but I think we were just kind of (…) too emotional for them, and just too in-your-face (…) Some of the bands [in those days] could have been contenders, but the mood of the time and media didn't encourage world domination like the Beatles, Stones, or even the Sex Pistols.[9]

U2 have created a space of their own, in their own country, because they have never wanted anyone else to tell them what to do. As always with U2, reinvention was the key word. So they were pioneers and reinvented what it was to be an Irish rock band. In the past if you were involved in an Irish rock band you could not remain in Ireland because the infrastructure was so poor you could not have gone far. U2 decided that, for them, it would be different. The fact that Windmill Lane was functional was obviously a big bonus, but they felt that they could make it from Dublin and be independent of anything that could hinder their slow but meticulous development. They were clever in their approach. They did not want to be part of the London rat race and find themselves at a loose end after a couple of singles. Everybody was cool in those days. They did not want to be cool, they wanted to be hot. Bono says: 'It was us against the world. We weren't gonna be part of any scene.'[10]

But U2 also recreated a conquering strategy of the world. Coming from a conquered nation that had bled profusely for freedom, they became conquerors of a new type that had not been seen before in Ireland. They conquered the world with a very loud and wonderful tool: popular music. That way, they could be seen and heard. And their contribution to Irish culture in the late twentieth and early twenty-first centuries is as important as was Joyce's contribution or Seán Ó Riada's, for instance. What I'm saying, in a larger context, is that (Irish) popular culture is as influential in the early twenty-first century as any other kind of culture.

To me, because U2's members were very much their own people and did not want to be part of any scene or any trend, their 'Irishness' was consequently exacerbated, or at least the band's origin. That is why I believe that 'Irishness' and independence in U2 are inextricably linked.

'Irishness'

Before I move on to U2, I need to answer some questions. Where does 'Irishness' stem from? What exactly is it? Does it stem from a sense of place rather than a sense of self? It is indeed very difficult to give a precise answer. 'Irishness' is linked to the question of nation and to the precise nature of the Irish themselves. It has always been there and has grown with the nation. It is what it is nowadays because of Ireland's history. To give a definition of it is rather difficult. I can only offer an outsider's point of view. I believe that a phenomenon similar to that of 'Irishness' exists in every country. 'The only unique thing about the Irish, perhaps, is their utter conviction that there is something unique about being Irish,' says Dennis Kennedy.[11] Perhaps he is right. However, I believe that the Irish have constructed an identity that resembles no other, an identity in which 'Irishness' isn't a mere word but represents the past and also the present, and the future. They have a history in which they had to fight for their identity, and reclaim it. The Irish identity is complex, watered down by colonisation in one way, different from its origins, but also enriched by it. I believe that any country that was colonised suffered deeply in its heart and soul. However, there were not many options and the Irish fought hard for their independence. They gained freedom through it but they also gained something more, something that resurfaced decades later. They became part of the world. That history is fairly recent. Therefore, it is quite understandable that trying to define 'Irishness' is a perilous exercise. Richard Kearney's interviews for *Across the Frontiers: Ireland in the 1990s*, with four people involved in the arts expressing themselves – the poet Paul Durcan, the film-maker Neil Jordan, the painter Robert Ballagh and Bono – is an attempt at defining 'Irishness'. It is a state of mind. The notion of 'Irishness' is very elusive. Yet I am convinced that every Irishman and woman feels connected to that notion of Irishness. It seems there are as many definitions of 'Irishness' as there are people on the island of Ireland. And that definition seems to change slightly with time as the country grows and changes. 'Irishness' today is modern. 'Irishness' means freedom and that's probably why U2 felt able to be Irish and become international rock stars. As John Waters put it: 'U2 are Paddys with attitude.'[12]

'Irishness' can be found inside and outside Ireland. It is nowadays an all-encompassing concept, gathering under its flag those who were born and bred in Ireland and those who were born and bred abroad, but who have Irish ancestors. The social anthropologist, Caroline Legrand, suggests that some people of Irish extraction, who are seeking their roots in Ireland, will automatically say their ancestors were forced out of the country, without any evidence, and this belief is a prevalent one, whereas there is evidence that many emigrants actually left Ireland seeking a better life abroad. Those people were not exiles, in the same way as others who indeed had been expropriated and forced to flee the country.[13] The glorification of the past is prevalent, an aspect that turned some Americans into supporters of the IRA. This was a dangerous game to play and was denounced by a couple of rock bands, notably the Northern Irish band Ruefrex. In their song, 'The Wild Colonial Boy', they ferociously denounced the support given by Americans to NORAID, the IRA's fund-raisers in the US: 'Well, I'm the Emerald Isle's own son / I was born on stateside, Wisconsin / And your troubles sound like Hollywood / They sound real good to me. / The rush to be Irish now is on / The queue is standing ten miles long / And would-be green men stand in line / To swap their stories tall.' The song ends mercilessly: 'What with collection time and all / With charities, functions and balls / It really gives me such a thrill / To kill from far away.'

U2 were also faced with the American support for the IRA. Bono talked to English music writer and reporter, Robin Denselow about the genesis of 'Sunday Bloody Sunday' and talked of his trying to change attitudes: 'They just didn't understand. When Bobby Sands was dying on hunger strike the American audiences were virtually throwing money on stage.'[14] 'Irishness' was used by some people to glorify the IRA. It was a distorted view of Ireland, the glorification of a struggle that had turned to terrorism. That is how some people viewed it.

For U2, it was different. They came from the inside. They saw the situation in their country and for them, only a peaceful struggle could overcome the Irish issue. They themselves denounced the IRA and a direct consequence was that they were considered traitors in some quarters. But people soon realised that: 'it wasn't that we weren't nationalists, or that we weren't supporters of their grievances.'[15] U2's sense of 'Irishness' therefore came from another place. The band have had the power to voice their concerns and point of view, unlike so many.

But U2's 'Irishness' was also revived when they went to America. Bono said that 'rock 'n' roll became a passport home'.[16] The relationship U2 have with America isn't as unusual as it may seem if looked at from the outside. Indeed a foreigner could easily wonder why U2 have such a close link with America. After all, the Irish have been emigrating to the US since the Great Famine in the nineteenth century and, for those whom emigration isn't a distant memory, have kept in touch with their roots and families. Others, whose ancestors emigrated long ago, have tried to trace back those roots, through the so-called 'roots-tourism' phenomenon.[17] If U2 have always felt so much at home in America, it is because of the 40 million or so Americans of Irish descent. That they did not have to emigrate to make it in the music business may have played a part in it and it is possible that a kind of empathy developed towards those who had to leave behind so much loved a land. Music is undoubtedly also a contributing factor. The fact that U2 play rock 'n' roll, a hybrid music, and the fact that Irish music was exported from Ireland with the emigrants, to be later reimported in another form (country music), is quite interesting. Bono is the 'White Nigger' (Richard Kearney's section on Bono is called that). The singer explained that he was called that by a black musician: 'I took it as he meant it, as a compliment. The Irish, as the blacks, feel like outsiders. There's a feeling of being homeless, migrant but I suppose that's what all art is – a search for identity.'[18] It is interesting that Kearney should have chosen that particular expression, and it appears that it is this ambivalence within the Irish identity of being of one place but of feeling uprooted in many ways, as if the ghost of emigration had colonised the Irish psyche, a wound that can never quite heal.

This is why U2's identity is a complex one and in no other place is it more complex than in the music.

In 1992, Bono talked to John Waters about the album *Achtung Baby*, about the Zoo TV tour, and about 'Irishness':

> On one level, I like to say, 'This is Irish. We are Irish. Completely and utterly '90s Irish.' It's just not about 'Irishness' or Ireland – it is, I believe, that Irish culture is much more than speaking as Gaeilge, or Gaelic football or all these things. That's why I say our music is about 'Irishness'.
>
> I think that there's something else much more interesting, and valuable, in the European context and I don't know quite what it is. Because we don't have that other stuff, and yet we feel very Irish. And feel valued for our 'Irishness' when we're away. So we must be something, because I don't have those badges. I don't go singing in every bar or do all those things that are supposed to make you Irish.[19]

For Bono, 'Irishness' is definitely a state of mind and it is definitely real. It is tangible but also intangible. It has many facets and can also create conflict: 'Even while on the island, [people] have had great difficulty agreeing on a definition of 'Irishness', disputes leading both to split hairs and split heads.'[20]

The Irish have a tradition of story-telling that is bound to 'Irishness' and Bono's gift of the gab as well as his gift of writing are things that are undeniably Irish.

Culture

It seems that U2 don't want to get too involved in the debate and live rather than explain their 'Irishness'.

And what we can say of U2 is that the place they were born in has had a tremendous impact on their music and on what they are as human beings. They are definitely a product of their environment and even if that seems obvious, it must be underlined.

Because of their chosen career, however, the area that seems to be the most illuminating to understand U2's 'Irishness' is cultural. I have chosen to analyse the effects of Irish culture on the band to see how it has, consciously or not, influenced the band.

Indeed, the influence of Irish culture on U2 and their music has undoubtedly allowed the band to actively take part in the cultural life of the country but it has also shaped their 'Irishness'. In fact, the consequences of that influence are seen to this day.

NATION AND IDENTITY

John Waters says very obviously but very wisely that: 'U2 have emerged from a place and a time – Ireland in the '70s – which was the product of a historical and evolutionary process, and that they are as faithful a representation of that place and time as it is possible to conceive of.'[21] He goes on to say that this fact is one of the reasons for U2's success and appeal and that this idea is the hardest to put across to the Irish. It is quite obvious that U2 holds an ambiguous place. It isn't, however, so obvious that the Irish don't understand what U2 represent in Ireland. They simply find it hard to accept the place U2 occupies within Ireland, when they are international stars and the Irish may feel that U2 do not belong to them, because of their success.

U2 were born in a nation that, for a long time, sought an identity lost through colonisation, or at least it seemed that way. When the Irish conquered their identity again, it was inevitably more complex and far more mixed than at the point of origin, and seeking to get back an identity that would be pure and free of any influence could only fail.

Larry, Bono, The Edge and Adam grew up in the 1960s and 1970s in a country that had become more stable economically but where it was made difficult for rock music to find a place. When they reached adolescence, the country had changed again and was more dynamic. Culturally, the country grew and changed dramatically, especially because it had become a much more consumer-orientated place, the influence of television advertisements being very strong. TV had a strong impact on the developing mass culture and the place of rock music changed.

However, Bono doesn't seem to agree with the fact that Irish culture was very much alive in the 1970s. In the 2000 TV programme, *From a Whisper to a Scream*, he observes: 'You have to remember where we came from or where I came from at least. We came from nowhere. We came from this place that was just grey concrete, lower middle class, a ghetto of non-culture. The thing I remember the most about growing up is violence.'

For the singer, the Irish culture in which he grew up doesn't seem to exist or rather is overshadowed by violence. He contradicts himself when one looks at some of the previous interviews he gave when he said that he grew up listening to the Dubliners.[22] It seems that his reaction was one of possibly unconscious rejection of the culture he grew up in, rather than a childhood or adolescence in a cultural desert. However, it is rather obvious that if you grew up in Ballymun, in a very modest home and area, your apprehension of culture was rather different from the people who grew up in more prosperous areas. Bono actually describes the place as a no man's land between three areas – Glasnevin,

Finglas and Ballymun – where one had to negotiate his passage between the gangs of youths by pretending to be from such and such an area depending on the gang one met.[23]

U2 was partly founded as a reaction to the violence encountered, to that cultural no man's land, or which was perceived as such. The Lypton Village was also built on that foundation, as well as the Virgin Prunes, since they encompassed the same people anyway. U2 created their own culture, which was necessarily soaked in that culture of origin. Therefore they could create a music that has a resonance and an appeal that are both national and international. How else can we explain the fact that Irish fans as well as foreign fans recognise themselves in the band and their music? John Waters is right when he says that U2's Irish identity is vital to U2's appeal. One can add that U2 evolved in and with an Irish nation and culture that has changed at a striking rate over the past 25 years. The band evolved with time. However, their Irish identity remained intact, despite the music having encountered a high degree of acculturation.

DESIRE FOR INDEPENDENCE
The second influence on U2 is the strong desire for independence.

Following the history of their country, the members of U2 wanted to be independent of the British music industry as early as possible. It's as if they rebelled against it and its influence first of all by basing themselves in Ireland and then by wanting to conquer America, which they looked upon as the territory to conquer, the success of which is astounding. U2's relationship with Great Britain, on the other hand, is rather ambiguous and could well reflect the some-time difficult relationship that Ireland has historically had with its closest neighbour.

RELIGION AND SPIRITUALITY
The third influence on U2 is religion and spirituality which have had lasting consequences on the band. Three out of the four members of the band were profoundly shaped by religion. That is not to say that Adam Clayton lacks any sense of spirituality. I don't think he would be in U2 if he didn't share at least a sense of spirituality with the others. But he has always stayed as far away from religion as he could. In other words, spirituality and religion are two completely different things. It is strange to notice that U2 don't represent the overall religious tendency of the Republic of Ireland. Indeed, only Larry Mullen is Catholic, whereas Bono is Catholic/Protestant and The Edge and Adam Clayton come from Protestant backgrounds. The fact that the members of U2 come from different denominational backgrounds is, of course, due to a chance encounter and we can

surmise that the U2 parents were open-minded enough to send their children to a non-denominational school. We can also safely say that each member of U2 was totally indifferent as to the religious denomination of the others. Indeed, the fact that they joined a movement such as Shalom shows they had found a common ground.

The influence of religion, wherever it came from, was transmitted naturally and the members of U2 did not actually rebel against it but embraced spirituality in an unusual way. Or maybe they did rebel against the religion of their parents by joining Shalom. Whatever the way, it never put into question their faith and if there was a rebellion, it happened for institutional rather than spiritual or ideological reasons.

At the end of the Shalom period, rock 'n' roll seems to have become a place where U2 could find a balance between what they did and their faith, and music was definitely therapeutic.

Spirituality has always lingered in U2's music, even in the 1990s and more recently. Faith is part of U2's core identity, as it is part of Ireland's identity, and even though Bono, for instance, says that he hates religion for what it did to the world, he has never rejected his faith in God.

THE TRADITION OF GENEROSITY

The fourth influence on U2 is the tradition of generosity. It is probably linked to the religious side of Ireland. It is, of course, difficult to generalise the particular influence of religion in the daily life of the Irish. However, they do have a reputation for being generous. There are many charitable organisations which are very active and efficient. Whether it is due to the size of the country or because the Irish are truly a generous nation (and I believe that the latter is true), Catholicism is linked to a culture of sharing and of help towards others. The poor are at the heart of this tradition and the Irish are always present when it comes to lending a hand. Is it surprising in that context that during Live Aid in 1985, they gave more money per capita than any other nation? This is only one example.

The members of U2 have chosen to pursue that tradition with the means at their disposal. Their Christian faith plays a big part in that and they represent a national and religious opinion which is deeply embedded in a history of poverty. During the launch of the United Nations' Human Development Report for 2003, Bono reminded the Irish that they: 'should be familiar with the problems facing developing countries; that we were part of that developing world not too long ago ... the crushing poverty that faces Africa – we are well placed here to understand that.'[24]

Bono did not hesitate to remind the Irish that their history was plagued with many shortages and a lot of poverty before the Celtic Tiger, but that they should also remember that the Irish always were a generous nation despite the poverty, and the economic success of Ireland should not make them complacent. The members of U2 want to continue that tradition which seems inherent to the Irish.

The idea of community is tied to religion and self-sacrifice. The commitment of the band within the community comes from that idea of helping others, whether it is taken in its largest meaning within society and in its more restricted meaning within the rock community.

ARTISTIC CREATION

The fifth influence on U2 lies in the realm of artistic creation. Despite what they say, Bono and Larry were immersed in their culture of origin from the moment they were born. The Edge and Adam, despite being born in England, were immersed in Irish culture from a very early age also. One cannot escape the culture in which one is raised, despite the sometimes profound differences that can exist between two countries. In this particular case, the differences were not as marked as in some other cases.

The Irish cultural tradition, may it be musical or literary, and even if it was acquired in an unconscious manner and runs through the band's music without necessarily being obvious, has had a very special influence on U2.

It is difficult to escape the rich Irish musical tradition. Nowadays, it is even richer, and is found all over the place, in the streets, pubs, shops, radio stations, TV, etc. The singers and musicians that play daily in Dublin's Grafton Street, for instance, the pubs where bands of the traditional or popular arena show off their skills and share their love of music, the TV and radio programmes about music, are all proof of the vitality of music in Ireland. That tradition is part of U2 which in turn are part of it, and the fact that they don't play traditional music as such doesn't really matter. They are still, if subconsciously, influenced by it and U2's music would not be the same without that influence. U2's cultural identity has undoubtedly benefited from that tradition to create a model for Irish rock. Bono took part in that tradition in his own way by recording the duet with Máire Brennan of Clannad 'In a Lifetime' in 1986. Later, in 1991, he wrote the song 'Wild Irish Rose' for the TV programme Bringing It All Back Home. He also took part in The Chieftains' 1995 album, The Chieftains and Friends, with the song they played together, 'The Long Black Veil'.

The influence of Irish literature and of the storytelling tradition is also one of the cultural effects that U2 have integrated in the creative process and the words of some of the songs have an undeniably poetic aspect that is far from the rock tradition and can only come from a strong literary and poetic one.

Like the previous example, Irish writers seem to have a permanent influence on Bono. On 30 April 1989, the singer took part in a charity event organised at the Abbey Theatre in Dublin, and for the occasion put to music two poems by W.B. Yeats, 'September 1913' and 'Mad as the Mist and Snow'. Another reference to Yeats and to the poem 'The Stolen Child' is found in 'A Sort of Homecoming', on the album *The Unforgettable Fire* and in 'New York' on *All That You Can't Leave Behind*: 'In the stillness of the evening / When the sun has had its day / I heard your voice a-whispering / Come away child / New York New York.'

There is the definite impression that this influence has remained hidden within the band only to appear in an ethereal manner in the lyrics and the music. The quest for a musical identity within the band went to the roots of rock, blues and gospel, from Robert Johnson to Bob Dylan, only to return to Ireland.

IRISH ROCK CULTURE

The sixth influence on U2 is Irish rock culture. Even though it barely existed when U2 was formed, it had an influence on them because some bands that originated in Ireland became very successful at home and abroad, though they were based in England. Thin Lizzy, Taste or Them are undeniable influences on more recent Irish rock musicians. It is, however, difficult to know which of them had the most influence on U2. When Bono talks about Stiff Little Fingers' punk rock or Van Morrison's *Astral Weeks*, which he calls legal drugs, one cannot help but notice the influence of early Irish rock. However, staying in Ireland also confirms the wish to reject a tradition which was forced upon the musicians and which made them emigrate in search of an international career. U2 definitely rejected that tradition and, in this way, invented a new one. Bono says that U2 neither found a place in the Irish musical tradition nor in the British rock tradition, which lacked passion, a characteristic that he describes as being quintessentially Irish and which is called soul within the black-American community.[25] By creating a new tradition steeped in Irish, American and British music, U2 found a place where they could flourish artistically.

REBELLION

The seventh influence on U2 can be found in the notion of rebellion. It is quite obvious that U2 wanted to bring a wind of modernity to the Irish rock world. That very attitude could be seen as rebellious towards the culture from which they have emerged. This traditional classical culture did not fit U2's idea of and wishes for artistic freedom. Larry, Bono, The Edge and Adam found it difficult to fit into the culture they came from when they were growing up. They were misfits in that regard and turned their backs on it for a while. Bono especially felt that that culture, whatever it was, needed to be rebelled against and that was what he did. He eventually found a place in rock culture, as did his friends and colleagues of U2.

However, they only rebelled against some aspects of Irish culture and the society they lived in. They were always religious, which was fine by Irish standards but they did embrace, for a while, an extreme side of religion. They may have rebelled after all against a form of organised and accepted religion by joining Shalom. They also have liberal ideas about sex, contraception and divorce, a point of view shared by many people of their generation and younger. But they have never adopted a provocative attitude like The Virgin Prunes and immediately joined the mainstream of rock music. Rebellion in U2's world was always free from aggressiveness, exacerbated sexuality or violence.

While rebelling in some ways against Irish society, they also rejected the more conservative aspects of that society; they embraced, however, the capitalist side of it. They helped the record industry in Ireland and greatly benefited from it. They are also exempt of tax on a big portion of their earnings in Ireland, under the 1969 tax exemption scheme for artists.[26] This must be underlined as one cannot help but wonder how much that particular aspect weighed in the initial decision to remain in Ireland. It was undoubtedly a factor but one could also argue that the members of U2 could not have known as early as 1979 or 1980 that they would be as successful as they are now. The question is therefore open to debate. But Ireland certainly gave U2 one more reason to stay.

AFFECT

The final influence on U2 is that of the affect, or the emotional. It is important to underline that aspect even though it could be perceived as misplaced in the light of the other influences. The bond that unites the Irish to U2 and U2 to the Irish comes from a very deep cultural tie where emotions hold a very important place. The band developed in what could be called a cocoon. Ireland was definitely that for the young U2. But the fans also helped the band in that aspect. It was as if they protected their young idols and wanted them to succeed almost as badly as they themselves did. By staying in Ireland, U2 were sheltered from some of the problems inherent to rock life in London. They also succeeded in creating a real umbilical cord with the country and its inhabitants, which to this day has not managed to be broken. As a matter of fact, they are always welcomed back as heroes when they play in Ireland and never forget to thank the fans for their support and their love throughout the years, because that is exactly that: there is tremendous love on both sides and that love has lasted. Interestingly, Paul McGuinness says: 'I sometimes compare us to a football team, the national football team that has to win the World Cup every four years and everyone expects it. U2 have been winning the World Cup regularly.'[27] But the relationship has also changed through time, and has become complex as U2 have become more and more popular and have become celebrities.

John Waters worries about that aspect and wonders if the image of the members of U2 shown in the press is actually a misrepresentation of what U2's meaning really is, which in turn prevents the Irish from understanding the band.[28] He also claims that Ireland tends to imitate other cultures and as a consequence, the country depends on what foreigners make of Irish popular culture. He gives the examples of The Clancy Brothers and The Cranberries who would both have been ignored in Ireland until they reached a certain amount of success in America. As for Adam Clayton, on the Late Late Show of 16 December 1988, he said it was the press that did not quite get what U2 was about and not the Irish, only to contradict himself in 1994 when he told John Waters:

There is the assumption, just because U2 have been successful, that everybody else who is making records is on the same road – and they're not. I think most people out there, they don't have much of an idea of how we've done what we've done. And why it is the way it is. They just see the effects of it. It either fits into their view of the state of the nation, or it doesn't.[29]

It looks as if Adam was reproaching his compatriots with not being in touch with U2, with really not understanding them. But is it because they became celebrities in the 1990s and therefore became more aloof and less approachable?

Bono, on the other hand, tends to say that he feels that he is approachable and that the fans know that. He feels that: 'We're not really believable as rock 'n' roll stars, though we've gotten much better at it.'[30] As a matter of fact, he doesn't travel with security and is pretty relaxed in that regard. I believe that things have indeed evolved positively from that point of view. The glamourous side of U2 in the 1990s may have hidden that approachable side of U2 but the Irish, in the end, are no fools. And maybe shoving U2 in everybody's face makes people truly fed up with them, which is again understandable. I think one thing is truly typical of U2's relationship with their compatriots: they will be sometimes adored, sometimes despised, often laughed at, but always respected. And amidst those contradictory attitudes, one common aspect emerges: everyone will want a ticket to a U2 show, even those who are not huge fans, who are not really that interested.

It seems, however, and here we will go beyond the polemics on the meaning of U2 or the lack of understanding of the Irish, that the latter do love U2 and also understand what their true meaning is: a contemporary image of Ireland, a band which, through its vision of music and art, was able to put Ireland on the rock map of the world, but also a band who helped Ireland to emerge as a modern and mature country. And the country which gave birth to the U2 phenomenon gave back respect and affection to the band; although we can also say that the other side of the coin is an increasing demand to acknowledge and emphasise that particular point. One example is the controversy over the price of the Dublin concert tickets during the Lovetown tour. The band was to play four concerts due to take place on 26, 27, 30 and 31 December 1989. When the tickets went on sale, the asking price was IR£20.50 for standing and IR£25.50 for seating. It seems that many people were shocked by the high prices. Accusations of hypocrisy and lack of respect for the fans who helped put U2 on the world map of rock 'n' roll flew. Paul McGuinness decided to remedy the situation and sent a declaration from Brisbane, Australia, to the magazine, *Hot Press*:

> U2 have had a policy over the years of giving good value: extra-tracks on B-sides, special guests at our concerts, low ticket prices. Our reputation for fairplay was so well established that we felt the proposed ticket prices were reasonable. In a town where it has cost up to IR£20.50 to see Bruce Springsteen in a field (...) and IR£65 to see Frank Sinatra in a football stadium, we felt that people would be interested in paying to see U2 and B.B. King performing together in a comparatively intimate setting (...) It seems that we have made a mistake. We will therefore be dropping the ticket prices to IR£16 standing and IR£18 seating.

It seems that being Irish and successful worldwide doesn't preclude anyone from the wrath of the Irish when it comes to fairness (in their eyes) or when it comes to their pocket for that matter. 'Irishness' comes at a price! 'Irishness' is therefore what shapes U2's identity in the first place.

'Irishness' in music

The important point to understand 'Irishness' in U2's music is to talk about some bands that have made a difference. The question is whether Irish music in its most general sense is the epitome of 'Irishness'. Is music instrumental in forming a sense of 'Irishness', and what is U2's contribution to that music in the strictly Irish sense and to the idea of 'Irishness' in Ireland and abroad?

Bono said in 1995: 'Back in the 1980s we were the loudest folk band on earth.'[31] He said it again in 2005.[32] It is interesting that he should put U2 in the folk category, but it does make sense in that the band's spirit is very similar to that of the first Irish rock band that springs to mind because they were the creators of Celtic rock: Horslips. Interestingly, Horslips had decided to base themselves in Ireland. They were the first rock band to do so, although they did not achieve the same success as U2. The first concert that The Edge ever saw was Horslips in Skerries, in north County Dublin, in the mid-1970s.[33] At the time, they were huge in Ireland, having broken into 'mainstream consciousness'[34] with another type of hybrid music, a mixture of rock and traditional music. It was a successful attempt at blending the two genres. 'Horslips were part of a younger generation who understood the communicative power of the electric medium and the potency of their Celtic ancestry,' says Mark Prendergast, Irish music author.[35] The drummer, Eamon Carr, who is now a journalist, revealed: 'Our wish was to provide an essentially Irish rock music, something distinctly our own, to galvanise each style with the other. We felt it was important to convey our 'Irishness' – a sense of our own identity and our heritage.'[36] What was important was that they defined Celtic rock and made it into a very successful phenomenon. 'Horslips changed the history of Irish popular music, and possibly much more besides. They acknowledged a hunger for an Irish music that would respect the permanent and yet be new, that would transcend all tradition and yet be real, everyday, spontaneous and true.'[37] Horslips' adventure lasted for about ten years, until 1980. And the relationship with U2? In a very interesting twist, Barry Devlin, the band's bass player, went on to direct several U2 promo videos. As well as that, after Horslips split up, the band had to go to court to regain their record rights which had been acquired in an illegal manner by a Belfast businessman. U2 actually gave financial guarantees for the case.

Although they were hugely popular in some places in America (upstate New York and other East Coast states, as well Chicago and San Francisco), Horslips' Celtic rock innovative sound suffered from a liking by some members of the West Coast sound. The result was that the purely Celtic instruments were abandoned on the album *The Man Who Built America* in 1978. Their attempt at 'breaking America' had failed. Was it because they had left behind what made them great, their true originality and Celtic roots? Whatever the reason, U2 were able to do what Horslips had not because they played music firstly that reflected what the band was good at, and secondly, they played a universally recognisable rock music on the one hand, that was tinted with Celtic spirit, on the other. It was instantly recognisable, yet the 'Irishness' in it floated in the sound of Edge's guitar or in Bono's lyrics. Americans undoubtedly recognised that, albeit unconsciously. That may well be why U2 have always felt at home in America, because of a mutual recognition process. Let's give John Waters the last word on Horslips' influence on U2:

Horslips are the most plausible fragment of ancestry to be found in recent Irish popular culture for U2. In the smallest sense first: their experience provided a map by which U2 manager Paul McGuinness could plan his baby band's assault on the world from Ireland, for which there were few other guides. More importantly, they provided a cultural model by which their putative offspring might seek truthful ways of self-expression out of their own.[38]

Another influential band was Clannad. Formed in 1970, the five members of the group are from Gweedore in County Donegal, are Irish speakers and are all related. They sang most songs in Irish and a 'Celtic spirit' permeates their work. What is interesting is the blend of folk, jazz and classical, later to incorporate rock music, that they used at will to create something truly original, 'a lucid experimental style from which emanated a youthful energy and a potent Celticism'.[39]

The song which was to become the single 'In a Lifetime' was written by Clannad and they were looking for someone to sing it with Máire Brennan. Bono was chosen. U2 had been fans of Clannad for a while and had used their 'Theme from Harry's Game', as post-show music for many of their gigs. The song also appeared on Clannad's 1985 album, *Macalla*. Máire Brennan's pure voice is balanced by Bono's raw singing, The promotional video was shot by Meiert Avis. Filmed in Gweedore, the images fit perfectly the idea behind the song, and add to the fleeting image of a mythological Ireland.

Bono was obviously interested in discovering (rediscovering) his Irish musical heritage with a band whose reputation is still very prominent despite their break-up.

Not that U2 were not interested in doing just that even before 'In a Lifetime'. *The Unforgettable Fire* album was recorded in Slane Castle, in County Meath, a very revealing choice. From then on, U2 would not necessarily record their albums in studios but very often on inspirational ground, in places that inspire them, houses for instance. They draw from those places something special that finds its way through the music, that goes beyond the simple echo or sound of a room. U2 have always recorded in Ireland, and that doesn't stem from a sense of having to do everything in Ireland. Something quite inexplicable, difficult to put in words, what could be termed a 'Celtic energy' in some places is quite powerful and U2 have undoubtedly felt it too. In that context, Slane Castle was a perfect choice to convey an ethereal atmosphere to the whole album, with Brian Eno's help. *The Unforgettable Fire*'s atmospheric music, the pictures of the band in front of an old (haunted?) Irish castle in ruins were essential ingredients to allow what would become the U2 myth to emerge. U2 may be a rock 'n' roll band but Irish ghosts travelled through that particular U2 landscape and Irish mythology was a very powerful influence.

The use of other places around Dublin is also interesting. Adam's home, Danesmoat, was used to record 'Heartland' from *Rattle and Hum*, and much of *Zooropa*.

The fact is that, wherever U2 have gone, whether it is Berlin, Miami or France, they have always returned to their roots to record some tracks, as if Ireland was a necessary step for the songs to be complete, not in a practical, but rather in a soulful way, a true inspirational ground. Indeed, when they went to Berlin to record some tracks, the sessions did not work as well as planned and only two songs came out of it, one of which remains the most emotional and heartbreaking of U2's career, 'One'. When they returned to Dublin, the album came together in Elsinore, a mansion in Dalkey, near The Edge's and Bono's homes. The atmosphere obviously suited U2's creative stride and their most extraordinary and least 'Irish' record was made there. Again, underneath the surface, 'Love Is Blindness' or even to 'Ultraviolet (Light My Way)', convey the same Irish passion that permeates the earlier work.

'Irishness' is therefore not only about words, attitudes and places but also about an atmosphere that is quite difficult to put in words or to explain. Irish legends are a potent reminder of the origins, even though we all know that they are just legends. Leprechauns and banshees serve as reminders of the love the Irish have for a good story. U2 are very good not necessarily at telling stories, but telling fragments of stories. They can blend those fragments with the music, making them into songs of great joy or sadness, from the dark or the bright side, stories of life, stories that matter, themes that we all identify with, and most of all, melodic qualities that could only have come from within an Irish context.

There is no doubt that music is a powerful means of conveying 'Irishness' because it doesn't need explaining. People hear it and feel it and simply soak up the atmosphere it creates. Tourists in Ireland go to pubs to listen to music. This is one of the aspects that is the most attractive to them.

Everything Celtic and especially Irish is very fashionable, although it has slightly changed over the last ten years, with the boom in the Irish economy and the Celtic Tiger. Dublin has become another big European city and may have lost what made it unusual. In 1996, when I talked to Keith Donald, originally from Northern Ireland, a renowned Irish saxophone player, former member of the band Moving Hearts, composer, and writer, who was the first popular music officer for the Irish Arts Council and later in charge of the now defunct Music Base, I asked him why people were so attracted by and interested in Celtic and Irish music. He said:

One of the reasons is that a lot of the folk music in developed countries has remained stagnant. For instance, German folk music, the music of the last century. There hasn't been a way for them to develop their folk music so that it makes a relevant statement in the late twentieth century. Irish tradition-al music has been the subject of constant development. And now there's a kind of global shrinking that we see, the advance of communication in the late part of this century. Irish music has kind of developed to the stage where it's ahead of the pack in world music terms. It has always been developed and its development has been because of a desire in this colonised country to protect what is uniquely Irish. I think that also happens in colonised coun-tries in Africa and I think because Ireland is in a unique position – it has been colonised and yet is part of the developed world – our music has not only survived but has become very strong.

I then moved on to U2 and rock music, and my question was as to the kind of impact, in his opinion, bands like U2 have had over the years on the promo-tion of Irish rock abroad and of Ireland as a country:

Huge, absolutely huge. If you stop anybody under the age of 40 in the street around the world and ask them what they associate with Ireland, it will either be sport or music. It won't be James Joyce, it won't be W.B. Yeats. It will be U2 and it may be The Cranberries. It might be Van Morrison. It can very possibly be Sinead O'Connor. It might be the kind of intangible things like greenness and purity and lack of industrialisation but I think music would be foremost in the consciousness of people.

Nowadays, music is still as important in the consciousness of people. And U2 has had ten more years to make an impact since that interview. They could be considered veterans in their chosen area.

Conclusion

That U2 should find themselves in a book about Celtic music such as June Skinner Sawyers', *The Complete Guide to Celtic Music*, is a real testament to their belonging, albeit in a warped way, to Celtic music. Talking about *The Joshua Tree* she says: 'The themes were hardly Irish (…) nor were the musical influences (…). Yet somehow the group's Irish spirit shone through. It sounded both Irish and American – but it also transcended nationality and music boundaries. In a way, this was soul music. Irish soul music.'[40] Bono says that the Irish have soul and that is very obvious in U2, despite the medium chosen.

'Irishness' in U2 is seen in a modern light. It isn't an old-fashioned concept. I wonder actually to what extent it is a concept at all. I believe that for U2, it has become real. The journalist Gavin Martin observes quite rightly: 'U2's success and their decision to remain based in their homeland has been a decisive factor in sealing the image of modern Ireland.'[41]

U2's sense of their place in the world is actually quite astonishing. They have built their identity around several poles, one of which is 'Irishness'. They define themselves as Irish, and their music is Irish rock. (Irish) rock, the idea of it, comes for Bono from an Irish definition of art, in the first place:

You put your hand in under your skin, you break your breastbone, you rip open your rib cage (…) Are you ready to do that? Or is rock 'n' roll for you just a pair of shoes and a haircut, or a certain sour existentialism or a certain sweet decay? That was one of my first definitions of art. Blood. That comes from Irish literature, that comes from Oscar Wilde writing *De Profundis*, that comes from Brendan Behan walking on the stage while his own play is being put on in front of an audience, telling people to fuck off. In Ireland, that pain of opening your rib cage, it's in us.[42]

Therefore, it would be logical to assume that, although, their attitude on the surface has changed over the years when it comes to spilling their guts in public, their songs bear the same openness and heartache to before. They still bleed on people's carpets when a U2 CD is being played. They still touch people's hearts and, whatever their genesis, they are written with the same Irish imagination and truthfulness as before. If there is a truth in U2 that can be found anywhere, it is in the songs.

And that's what we're all interested in, in the end. The songs, the music and the words, are U2's life blood. That's what they're meant to do. The question is: how do they do it?

3

IMAGINATION

Imagination is at the heart of the creative process and therefore at the heart of U2. When an artist creates a work, he/she needs to use imagination to make it come to life. U2 are in no way different.

To imagine, to dream up, to reinvent are all verbs that the band are fond of. They are essential to their well-being and to their creative power. U2 need to constantly reinvent imagination, to always bring it forward so that the process of reinvention becomes credible. And this credibility is the key to success, but there is also the ability to imagine otherwise. Before and after the release of *How to Dismantle an Atomic Bomb*, I came across a few articles where Bono was saying that the least U2 could do to thank the fans for giving them such an incredible life was not to make a crap album. Their credibility is therefore still at stake even after 25 years of a career.

U2 must, however, follow a certain way of creating imagination which in the rock world has its own rules, and 'the band is a dream full of images that it uses both as its own body as well as a psychological envelope'.[1]

Modus operandi

In many interviews, the members of U2 have tried to explain how a song is born. They describe a process that is specific to the band. They all gather in a recording studio and play until a musical trend starts emerging. They can be influenced by the music they are listening to at that moment of improvisation. Most of the time, the music will be written before Bono puts words to it. Each member of the band will take part in the musical creation but Bono writes 95 per cent of the songs, the remainder being The Edge's, or his and The Edge's work.

If we move beyond this simplistic description, one must be aware that not many bands work in this way. They will arrive in the studio with something already composed or written and with a precise musical direction. U2 start improvising before arriving at something which will be for them an interesting piece of music.

The creation of a song is a moment of intense pressure and the most important moment, for it defines in essence what U2 are, a rock band creating songs with one objective: to make music that reflects its musical quest at that particular time, but that also reflects its role as witness of an era, a social or political climate, or that reflects personal events and more intimate themes. Bono sees himself as a 'travelling salesman (…) I sell songs from door to door, from town to town. I sell melodies and words'.2

The Holy Grail of a rock band is the sound. Searching for it may be a vain quest for many, but the members of U2 were inspired when they found it. This is the first common denominator between rock bands. U2 are therefore in no way different. Influenced by classical rock bands and musicians (the Rolling Stones, the Beatles, the Who, Bob Dylan, Roy Orbison,) and less classical outfits who were/are as talented (David Bowie, Patti Smith, the Ramones, Joy Division, Television), inspired by Irish musicians such as Van Morrison, Rory Gallagher, Thin Lizzy or Stiff Little Fingers, U2 will admit to many different influences. The myth that they themselves kept alive for a while was that U2 came from nowhere, that their musical roots were 'somewhere in space'.3 That they were bad at playing other people's songs and that they decided very quickly to write their own is more credible. The Edge admits that 'from very early on, it became clear to us that we had no idea about songwriting technique. Our way into songwriting was to dream it up. We'd try to imagine how others might do the song, the Clash or Lennon or The Jam. Instinct was everything for us, and it really still is.'4

However, they quickly found a way by looking at others and taking inspiration from sources such as punk. In the Irish television programme, *From a Whisper to a Scream*, Bono observed about Stiff Little Fingers and punk:

One of the best rock 'n' roll concerts I ever saw was Stiff Little Fingers. And apart from the music, the atmosphere adds another colour to it which is violent. [Punk] was like a cultural revolution. It was like China (…). You couldn't have long hair, you couldn't wear flares but it was an interesting feeling because it was the beginning of punk-rock. That's where the idea formed in me that music is a life or death experience, which it sounds mad to say. Honestly, that's how we felt about it. It wasn't entertainment.

The musical genesis of U2 cannot be detached from a desire to escape a place that they did not feel comfortable in, that prevented them from being themselves.

In a classical manner in the world of rock, they are self-taught. But they were successful in finding a sound that other bands found inspiration in. Two elements are combined: finding a sound through improvisation but also being aware of the band's musical limitations. Adam Clayton explains this quest for a sound:

> I think we've always found a difficult way to write which is a lot of times we start with band improvisation and it's really us looking for a sound. It's not us looking for a song initially (…) Once we find that sound, it produces a feeling and then Bono has to try and fit (…) some lyrics around that idea. It's a long process but it means the integrity of the musical idea and the emotion that that sound has produced is preserved right through to the end.[5]

This quest is obviously a constant feature of the band and falls within the scope of reinvention. However, U2 agree that there is a general trend but no precise rules. They may talk for hours about a song or else improvise for hours. The Edge says:

> U2 songs can come together very fast with everyone in the room and it's all very exciting, and you've got something very quickly. And sometimes it's a very frustrating process; you know there's a great song there somewhere and you just gotta try and get to its essence and in some ways trying to keep your hands off it as much as possible, and let it come through, and that can mean lots of going down blind alleys or whatever you have to do to get there, and that's what I do a lot of times is just try and get a song to the point where it will take flight. There's no formality to it. It's very much a trial and error thing.[6]

The band members are also aware of their strengths and weaknesses. They say that they work much harder than other bands and in the mid-1990s, they still admitted to having to improve on what they had already done. Striving to be the best and not only the biggest is one of U2's main concerns.

Another point that can be discussed is more spiritual and pertains to creation as being a quasi-divine experience, in fact creation as needing divine intervention to exist. This idea can be found many times throughout U2's career, and it seems like an almost unavoidable theme, considering the place spirituality holds in U2's life. In 1984, The Edge observed:

It's not me, it's not U2 that's creating this great art. That's why I can be so arrogant or seemingly arrogant about what we do because I don't believe it's us. Essentially, I think there's something that works through us to create in this way.[7]

Some ten years later, Larry comes back to that point by telling journalist, Bill Flanagan: 'None of us understands where this music comes from. If one of us wrote a book about the band, he wouldn't be able to explain it. I believe that it comes ...'[8] (He apparently pointed to the sky while saying this last sentence). Creation in U2 is, it seems, a divine mystery that is quite inexplicable. Whatever one's point of view, it fits perfectly within the religious beliefs and spiritual awakening of the band's members. But what they are looking for in a song is also an emotion. Bono says:

Feelings are stronger than ideas or words in a song. You can have 1,000 ideas, but unless you capture an emotion, it's an essay. That's probably what I would have done if I wasn't in music, but that's not songwriting. Songwriting comes from a different place. Music is the language of the spirit. I think ideas and words are our excuses as songwriters to allow our heart or our spirit to run free. That's when magic happens.[9]

The second phase of writing a U2 song is fitting the lyrics in. Bono was for a long time ill at ease when it was his turn to write the words, as he wanted words that would be meaningful. In 1984, he revealed that: 'Writing songs scares the living daylights out of me.'[10] He had a tendency to improvise songs rather than writing them on paper. His *modus operandi* changed drastically over the years and improvisation was replaced by pen and paper (or computer tactic).

But for the singer, writing lyrics goes beyond a mere song with a meaning. He talks of words as music, almost as poetry. I love the way Bono uses words. It is very unusual, undoubtedly very Irish. It is cleverly done and there are always surprises. That's why I love reading Bono's lyrics even before I hear a new song. He talks of the rhythm of the words, of the way they fit together. He compares this process to painting where the emotions are visual. In fact, surprisingly, he makes the words into very powerful images, into something concrete and that loses its abstract meaning (not all the time, however!). It is an instinct that must be intellectualised. He calls it 'songwriting by accident'.[11] What he suggests here is that the best songs aren't necessarily the ones you spend a lot of time on, but may be those which are born almost naturally, without too much effort.

Bono's style of writing is quite complex and rhetorical figures abound. Biblical metaphores, inversions, changed phrases or idioms, all of them contribute to a style that is rarely colloquial, often abstract and poetical. The songs tell stories, or rather bits of stories, moments experienced by the protagonist of the song or indeed by Bono himself.

However, the concept of song appeared quite late in U2's career. According to The Edge, in the beginning, Bono chose to write songs in a 'more expressionist' way, and if he mainly held on to atmospheres, from *The Joshua Tree* on, 'the songs were very much thought of, written and produced as such'.[12] The style, however, often remains suggestive rather than explicit. That is why the songs' interpretation is so difficult. This is a common problem and if you go to any U2 website where there is an attempt at song analysis, you will notice that there are different interpretations. Some words appeared very late in the songs. For instance 'baby', a term so often used in a pop song that you don't even acknowledge it anymore, only reared its common head at the time of *Achtung Baby*. Flood, one of U2's favoured producers, says of 'Ultraviolet (Light My Way)':

There was a lot of debate and a good deal of laughter, about Bono actually coming out and going 'Baby'. It was less to do with the political correctness of it than whether he could actually get away with singing 'Baby, baby, baby/Baby, baby, baby' and so on. That was very funny for a long time. But he got away with it alright.[13]

Bono has also borrowed, and that is more interesting, from writers and poets or famous people in other areas. In 'Trying To Throw Your Arms Around the World,' the sentence 'A woman needs a man like a fish needs a bicycle' is borrowed from the feminist Germaine Greer. 'Days run away like horses over the hill,' at the very end of 'Dirty Day' is the title of a poem by Charles Bukowski. In 'A Sort of Homecoming', the line 'O Come away / O Come away / O Come away / Say I' is inspired by the Irish poet W.B. Yeats and his poem 'Stolen Child'. I could go on, but what is more interesting is the subversive use of every day, ordinary words which serve an extraordinary means of communication – rock music. The ordinary becomes extraordinary thanks to the music, and if rock songs are not poems, they are 'implied narratives', with a character, the singer, who has 'an attitude, in a situation, talking to someone, if only to herself'.[14] The closest a rock song comes to poetry is in its poetic effect. This is quite obvious in some U2 songs. For instance, 'The Unforgettable Fire': 'Ice / your only rivers run cold / These city lights / They shine as silver and gold / Dug from the night / Your eyes as black as coal / Carnival, the wheels fly and the colours spin / Through alcohol red wine that punctures the skin / Face to face in a dry and waterless place.' But the poetic effect of a rock song is at its most powerful when the words and music combine in performance: 'A poet chooses words for reasons to do with meaning and sound,'[15] according to Simon Frith. It is quite clear that Bono loves the sound of words, the music of words. He attributes to his Irish origins the attraction they hold. The construction of a text is essential to its life but also to communication. The singer obviously chooses his words carefully, to convey the right meaning, and in that his approach is very similar to that of a poet or a writer.

However, he has to work within constraints of a particular kind. A rock song can only have a poetic effect when put to music and performed. If you take it out of that framework, it rarely is poetry and is too often dull and uninteresting. But the genre only lends itself to poetic impressions and can be compared to poetry in very rare cases. More appropriately, songs appear almost as short dramas, acts in plays, and the use of ordinary words is a quest for perpetual enrichment of the song and of the effect those words are going to have during performance: 'Song, like drama, is about the invention of characters and stories. People … are at its centre.'[16] Despite a some time obscure narrative, Bono invents characters and puts them on stage in the lyrics but also during concerts. An obvious example is the Fly character.

The difficulty of writing a song for Bono seems to lie in the use of appropriate words, from a semantic point of view but also from a musical and rhythmic point of view. An interesting example of a U2 song spoken rather than sung shows that the sound and rhythm of the words is in the performance. In the 1997 TV programme about the PopMart Tour, the American poet Allen Ginsberg actually recites the song 'Miami' while the song is playing in the background. He stresses some words more than others and makes the song into an interesting piece of theatre.

Bono is adamant, however, that rules should be bent occasionally when it comes to songwriting: 'Songwriting really is a mysterious process … because we're asking people to expose themselves. It's like open heart surgery in some way. You're looking for real, raw emotions, and you don't find that by sticking to the rules.'[17]

The music and words go together in a rock song and the members of U2 share in the creative process. As Adam puts it: 'We're tough guys. We know we'll get there eventually. A lot of it is perspiration. You just have to put in the hours and do your time.'[18]

If they do their time in the studio to create songs, they cannot do it on their own. They are surrounded by people who are professionals in the field, notably the producer, the sound engineer and designer. Not surprisingly, these people have been working with U2 for many years. We can call them the mediators. I borrowed the term from the French sociologist Antoine Hennion whose exhaustive definition encompasses all the people and all the instruments that are linked to music (they may be the singers, producers but also music sheets or the media) who intervene between its creation and its production.[19] I use this term to designate the people who have worked closely with U2 and have played a crucial role in the creative process.

The Mediators

Let's start with the producers. Steve Lillywhite, Brian Eno, Daniel Lanois and Flood have, alternatively or together, worked on U2 albums. Their work is to direct and supervise the sessions but also to make recording 'a form of composition in itself, rather than simply a means of documenting a performance'.[20] A producer would therefore be a collaborator and he becomes an integral part of the recording process. He must understand the vision and desires of the band, so that the final result is what the band wants. The four producers have all been part of the U2 phenomenon, bringing different styles and approaches and therefore taking part in the reinvention process.

Steve Lillywhite first produced U2's second single on Island, 'A Day Without Me / Things to Make and Do', released in August 1980. The aim was to actually see if he and the band would click. He went on to produce the first three U2 albums. He also took part in the mixing of some songs on *The Joshua Tree*, *Achtung Baby* and *All That You Can't Leave Behind*. He produced U2's 2004 offering *How to Dismantle an Atomic Bomb*. Steve Lillywhite could be described as a permanent feature of the band, as much as Brian Eno and Daniel Lanois.

The pair came on board at the time of *The Unforgettable Fire*, when U2 were looking for a producer with a different approach. The story goes that Bono pestered English musician and producer Brian Eno so much that the latter relented and agreed to meet. The choice was inspired, as *The Unforgettable Fire* is magnificent. I still enjoy listening to it, over twenty years after its release. Brian Eno, who brought Canadian musician and producer Daniel Lanois on board, was true to his reputation and changed everything, helping the band to complete its first transformation. Choosing Slane Castle as a recording venue is ample evidence of U2's desire to explore new sounds. And isn't that what it's all about, finding a fresh sound? That has always been U2's aim. Brian Eno's view of the band in 1984 is also very important to understand why it worked so well:

> My first impression of U2 and my lasting impression of U2 was that they were a band in a way very few people are bands now. The music was the result of those four people, not four instruments. It was those four people in particular angles and differences of approach that they brought to the music.[21]

Brian Eno sees the band as individuals who create music reflecting each of their personalities. Here, U2's cohesion on an artistic and on a human level appears as the cornerstone of the band. And this is a fundamental aspect of the band's success.

The Unforgettable Fire was one of the first steps towards a reinvention policy that would become U2's trademark. Brian Eno and Daniel Lanois produced other U2 albums, *The Joshua Tree*, *Achtung Baby*, *Zooropa* and *All That You Can't Leave Behind*. They also collaborated on *How to Dismantle an Atomic Bomb*.

The fourth producer to work with U2 is Mark Ellis, nicknamed Flood. He was firstly sound engineer on *The Joshua Tree*, *Achtung Baby* and *Zooropa*, having co-produced the latter with Eno and Lanois. He was in charge of the most tech-no-trip-hop-pop album, *Pop*, and the least U2-like. Don't get me wrong – I actually love the album but it is difficult to categorise it when it comes to a genre. That's what makes it so interesting, I guess. But Flood put his signature on it, through the pop rhythms that permeate the whole work.

I have asked myself what kind of influence all those producers have had on U2 albums and what their responsibility is in the making of the albums. Their presence is an essential element in the creation of a musical work and their influence is strong. But this collaboration must bear fruit. U2 are obviously in charge here. They are very independent and would probably not tolerate too much interference. If the producer and U2 don't click, then he is replaced. That's what happened on *How to Dismantle an Atomic Bomb*. The Irish quartet started working with Chris Thomas but it did not work out and they went their sep— ways. Bono says:

> It started out to be a rock 'n' roll album, pure and
> ed that Edge wasn't sitting at the piano or twidd
> because he is one of the great guitarists. Halfwa
> because it turns out you can only go so far with ri

dimension. Now you've got punk rock starting points that go through Phil Spectorland, turn right at Tim Buckley, end up in alleyways and open onto other vistas and cityscapes and rooftops and skies. It's songwriting by accident, by a punk band that wants to play Bach.

Being a U2 producer mustn't be fun every day! So Steve Lillywhite was back for more. And that is what makes U2 an unusual outfit. They always work with the same people because there is an obvious mutual understanding and respect. That is not to say that it is plain sailing all the way through to the release of the album. There have been incidents between the members of the band and the producers that have probably cleared the air. Brian Eno recalled how he nearly wiped out 'Where the Streets Have No Name' from his mixing table, because the band were driving him crazy with it, only to be stopped in the nick of time. But this seems to be part of the creative process: perspiration and sometimes shouting matches.

Perpetual reinvention is high risk, indeed, but it is also an essential step for creativity. U2 have always rejected things that were easy. The producer must therefore follow in their footsteps, but he can also intervene. He must lead the project to its conclusion while giving his opinion but most of all his advice to guide the band to the exit.

He is as essential as the chief sound engineer, in this case Joe O'Herlihy, as well as the designer, Steve Averill. The only difference is that O'Herlihy and Averill have worked on all the albums. So the staff are faithful. This aspect is inherent to U2's philosophy. I am still in two minds about whether U2 is 'assiduously designed', as according to Michael Ross.[22] As much as it is true of the 1990s, the 1980s are problematic. I don't think that U2 was designed completely on purpose, even if rock 'n' roll is also based on image. But I will come back to that. One thing is definitely clear, however: U2 have always wanted to be in control of everything. That control has obviously created some tension in the creative process and Bono told a French journalist in 2000:

For me, belonging to a band means shouting abuse at one another constantly. It's like a lovers' quarrel, intense and passionate. First of all, we don't make any concessions when it comes to work. And celebrity eventually makes you look ridiculous. You could think that in such a context everyone's ego inflates dramatically. Mine ended up exploding or rather imploding in the pathetic face me. As you get old, why would you want to bother with all the tension ws that come with being in a band? That's a good question.[23]

Bono talks about the question from a general point of view and this illustrates the fact that even U2, maybe U2 more than others, have rows of biblical proportions when in the studio.

It is obvious that U2's work is created in blood, sweat and tears. Is it the price to pay for originality and renewal? The musical passion in U2 is undoubtedly the catalyst for inspiration. But the band have to go through moments of doubt and friction to create their music. This sounds very much like a cliché: an artist has to suffer for his/her art. But U2 seem to belong to that cliché. Their musical limitations, as the members of the band have often called those, make them choose different creative strategies.

But another problem arises linked to creativity and what it should be. U2, just like some of their talented contemporaries, are faced with the crisis of art versus commerce and those two aspects are glaring contradictions in the music industry.

Art and Commerce

This dichotomy between art and commerce in the world of rock is very regularly debated by academics and otherwise. The question is not new and the debate has always been heated. The question is how to reconcile a mass product and a work of art? How to accept them as polar extremes? How to fuse them? Must a work of art necessarily belong to an elite? Can it not also be made for and belong to the masses?

This particular debate was actually opened in the 1930s by the German philosopher Theodor Adorno of the Frankfurt School.[24] He mercilessly criticised popular music in general and jazz in particular. His theory is based on three major points: musical production as a reified form, musical standardisation and its instrumentalised reception put in the service of the interests of the ruling class. Culture had become an industry and capitalism, according to Adorno and his colleague Horkheimer, used the culture industry as a domination tool. The culture industry produced commodities, in other words things to be bought and sold, which allowed the companies which produced those commodities to make a profit from them. This led to a very high level of standardisation, meaning that every piece of music is brought in line with the next from the sound point of view and the themes dealt with. It also created a new kind of listener, a consumer of those cultural products, who wasn't discerning and who was passive. In other words, at the heart of Adorno's theory lies the issue of musical standardisation and its link with capitalism as a system which creates products meant for immediate consumption. Adorno set popular music against classical music, which for him was the ultimate art. He also pinned the listeners of both genres against one another and considered those of popular music as being distracted and not pay-ing attention, obeying emotions rather than listening in an intellectual manner.

There tends to be a very strong standardisation in some pop songs. The boy bands trend is an example of it but is by no means isolated. It happened before and will happen again. Every era has its standardised products starting with Tin Pan Alley.[25] But much criticism has befallen Adorno over the years. The most common one is the fact that he put all popular music in the same bag, without taking into account each of the specific aspects comprising the genre. He also always compared it to classical music, which leads to a distorted value judge-ment, whereas it should not happen because one cannot compare what is not comparable. Classical and popular music are two different genres and people can enjoy both. Moreover, the era which Adorno was born in, as well as his social background (German intellectuals with a great musical culture), is a problem in that one wonders if he was actually able to apprehend the changes that took place in the realm of music at that time. According to sociologist, Brian Longhurst, popular music must be thoroughly analysed to be evaluated in the right way in society, and Adorno's theory doesn't offer that kind of analysis.[26]

U2 and every other rock artist have been faced with this dichotomy of art versus commerce. At the beginning of the 1990s, Bono observed: 'I think rock 'n' roll has more contradictions than any other art form. Whether it's been art and commerce, idealism and nihilism, it goes on and on – a fuzzbox versus a gospel choir.'[27] The band works constantly at the heart of this contradiction and rock 'n' roll is probably the place where those two opposites of art and commerce are the most visible. On the one hand, a band will not be recognised for its achievement and talent without having first obtained the critics' accolade, without being recognised as belonging to the great names of rock. On the other hand, that same band will not be recognised as being successful without selling millions of records and without having played hundreds of concerts to hundreds of thousands of fans.

Ed Power, in an article for the *Irish Independent*, berates U2 for being suc-cessful and for being, according to him, untalented. He places Echo and The Bunnymen above the Irish band:

> Several years ago I interviewed Ian McCulloch, the lead singer of Echo and the Bunnymen, a Liverpool group once predicted to be bigger than U2. Asked if the band regretted not having approached touring with the same careerist determination as the Dubliners, McCulloch shrugged and said the Bunnymen had decided to go to Paris instead and cut an experimental record with classical musicians.

The resulting album, *Ocean Rain*, enraptured critics but suffered mediocre sales. Today an Echo and the Bunnymen show would probably struggle to fill Croke Park's dressing rooms.

Fortune, it is clear, favours neither the bravest nor the most extravagantly talented. The smart ones are its darlings and they don't come any cannier than U2.[28]

Ed Power is perfectly entitled to his opinion and I am actually glad that there are people who don't like U2. Indeed they were clever, they toured incessantly and built an audience over the years that remains faithful to this day. He doesn't ask himself, however, why people still love U2, why the band is still relevant nowadays. He doesn't recognise the fact that they have cut some amazing albums and that they have been recognised by the most difficult of critics as having achieved something quite astounding. The fact that they were inducted in the US Rock 'n' Roll Hall of Fame on 14 March 2005, did not seem to bother him. I have nothing against Echo and The Bunnymen and they were a fine band. But their goal and audience were different and it is impossible to compare the two bands. Not only are U2 talented but they are ambitious. Those two aspects are not mutually exclusive. It ultimately boils down to a question of taste. But one must recognise, despite their not liking U2, that they are actually almost as influential as the Beatles and that no one can last this long without talent.

I agree with Ed Power on one point. U2 are extremely clever and cunning. U2 is a trademark that they control. This brand must be sold while putting forward the artistic side of it. Paul McGuinness says: 'What we sell is the experience of buying a designed, branded artefact that is not just a piece of software but also represents, in tangible form, the values of the band.'[29] In spite of its nature, image has to become fuzzy in front of musical qualities. U2 are masters of media hype without appearing so (with the exception of *Achtung Baby*). One of the band's strengths can undoubtedly be found in that game of appearances.

Authenticity

The idea of authenticity is therefore not far when one discusses that particular point of art versus commerce. And when one discusses U2. It is a notion that has been part of the band's appeal since the beginning. But the problem is first to define what authenticity is and how U2 have used it throughout their career.

Authenticity has enormous symbolic value. In its most classical sense, an authentic work must be a mixture of originality, sincerity, integrity, hard work and self-sacrifice. Without it, it cannot pretend to hold a higher place in the rock field.

The concept of musical art in the rock world is largely built around this controversial but essential notion of authenticity. It is indeed difficult to agree on it but authenticity is crucial to the rock aesthetic and to the way the latter is perceived.

Philosopher Walter Benjamin, also from the Frankfurt School, was interested in the aura of a work of art and in the idea of it being unique. According to Benjamin, if the work, for instance a photograph, is reproduced, it loses its authentic character because the here and now of the original constitutes its authenticity. So, by extension, a musical work, if it is reproduced thousands, or even millions of times, loses its authenticity. My question is: is it really the case and can it be applied to rock? Do classical music works also lose their authenticity because they have been using the medium of music reproduction for decades now, and have been distributed around the world millions of times? The answer is quite obvious to me. In the case of rock, it is possessing its own authenticity thanks first of all to the search for a sound, therefore for something original, something that will become the trademark of the artist. Don't we talk about a U2 sound, for instance? The work also has unique qualities if it follows the criteria mentioned above and possesses the characteristics accepted in the world of rock and constructed by it, even if it is reproduced a million times. It may well be that its authenticity is enhanced and its aura becomes even more powerful. One can only imagine how many times a U2 song is played on the radio, on TV, or in somebody's house around the world, and probably at the same time. These works can be reproduced ad infinitum without losing their original value.

For rock fans, their favourite band's authenticity is without doubt. There is a real rock tradition that has developed over the years and cannot be detached from its reproduction.

Another aspect of authenticity can also be found in longevity. People still listen to the Beatles, long after the break up of the band. Selling millions of records is not a problem in itself if the artist has proved his/her worth elsewhere, if he/she has been around for a long time, has been supported by the music industry in award ceremonies, for instance. When it is the fans themselves who choose their favourite artists, it is another kind of support, the most important one. Over the years, U2 have received accolades from the music industry and from the fans. For instance, between 1983 and 2002, the Irish band won 27 awards of various kinds, including fourteen Grammy awards and eight Brit Awards.

This authentic label has followed U2 like a shadow and seems to be a lasting feature, in spite of musical changes and image overhauls.

Words like integrity, sincerity, honesty, ethics have been part of the band's image since the beginning and mostly in the 1980s. Those categories are part of the U2 phenomenon, and U2 are perceived as possessing morals that some other bands don't have. A most recent example shows that this is still the case. The tickets for U2's Vertigo tour went on sale at the end of January/beginning of February 2005 (depending on the location). Most concerts were sold out within hours (50 minutes for the Dublin shows). Some fans had access to pre-sales if they had paid their rather hefty $US40 contribution to the U2.com website. But it did not work out as planned and some fans were understandably disgruntled at the technical blunders that marred the pre-sales. However, this may have been only a minor hitch had some fans not shown their discontent concerning the prices of tickets. One of them said:

> I am really surprised that U2 is charging $160 plus service charges for tickets to their concerts. They tout themselves as a benevolent band, and yet they charge top dollar. Even though I can afford to, I won't be going. I won't pay that kind of money to see any band.

Another concurred:

> Couldn't agree more! I've loved U2 forever but I'm beginning to loathe them now. They're such marketing mouthpieces it's disgusting me. Paying $40 to get 'early access to good seats?!' Whatever! I logged on at 10 am sharp yesterday and NONE – I mean NONE – of the GA tickets [tickets set aside for subscribers] were available. I, already freaking, paid 40 bucks to get first dibs and now I have to rush to get good seats? If you're a fan club member, you should just be able to buy two tickets through the fan club – no hassles, no ticketmaster, no dumb passwords . . . like how REAL bands do 'em – like Pearl Jam's tenclub.[30]

One can understand the anger of the fans who were let down. And the prices for the tickets were definitely high. But not as high as for concerts by some other artists. The first fan I quoted put his finger on it. He said that U2 were a 'benevolent band'. That he should think of them like that is ample evidence that the ideas of integrity and morality are very much present in the fans' minds. But what they seem to forget is that U2 are not a charitable organisation. They are musicians who get paid for what they do. Would anyone be happy to work for free?

Therefore, integrity, honesty and sincerity very much became part of the band, and they refer to the music first and foremost, but also to the individuals.

They reflect the originality of the work, but also the powerful performances and the emotions that go with it.

At the heart of it all is performance. It is traditionally associated with rock authenticity and U2 are the epitome of it. Adam Clayton is adamant that: 'A concert is the most authentic form of music. Records were invented a long time after music. Ask Beethoven.'[31] The musicians play live, they are on stage, people can see and touch them. But what they say and what they do outside of music is also important. The fact that U2 have supported organisations like Amnesty International or Greenpeace throughout the years makes a difference in the perception the fans have of them. They are authentic in music and outside of it. But music is the founding element of this authenticity.

The debate is ongoing within the rock community and there is still a problem: the independent ghetto. The artists belonging to that side of the music industry must follow a particular type of behaviour. It is an ethics which U2 have always fought against. Independent artists too often consider artistic integrity as being incompatible with the sale of millions of records and commercial success. If a musician decides that he/she must develop commercially and is subsequently successful, he/she will lose his/her credibility in 'coolsville'. If he/she stays where he/she is, he/she will never get out of this ghetto. And the only way for him/her to preserve his/her credibility is to have posthumous success.[32]

U2 have always refused that simplistic blend between the independent ghetto and authenticity:

It's one of the things that makes Bono most visibly angry. The basic premise seems to be that once you're successful, you've sold out. Automatically. It doesn't apply in sport. It doesn't apply in the movies. It doesn't apply in poetry. And yet in rock 'n' roll, it's a common assumption that amounts almost to an article of faith among those who claim the ideological high ground: the very fact that an act has become successful means that they must have lost touch with the street.[33]

In 2005, Bono came back to that point, albeit from a different angle:

[The indie music scene] was a bunch of lies sold to people. It made our life in U2 a lot less interesting and a lot more lonely – even just in terms of who we were sharing hotels with. All the bands who were broken up by that indie 'cultural revolution', they're not there anymore. It was a 'cultural revolution' disguised as 'street cred'. This is the lexicon of what we lived through during the

'80s, the excuse used for not having a good song. We were smart enough to
go to America and bypass that. We took a few blows for that and a few connected.[34]

For U2, the problem is ultimately not to sell millions of records but to apply
a form of ethics to their behaviour and to their music. Bono actually keeps
repeating that if U2 made two crap albums in a row, they would be out. They
don't want to be the biggest as much as the best. And being the best involves
working in an artistic but also in an intellectual manner to apprehend the world
as it is today. U2 must be relevant all the time.

The notion of art for art's sake is the question raised by the independent
world. But this notion is rather difficult to entertain when it comes to a way of
expression destined for a mass market. Larry is very conscious that one can
become complacent: 'There's a thin line between art and art for art's sake and
you have to be careful with that.'[35] He is talking here more specifically about the
album *Passengers*, recorded with Brian Eno in 1995. It can be called an experimental record but Larry doesn't like it that much because he finds it pretentious.
A means of communication like rock 'n' roll is a form of entertainment first and
foremost but it is more suitable to delivering an artistic or even a political message, because millions of people have access to it. The members of U2 never
rejected that idea of mass communication, their goal being to reach the top.
Their ambition could not have been fulfilled with any other type of music. They
basically wanted to be heard. They therefore chose to work within the system
without becoming slaves to it, while retaining a great measure of independence,
and while using it to their advantage. As it is, their records are artistic and commercial successes and they still can pull crowds to their concerts. They in fact
have a lot of clout.

U2 have used two different types of authenticity, the classical model and the
ironic model. There is indeed a screaming difference between the two. The first
model takes place at the level of space and time. That includes belonging to the
origins, for instance being part of the first wave of musicians who created a certain style of music, and for later generations, being directly inspired by them,
denouncing inauthenticity, refusing to sell out, rejecting the commercial aspect
of music, in short romantic notions of purity. Its origins are found in the
Romantic movement of the nineteenth century. The second model allows an
artist or band 'to be set apart not only from the commercial machine within
which it operates but also from its own practices',[36] because they can laugh at
themselves while pretending to have been swallowed up by the system. The U2

of the 1980s is at one end of the spectrum while the U2 of the 1990s is at the other, without any transition between the two.

In the 1980s, U2 were seen as a truly authentic band, whereas in the 1990s, the change was drastic. They wrapped themselves in rhetoric and embraced what Lawrence Grossberg called an 'authentic inauthenticity' in other words, a form of postmodern authenticity which is 'purely ironic.' Grossberg continues: 'If every identity is equally fake, a pose that one takes on, then authentic inauthenticity celebrates the possibilities of poses without denying that this is all they are.'[37] U2 used irony as a stage prop, first of all towards themselves and then towards others. They used the system as a springboard to embrace another form of authenticity, the ironic form. Bono said that they: 'played with all the ideas of authenticity in *Rattle and Hum*.'[38] U2 indeed sought a classical form of authenticity at the end of the 1980s, going back to the roots of rock, to the origins of rock. But, paradoxically, that was when they were seen as the least authentic. As long as they stuck to America merely as a place of inspiration mainly with *The Joshua Tree* album, everything was fine because they were themselves. However, as soon as their music sounded far too close to the roots of rock 'n' roll, all hell broke loose and their authenticity was in doubt. Why was that? Probably because they started imitating their idols long after they had themselves become rock stars. In other words, their path was the reverse of any classical rock band, who is first inspired by its rock heroes and then finds its own sound and songs, through the appropriation of one or several styles. *Rattle and Hum*, however criticised, sold in excess of ten million copies all the same. But U2 were conscious of the mistake. They therefore must reinvent a new form of authenticity although Bono, in a manner of paradox that has become almost normal, said that authenticity was not the most important. In 2001, there was a new era, new contradiction. Bono told a French journalist: 'The most important thing is to be authentic.'[39] But before he came back to 'authentic authenticity', the discovery of what technology could offer music made those beliefs redundant: 'This was one of the things that to me exploded the idea of authenticity (...) I started to see Kraftwerk as some sort of soul group.' Indeed the musical possibilities offered by technology are vast and U2 revelled in them for a while. However, the basic rock instruments remained the same. Despite the technology, U2 remain a rock band and the reasons for the lack of transition between the two models of authenticity are found in the spectacular reinvention of the 1990s. They very simply wanted to reappropriate a phenomenon that had escaped from their grasp. But U2 also remain something more than a mere rock band, rather an Irish rock band. Ireland is at the heart of the phenomenon and represents a form of authenticity. Bono talks of himself as: 'an Irish person who has worked hard to sort of musically try and reinvent what it is to be Irish (...) because people listen to U2 and say, "What you do is Irish yet by the look of it, it's not." It's a spirit.'[40] Ireland's reputation as a musical nation has undoubtedly something to do with it and I wonder if some of it has not rubbed off on U2.

Finally, the fact is that U2 reverted back to something akin to authenticity in the 2000s. The ironic stance was but a phase that the band went through and Bono is adamant: 'That particular era is over. Irony doesn't work anymore. The people I meet in pubs and clubs want a more direct approach.'[41] Indeed the band seems to have been a sign of the times in the 1990s but later on, musical passion which is simple and bare was back, along with an authenticity akin to that of U2's beginnings. In fact, U2 have never abandoned authenticity, just played with it.

Songs

To move on to the themes dealt with in the songs, I have already talked about the importance of words for Bono. I believe that a rock song is incomplete without words. Some people would be more interested in the music but the words make up 50 per cent of the song and most people will be interested in the meaning of such and such a song. What does Bono mean when he sings 'Until the End of the World' or 'Crumbs From Your Table'? Why does he say this or that?

There are four main themes that come back regularly in U2 songs: spirituality, love and eroticism, Ireland, and politics. There are also personal themes like the death of Bono's mother or father. Because it is often difficult to put one song into one category, I've chosen to talk about them in a general way, taking extracts and therefore being, I admit it, completely biased.

SPIRITUALITY

The theme of spirituality literally permeates U2's work, like an invisible thread. It gathers under its heading God, religion, the Bible, the crisis of faith and redemption. Bono's beliefs are very much in evidence in the songs with a spiritual theme but he rejects the idea of religion: 'I reject religion, the idea of religion, when it creates conflict between two people. There is a confusion between religion and spirituality. Music has always been spiritual.'[42] Whether the singer calls upon Jesus to try and make sense of the Omagh bombing on 'Peace on Earth', or whether the theme is dealt with in a more ostentatious way in the album *October*, the place of God and spirituality in the band is essential to its life and to its music. The approach over time is, however, different. Growing up, becoming more mature, had an obvious effect on the way Bono writes. But what is more interesting is that U2 were always accepted as talking about God. What they never did was preach and that is why people who don't share their views don't see them as a threat. Despite the fact that they are believers, they are also rock stars. They drink and smoke and curse and don't come across as proselytisers. They do have a clean reputation and live ordinary lives outside of rock with their families. Adam Clayton, the least religious member of U2, is the only one who had a brush with the law and the tabloids, first for possession of cannabis in 1989 and second, because he was engaged to supermodel Naomi Campbell for a while. However, most of the time U2 keep a tight grip on their affairs, personal or otherwise, and in February 2005, The Edge and his wife took an injunction against newspapers to prevent them from running a story on a member of their family who was unwell. U2 also come from Ireland, a very Catholic country, and although most of them are Protestant, they were still raised in the Catholic or in the Protestant faith. It has definitely left its mark. Even if religious faith can appear as a paradox in the rock world, U2 never seemed to care. Going to Mount Temple School also opened their eyes to other possibilities.

But U2 never belonged to the Christian rock movement, even if they might have felt isolated for a while. Rock 'n' roll can be very spiritual and Elvis Presley was the first rock star but he was also a devout Christian. Steve Stockman believes '[U2] formed a band and discovered a fervent evangelicalism at the same time without getting caught up in some kind of dualism was only possible because of their location'.[43] I would agree with that and I wonder had they come from any other place what their difficulties would have been. The Shalom period had a remarkable influence on the band's creativity, with The Edge, Bono and Larry being pulled between their faith and their love of music. *October* is spiritual, poetic and full of doubt as to the future of the band. The song 'Gloria' represents the dilemma, the hesitation, the struggle of conscience. When Bono sings 'I try to sing this song / I, I try to stand up / But I can't find my feet / I try, I try to speak up / But only in you I'm complete', he seems to be desperately looking for a place where he could reconcile the two aspects of rock and spirituality. It is a prayer that may find an answer in the following lines: 'I try to sing this song / I, I try to get in / But I can't find the door / The door is open / You're standing there / You let me in.' This is probably one of the first references that Bono makes to the Gospels in the Bible, a reference to Gospel 7:7-8 according to Matthew which says that whoever knocks on the door will be welcome, whoever asks will receive. The chorus in Latin, '*Gloria in te Domine / Gloria exultate*', turns the song into a religious experience at least for U2, almost a celebration of the Eucharist. But Bono also said: 'It is a love song. In a sense it's an attempt to write about a woman in a spiritual sense and about God in a sexual sense. But there certainly is a strong sexual pulse in there.' Here we go: God, love, sex. These things are almost interchangeable for Bono and the truth is, he may be right. Even John Waters, when he talks about 'Gloria' says:

> The song had an unaccountable joyfulness about it, which because of the content made me uneasy. With hindsight it was my own positive response to it, in the knowledge of what it was, that made me uneasy. There were plenty of other pop songs with that title, but this was the least ambiguous. 'You probably wanted it to be about a waitress,' Bono joked to me a dozen years later. What I wanted was the song to be about what the song was about, but to be able to pretend I thought it was about a waitress.[44]

No U2 song is purely about this or about that. There is always something else underlying it and that is what make U2 lyrics so interesting and also so difficult to understand sometimes.

Almost all the songs on *October* talk about spirituality. 'With a Shout' is blatantly religious, Bono singing the word Jerusalem like a hymn to God.

> I wanna go / To the foot of Mount Zion / To the foot of He who made me see / To the side of a hill / Blood was spilled / We were filled with our love / And we're gonna be there again / Jerusalem Jerusalem.

Bono says that he is inspired by the Psalms of David most of all:

> In an odd way the walls of Jerusalem, or the walls of Jericho, were a great image for punk music, and the idea that went with it, that music could shake the foundations. The Psalms are amazing about music. They're all about bang that drum, whack that cymbal and, you know, dead bones rising up. Music as a wake-up call for the spirit – I think that was what we were driving at.[45]

Bono actually sees David as 'the first blues singer'.[46]

The Edge's, Larry's and Bono's experience within the Shalom community gave them a lot, however difficult it had become at the end. The study of the Bible was very useful in the end because it became an endless inspirational ground for Bono.

The truth is that in every album after *October*, there is at least one song with a spiritual theme. On *War*, 'Drowning Man' is an outstretched hand from God to a man who is drowning: 'Take my hand / You know I'll be there / If you can, I'll cross the sky for your love.' The song is written from God's point of view but also from David's point of view talking to God: 'And I understand / These winds and tides / This change of time won't drag you away,' and God's response is: 'Hold on, hold on tightly / Hold on and don't let go of my love.' Bono describes it as a psalm. '40', the very last song on the album, is directly taken from Psalm 40, with a bit of Psalm 6 in it. From 1983 until the end of the decade, U2 finished all their concerts with that song, a beautiful finale. Another song that has become very famous is 'I Still Haven't Found What I'm Looking For.' The Edge describes it as a Gospel song. It is a song about uncertainty and the crisis of faith: 'I have climbed the highest mountains / I have run through the fields / Only to be with you / Only to be with you / I have run I have crawled / I have scaled these city walls / Only to be with you / But I still haven't found what I'm looking for.' But the most interesting event in the history of the song is when it was appropriated by a Harlem gospel choir, the New Voices of Freedom. They had sent their version of the song to Island Records which in turn contacted U2. In the movie *Rattle and Hum*, U2 go to the choir's church and they sing together. The result is a classical moment in U2's career but also the realisation that the song is exactly that, a gospel song, offered a new meaning. This was even more true when the choir appeared on stage with U2 on 28 September 1987 in Madison Square Garden.

There are many biblical references in U2 songs from 'Pride (In the Name of Love)', to 'The First Time', and the unlikely 'Trying to Throw Your Arms Around the World', plus many more. What is important is that spirituality is still a theme that is essential in U2's work. *How to Dismantle an Atomic Bomb* contains at least one spiritual song with such a theme, which is 'Yahweh'. 'I had the idea that no one can own Jerusalem, but everybody wants to put flags on it. The title's an ancient name that's not meant to be spoken. I got around it by singing. I hope I don't offend anyone,' says Bono.[47]

LOVE AND EROTICISM

The theme of love is probably the most common in rock songs. It would have been strange had U2 not delved into the labyrinth of the most important and potent human emotion. And it is in fact difficult to separate it from spirituality, in Bono's mind. He is actually right. Love is a spiritual experience and it is quite logical that it cannot be separated, in the mind of a believer, from God's love.

In U2's world, ballads are called 'salads'. It is a difficult style and Bono says that he doesn't want to hear a U2 love song on the radio and go red in the face.

Simon Frith observes that: 'It is not that love songs give people a false, sentimental and fatalistic view of sexual relationships, but that romantic ideology requires such a view and makes love songs necessary.' Such an ideology is difficult to ignore and it may well be the reason for the love song's existence. Too often though, this romantic ideology is followed to the letter in those songs which therefore don't play a positive role. Very often, it is the plight of a lover left behind and who is desperate to have his/her love interest return. The U2 approach is quite different. Most of the love songs are bitter-sweet, the difficulty of understanding what love truly is being another part of the theme. One of the U2 love songs on *How to Dismantle an Atomic Bomb*, 'A Man and a Woman', is an interesting example of those two aspects. The chorus is a question about love between a man and a woman: 'I could never take a chance / Of losing love to find romance / In the mysterious distance / Between a man and a woman / No I could never take a chance / Cos I could never understand / The mysterious distance / Between a man and a woman.' Throughout the song runs uncertainty, doubt but also the joy of being together and of sharing moments. The bitter-sweetness is ever present. The last verse is a typical example of it: 'Little sister / I've been sleeping in the street again / Like a stray dog / Little sister / I've been trying to feel complete again / But you're gone and so is God.' God is always linked to love. Love is represented by the woman and God is love. The protagonist in the song can only feel complete through this woman who is inextricably linked to God and His love. This is not the first time U2 combine the two aspects and one song about redemption springs to mind. 'When Love Comes to Town' features B.B. King, one of the greatest blues musicians in the world. When the Irish band met him for the first time in Dublin, he was interested in recording a song with them. It turned up on *Rattle and Hum*. B.B. King was impressed by Bono's skill as a song writer and commented that they were 'heavy lyrics,' wondering how someone so young could write in such a way. Bono sings: 'I used to make love under a red sunset / I was making promises I was soon to forget / She's pale as the lace of her wedding gown / But I left her standing before love came to town / I ran into a juke joint when I heard a guitar scream / The notes were turning blue I was dazing in a dream / As the music played I saw my life turn around / That was the day before love came to town.' The power of love can free from temptation and God is the final redemptor. In the same vein, 'Love Rescue Me' written with Bob Dylan talks about the same type of character, a sinner looking for love to save him: 'In the cold mirror of a glass / I see my reflection pass / I see the dark shades of what I used to be / I see the purple of her eyes / The scarlet of my lies / Love rescue me.'

But the theme of love started out very early in U2's career, though not in an obvious way. It was very cleverly disguised, which was probably at the root of the idea that U2 did not write love songs and were more interested in politics. As early as 'An Cat Dubh' on Boy, love is on the agenda. The song is about a brief fling Bono had while he was already going out with Ali and they were going through a rough patch. 'Another Time Another Place' on the same album also suggests an adolescent sexual relationship, although more dreamed about than real. The song evokes the world of teenage fantasies: 'In my sleep I discover the one / But she'll run with the morning sun.' Two other songs have been appropriated by the homosexual community, 'Stories For Boys' and 'Twilight'. The gay community believed that the first one was a love song to a man, a non-macho song, whereas Bono simply thought of it as escapism, although he did not deny that it could have several layers of meaning. The second could indeed have appeared very ambiguous in America: 'The old man tries to walk me home / I thought he should have known.' 'Old man' means father in Ireland, whereas in America, it is taken in the literal sense.

Love songs become more common as time goes by. 'Two Hearts Beat as One' was written by Bono for Alison during their honeymoon; 'Promenade' evokes their life together when they lived in Bray; 'All I Want Is You' doesn't need any interpretation. There are other love songs about the general nature of love, for instance 'With or Without You', which deals with the difficulties faced by some relationships.

However, the subject of love reaches its darkest and most difficult aspect on Achtung Baby. The love songs on the album analyse love and erotic relationships from a pessimistic and dark viewpoint, a mixture of pain, love, unfaithfulness, betrayal, separation but also God and the crisis of faith. It is not, however, surprising that the dark side of love is shown in such a way, as there were many things going on at the time in the lives of U2's members. The Edge's marriage had disintegrated and the band were at a crossroads when they recorded the album, nearly splitting up in the process. It is easy to see here the creative process at work and life's influence on it.

One of the things that is most obvious here probably for the first time is this mixture of love and eroticism. With Achtung Baby, Bono was suddenly sexy and had become a sexual object. The songs talk about the dark side of love, at times blended with God. 'Until the End of the World' is such a song. Images of sacred moments or moments of betrayal are mixed with erotic ones: 'Last time we met it was a low-lit room / We were as close together as bride and groom / We ate the food and we drank the wine / Everybody having a good time / Except you / You were talking about the end of the world […] In the garden I was playing the tart / I kissed your lips and broke your heart / You, you were acting like it was the end of the world […] In my dream I was drowning sorrows / But my sorrows they learned to swim / Surrounding me, going down on me, spilling over the brim / In waves of regrets, waves of joy / I reached out for the one I tried to destroy / You, you said you'd wait until the end of the world.' Bono says: 'That's about a man playing the tart. I don't think I know many women who are tarts, but I know a lot of men.'[48]

Women, you might have noticed, never get treated badly in U2 songs. Even God has a feminine side in Bono's mind: 'I've always believed that the spirit is a feminine thing.'[49] And in the song 'In the Name of the Father', written by Bono, Gavin Friday and Seezer, he sings: 'In the name of the Father / And his wife the spirit.' Women are put on a pedestal by Bono, his mother's untimely death being undoubtedly one of the reasons. If anything, in some of the songs on *Achtung Baby*, it is the man who gets the raw deal. On 'So Cruel', it is the man who is the victim of a woman. It is the reverse of the classical torch song, described as a 'lament sung by a woman who desperately loves a commonplace or even brutish man.'[50] Bono sings: 'Desperation is a tender trap / It gets you every time / You put your lips to her lips / To stop the lies / Her skin is pale like God's only dove / Screams like an angel for your love / And then she makes you watch her from above / And you need her like a drug.' The man is manipulated by the woman's sexual power. He is incapable of pulling himself out of this relationship and despite his best efforts, he comes back to her. The short chorus, 'You say in love there are no rules / Sweetheart, you're so cruel' as well as the lines 'She wears my love like a see-through dress / Her lips say one thing, her movements something else' represent the woman's character – cruel, unreliable and unfaithful. She can only betray him and the duality between love and lust is well depicted in the song. However, unlike the classical torch song, this one ends with the man seemingly deciding to leave the woman: 'To stay with you, I'd be a fool / Sweetheart, you're so cruel.' The only thing we don't know in the end is whether he actually acts on his promise or not.

The woman as a domineering object of desire is also found in 'Mysterious Ways'. She is ever present in spirit and in flesh, teasing and tantalising. 'She moves in mysterious ways' sings Bono and during the Zoo TV tour, she is made real by the dancer who comes on stage. He tries to touch her but cannot reach her. She is so close and yet so far. If she is the spirit, then she is inaccessible. However, he cannot be without her and remains prisoner of the promise.

The most loved song on *Achtung Baby* must be 'One'. Bono says of the song:

'It amazes me when people tell me they played it at their wedding or for comfort at a funeral. I go to myself, "Are you crazy? It's about breaking up." '[51] But the music belies the actual theme of the song because in a lot of ways, it is comforting. However, when you look closely at the words, you know that it is exactly about what Bono says. It is about the guilt one feels when one ends a relationship. It is about the pain, despite the haunting chorus. It is bitter and one has but to look at the following lines to feel the pain: 'Have you come here for forgiveness? / Have you come to raise the dead? / Have you come here to play Jesus / To the lepers in your head? / Did I ask too much, more than a lot? / You gave me nothing, now it's all I've got / We're one but we're not the same / Well we hurt each other then we do it again / You say, love is a temple, love a higher law / Love is a temple, love the higher law / You ask me to enter but then you make me crawl / And I can't be holding on to what you've got / When all you've got is hurt.' However, the song has another dimension, that of the band itself and the fight for its artistic survival. A U2 song is never black or white and there are many layers of meaning, including in 'One', the spectre of Aids, a theme which has become close to Bono's heart.

Ireland

Ireland is like an invisible thread running throughout the songs, even those which don't have anything to do with Ireland. U2 never forget where they come from and it comes through at regular intervals.

But the band have also talked about Ireland in a more straightforward manner, both politically and personally. They have been inspired by Irish traditional music, despite the fact that they play rock 'n' roll. I don't think it is possible to ignore such an influence and even Bono said that he was influenced by the Dubliners and Luke Kelly. Their collaboration with traditional musicians (from Clannad to Christy Moore to the Chieftains) has undoubtedly allowed them to understand and appreciate their musical heritage.

Ireland north and south of the border has been dealt with in U2 songs but in different ways. Songs about Northern Ireland have definitely more than a political flavour while the Republic is dealt with in a more personal way.

Two songs written seventeen years apart deal openly with the conflict in Northern Ireland, in completely different ways. 'Sunday Bloody Sunday' and 'Peace on Earth' come from different directions. The first is partly about the 1972 events in Derry but also about the events that took place in Croke Park in 1921. The second is about the Omagh Bombing of 1998. The genesis of the two songs is equally different.

The Edge is at the heart of 'Sunday Bloody Sunday'. He wrote the music to the song while Bono was on honeymoon. The members of U2 wanted to write of the conflict in Northern Ireland but did not quite know how to go about it. They did not want to take sides though. They refused to be politicised and preferred a humanist stance. The lyrics could be construed as revolutionary to some. Indeed the military drumming style at the beginning is misleading, for this is a song about surrender. When U2 were playing a gig in the 1980s, Bono used to always say beforehand: 'This song is not a rebel song.' He was also trying 'to link what was happening in Northern Ireland to the original blood sacrifice and subsequent resurrection on Easter Sunday.'[52] Spirituality is never far from U2 and God's presence is omnipotent, especially in a song like this. What is interesting is people's reaction to the song. Fans from many countries seem to have become aware of the Northern Ireland conflict thanks to the song. Some have told me that it would have been difficult not to want to know what it was all about. And of course, during the concerts, when Bono used to say: 'You know the words, sing no more!', the crowd would respond quite readily. It was also the awareness that the singer talked about: 'It was only when I realised that the troubles hadn't affected me that they began to affect me. The bombs may not go off here but they are made here.'[53] Of course, the extract in the commercial video 'Under a Blood Red Sky' has become a classic in U2's career. Bono carrying the white flag while Larry is playing drums, bringing it to the crowd, telling them to 'hold it and let it fly' and then urging them to 'sing no more!', has become the stuff of legend.

Denouncing the IRA from the stage brought its worries as threats were made against the band, and the members of U2 had to have their fingerprints and toeprints taken in case of kidnapping. That, however, did not deter Bono from talking against mindless violence and a major event brought a new dimension to 'Sunday Bloody Sunday'. On 8 November 1987, an IRA bomb killed thirteen people in Enniskillen in Northern Ireland during a remembrance day parade and injured many more who had come to commemorate the soldiers of the North fallen during the Second World War. That day, U2 were to play Denver in Colorado. And they did play but those who saw the movie *Rattle and Hum* or were present that day will never forget Bono's rage when the band played the song. His speech during that part of the concert could have darkened the whole show:

And let me tell you something. I've had enough of Irish Americans who haven't been back in their country for twenty or 30 years, who come up to me and talk about the resistance, the revolution back home, and the glory of the revolution and the glory of dying for the revolution. Fuck the revolution! They don't talk about the glory of killing for the revolution. Where's the glory in taking a man from his bed and gunning him down in front of his wife and children? Where's the glory in that? Where's the glory in bombing a Remembrance Day Parade of old age pensioners – their medals taken out and polished up for the day? Where's the glory in that? To leave them dying or crippled for life or dead under the rubble of a revolution that the majority of the people in my country don't want. No more!

The song took an unexpected dimension that day. In Bono's words: 'It was almost like the song was made real for the day, in a way that it was never going to be again.'[54] The song's impact would never be the same again. In 2001, the band played it again but in a different and more positive manner, and Bono even commented in Pittsburgh on 6 May: 'If you're Irish, you got something to sing about in this song', when somebody passed him an Irish flag: 'There was a time when you couldn't hold this flag so high', and finally, he invited the crowd to: 'sing in the presence of love, sing in the presence of peace.'

'Sunday Bloody Sunday' may have been controversial but it remains a symbolic song for the fans of U2 because it made them a politically conscious band, a side that a lot of fans found appealing.

'Peace on Earth' is very different and probably the most despairing of U2's career. It is a homage to the victims of the Omagh bombing of 15 August 1998, in Northern Ireland which killed 29 people and injured many more, some of them very seriously.

Bono's reaction when he heard about it was immediate:

[This song] was written literally on the day the Omagh Bomb went off, right then. Nobody could actually believe it. In Ireland, when they read out the names of all the people who died on the six o'clock news, the city just came to a complete standstill … people were just weeping – in cars, on O'Connell Street, all over the place. It was really a trauma for most people – because not only was it the destruction of the lives, it was the destruction of the peace process, which had been put together with sticky tape and glue and tacks and a lot of faith. It seemed to be destroyed. It would be hard to describe to people who are not Irish what that felt like, that day. It was certainly the lowest day of my life, outside of personal losses. I couldn't believe it, that people could do that.[55]

The song reflects the singer's mood. Despair, powerlessness, disgust are quite evident in it, as are sorrow and pain, the feeling that one has had enough and despairs of ever seeing an end to violence: 'Heaven on earth, we need it now / I'm sick of all of this hanging around / I'm sick of sorrow, sick of the pain / I'm sick of hearing again and again / That there's gonna be peace on earth.' One can wonder if this song is not the most agnostic that Bono ever wrote, as Irish journalist, Niall Stokes suggests.[56] There is undoubtedly a crisis of faith here, when Bono sings: 'Jesus could you take the time / To throw a drowning man a line? / Peace on earth / Tell the ones who hear no sound / Whose sons are living in the ground / Peace on earth.' And he knows that there will not be an answer, not for now anyhow: 'Jesus this song you wrote / The words are sticking in my throat / Peace on earth / Hear it every Christmas time / But hope and history won't rhyme / So what's it worth / This peace on Earth.' Faith seems to be futile in the face of such mindless violence. But the homage to the victims is very poignant when Bono sings 'Sean and Julia / Gareth, Ann and Breda / Your lives are bigger than any big idea.'

These two songs deal with the same subject: the conflict and violence in Northern Ireland, whichever side it comes from. However, 'Sunday Bloody Sunday' deals with an historical event and is approached in a particular way: the ideas of surrender, forgiveness and neutrality are very much present. 'Peace on Earth' was written in the aftermath of Omagh and is much more emotional. There is therefore a real opposition between what is historical and what is a news item. The rage in 'Sunday Bloody Sunday' is softened by moments of hope: 'Tonight, we can be as one', the presence of Jesus being a soothing one. 'Peace on Earth' doesn't bring such relief. Even God seems to be deaf and not responding. The two songs are clearly opposite even from the musical point of view. Where 'Sunday Bloody Sunday' sounds like a military march, 'Peace on Earth' sounds like a Christmas song and becomes almost ironic. How can one indeed reconcile Christmas, its carols, family gatherings and festive mood with the horror of a massacre such as that of Omagh?

Other songs have been written about the conflict such as 'North and South of the River', a collaboration with Christy Moore, or 'Please'. Bono says that the latter was written for someone in particular (the singer doesn't say for whom) but: 'someone who really needs to have their face in the mud before they feel they have a licence to dress up in the garb of rhetoric and all that.'[57] It certainly could have been addressed to John Hume or David Trimble or anyone from either side of the sectarian divide. It was written with the end of the cease-fire in Northern Ireland in mind and the summer of conflict that ensued, with Drumcree as its lowest point. On 9 July 1995, in the small market town of

Portadown, the local lodge of the Protestant Orange Order, which parades every July, demanded that they be allowed their traditional march to take place on the way back from their annual church parade at Drumcree, despite the Royal Ulster Constabulary (RUC) preventing it from happening, thus going against the wishes of the Catholic residents of the Garvaghy Road. The stand-off continued the next day. On 11 July, the march was allowed to proceed without the bands. However, Ian Paisley and David Trimble both held their arms in the air when reaching the centre of the town, a gesture which did not please the Catholic residents of the Garvaghy road, to say the least. The following year, according to legislation allowing him to re-route the parades on the basis of public disorder, and in light of what had happened the previous year, the Chief Constable of the Royal Ulster Constabulary took the decision to re-route the Orange Order parade from the Garvaghy Road in Portadown. The decision created a wave of violence between 6 and 10 July 1996, culminating in 90 civilian injuries and the death of a Catholic taxi driver, amongst other incidents. On 11 July, the Chief Constable bowed to the Orangemen's pressure and the parade was allowed to proceed, much to the dismay and outrage of the Garvaghy road residents, but it also provoked considerable violence in Nationalist areas, sparking off many debates about the role of policing and the impartiality of the police force. However, 'Please' is very cleverly written and not as obvious as 'Sunday Bloody Sunday'. It is a very bitter prayer and the disillusionment that seeps through is palpable: 'Please ... please ... please get up off your knees / Please ... please ... leave me out of this, please.'

Bono also writes about Dublin, and Ireland in general. From *Boy* on, it has been a topic very cleverly disguised in the songs. Some of them are, however, more obvious than others. 'The Ocean' references Oscar Wilde and his *Portrait of Dorian Gray*, as well as the caravan Bono's family owned in Skerries; 'Shadows and Tall Trees' is about Ballymun; 'The Electric Co.' talks about Saint Brendan's psychiatric hospital in Gormanstown, where they used electric shock treatment. Other songs deal with the drugs problem in Dublin such as 'Bad' or 'Running to Stand Still'. Bono observes:

> If you can't change the world you're living in, seeing it through different eyes is the only alternative. And heroin gives you heroin eyes to see the world with. The thing about heroin is that you think that's the way it really is, that the old you who worries about paying the rent is not the real you.[58]

As I've mentioned previously, the Irish literary tradition has also inspired Bono.

Poets and writers are present throughout the lyrics, sometimes not in an obvious way, but his writing has something of Ireland in it. He mentions Sean O'Casey, Yeats, Patrick Kavanagh and mostly Seamus Heaney as having inspired him.

As for the Irish musical tradition, few songs have been inspired by it. However, its spirit runs through. 'Tomorrow' or 'Drowning Man' are beautiful examples of that inspiration, with the use of violin and Uileann pipes. The first was actually re-recorded for the 1995 *Common Ground*, put together by Donal Lunny[59] and featuring Irish musicians playing Irish traditional music. Ten years previously, the duet with Clannad 'In a Lifetime' became a hit but Bono's reaction was mixed: 'I'm almost embarassed about this being a hit because it's so emotional ... but I'm very proud of it.'

The Edge was himself inspired by Irish history when he wrote 'Van Diemen's Land' (also the title of a rebel song), a homage to John Boyle O'Reilly, a member of the British army in Ireland, who became a poet and a Fenian. He was arrested in 1848 for writing subversive texts that had the potential to shake the government. He was sentenced to hard labour and sent to Tasmania (called Van Diemen's land in the popular culture) for twenty years. For The Edge, Boyle O'Reilly was a political prisoner. But the song itself isn't rebellious. It rather depicts the suffering and injustice that people fighting for their freedom had to endure.

Politics

The penultimate topic is politics. I want to briefly mention some of the songs that have made U2 famous for their political stance. The first ones appeared in 1983 with the album *War*. Apart from the Irish situation, other issues were evoked. For instance, 'New Year's Day' sounds like an ordinary love song at first glance but was actually inspired by the Polish leader Lech Walesa and the union Solidarnosc. Bono said of its impact: 'The fact that "New Year's Day" made the top twenty indicated a disillusionment among record buyers with the pop culture in the charts. I don't think "New Year's Day" was a pop single.' He went on about the album: 'It was an unsettled time. You looked around and there were conflicts everywhere. We saw a lot of unrest on TV and in the media. We focused on these.'[60]

On *The Unforgettable Fire*, 'Pride (In the Name of Love)' is the most well-known song. It reached number three in the British charts, and it is a homage to Martin Luther King. Another song on the album, 'MLK', is about him also. These have undoubtedly contributed to the reason why U2 are seen as a political band.

The Joshua Tree was their most American album but it was also a very political record. It showed the beautiful but also the ugly face of America. U2 had by then developed an interest in international political issues. What is interesting is that the 1990s produced on the surface far less political songs than the previous decade. The reason is, of course, found in the band's image overhaul. But politics were present in the concerts, and *Zooropa*'s sleeve was, if anything, political. The blurred faces of dictators was evidence enough. Even on *Pop*, one can find a couple of well-disguised political songs like, 'Walk On', a homage to Aung San Suu Kyi, the Burmese leader and 1991 Nobel Peace Prize winner. And on *How to Dismantle an Atomic Bomb*, 'Crumbs From Your Table' and 'Miracle Drug' are reminders of Bono's fight against Aids and poverty in Africa.

Up Close and Personal

The singer says that *How to Dismantle an Atomic Bomb* is a much more personal than political album. Indeed, one can feel that listening to the album. Bono's father, Bobby Hewson, is very present. 'Sometimes You Can't Make It On Your Own' is a homage to him, to the man he was. It may actually strike a chord with a few listeners. On the previous album, 'Kite' was also about Bobby. At the time, he was ill with cancer. The topic of fatherhood is beautifully evoked, Bono himself being a father to four children. The duality of Bono as a father but most of all as a son is the central theme: 'I'm a man, I'm not a child / A man who sees the shadow behind your eyes.' As we grow, we understand our parents better. We stop judging them, and wonder how we will be later in life. Bono knows his father is ill and has to face Bobby's mortality, as well as his own. But there is also the feeling that when he passes away, the singer will always regret not having talked to him more, maybe not having understood him better.

Bono's mother is, however, one character that comes back regularly in his writing. Take the songs 'Tomorrow', for instance, or 'Lemon', or even 'Mofo'. The common denominator is Bono's mother's passing and her absence, a gaping wound that has never quite healed. The lyrics are very poignant, even when the music belies the real emotions. Those are found for example in the words: 'Mother, am I still your son / You know I've waited for so long to hear you say so / Mother, you left and made me someone / Now, I'm still a child and no one tells me no' ('Mofo'). The singer seems to have blocked a lot of memories from his childhood, when his mother was still around, possibly because of the pain it might revive, for instance when he told Michka Assayas, French author and journalist, that he couldn't remember if his mother liked music and suddenly recalled that she liked Tom Jones, for instance.[61] Painful memories make for beautiful music and raw emotion, and nowhere is it more obvious than in those songs of loss and sorrow.

The Ethics of Aesthetics

One more aspect has to be dealt with in this chapter, linked to the creation of the songs. It is essential indeed to talk about the ethics of aesthetics in rock and in U2. If it is, as sociologist Bertrand Ricard puts it when he talks of amateur bands, a 'form of social link founded on a shared and proselytist aesthetic vision',[62] then U2 are surely part of this. I have always thought of U2 as one of the biggest bands in the world with the spirit of a garage band. They still have an aesthetic ideal that they share with any young band. It may be another reason why they are still successful. They still want people to enjoy and understand their music. Like any other band, they must seek an ethics that includes reason and aesthetics, with a certain morality.

Bertrand Ricard believes that the reason for young people getting together to create a rock band is at first an aesthetic reason. But it could also be because of friendship or because it is a means to escape from a way of life that isn't suitable. There are, in fact, many reasons.

U2 was founded partly to escape a form of ghetto and partly because U2's members wanted to find a way of expressing themselves in an artful way. Their ethics of aesthetics was that of any young band, but they kept that spirit alive, as well as an eminently communal way of thinking. Had they not followed those principles, I am certain that they would not have kept on working with the same people since they started their career

U2's identity is understood and shared by the public. So is their ethics of aesthetics. Within the band itself, the ethical codes seem to be respected by all: respect for oneself and the band, work goals to achieve, preservation of the aesthetic ideals, development of the life of the band. Thus, norms and rules were created in the microcosm inhabited by U2, which have to be obeyed for the band's survival, and this is inextricably linked to the quality of the artistic work.

One ethical rule is that no album is created for commercial purposes only. It has to have qualities that the band and their audience appreciate. The songs have to be great, as opposed to just good. Another rule is that one has to seek something original, to reinvent oneself constantly. This is where imagination plays its biggest role.

To imagine and to think are two verbs that are essential in U2's vocabulary. The band want, indeed need something new. This is another key to their success. However, they also have to obey certain rules that belong to the medium itself. A rock song, notably a single, cannot be too long, has to have a chorus for instance. But also the creation of an identity is essential to a band's survival. This particular identity will allow it to have its own vision and to imagine otherwise.

This imagination can also be put to the service of others through 'ethical-poetical imagination',[63] capable of seeing and understanding the other, an ethical imagination which is 'a call of the other to be heard, and to be respected in his/her otherness'[64] and a poetical imagination which is 'inventive making and creating ... The imagination, no matter how ethical, needs to play.'[65]

During an anti-fascist evening organised by actress Vanessa Redgrave at the Thalia Theatre in Hamburg in 1993, The Edge and Bono sang 'One', accompanied by the Bengali-Indian musician Ravi Shankar. Bono gave a speech afterwards where he said:

If we want to challenge hatred, empathic imagination is central. We need to paint pictures and see them move. I think of the still frames of Helmut Hartzfeld who changed his name to John Hartfield to protest against the original nazis. I think of Berlin Dadaists whose movement unzipped the starched trousers of the fascists, exposing them as serious – painfully serious – dickheads. Close to the poison you'll find the cure. As well as an antidote, humour/laughter is the evidence of freedom (…) It was from a Mel Brooks movie called *The Producers* that U2 took the name of their last album. In the bizarre musical an SS officer is met with the greeting, 'Achtung, baby!' to which he replies, 'Ze führer would never say baby!' Quite right. The führer would never say baby. We are writers, artists, actors, scientists. I wish we were comedians. We would probably have more effect. 'Mock the devil and he will flee from thee.' 'Fear of the devil leads to devil worship.' Anyway, for all this: imagination. To tell our stories, to play them out, to paint pictures, moving and still, but above all to glimpse another way of being. Because as much as we need to describe the kind of world we do live in, we need to dream up the kind of world we want to live in. In the case of a rock 'n' roll band that is to dream out loud, at high volume, to turn it up to eleven. Because we have fallen asleep in the comfort of our freedom.

Rock and roll is for some of us a kind of alarm clock. It wakes us up to dream! It has stopped me from becoming cynical in cynical times (…)

While rock has applied this ethical-poetical imagination in raising awareness of social and political causes (and U2 have done the same), the Irish band also applies it to its creative process. And through the songs, this empathic imagination steps into the real world, allowing the vision U2 have of it to come through. Imagination can reach far and wide, at the musical level, but also at the social level. But U2 must also reinvent imagination through artful deceit, which may cause problems when it comes to some fans, for instance. In the early 1990s, some early fans started thinking that the band had sold out, that they had become insincere or inauthentic, that the new values they displayed did not fit their earlier philosophy. The issue here is the line that separates artistic creation for oneself from artistic creation for others. It seems to be most prevalent in rock and pop music. I often wonder if the songs some bands or singers sing are what they really want to sing, or is it just for the sake of selling records? The question of this separation has been high on U2's agenda since the beginning of the 1990s. Indeed, the issue is even aggravated by the fact that the medium of popular music centres around the fan, his/her tastes and his/her expectations. Talking to the fans of U2, and being one myself, I realise that we all have different expectations, so it would be difficult for any band to satisfy everybody. When U2 decided to change at the turn of the 1990s, the problem was not only to change the image they had but also to take imagination and bring it elsewhere. In other words, it was essential to reinvent the music, which is the essence of the band. And the music would actually dictate the change of image. Through this quest for new artistic ground, there is also a quest for a new form of imagination that encompasses all the aspects of rock creation, where '[it] shows imagination turning into something concrete'.[66]

For inspiration comes from the real world, may it be love, spirituality, politics or more personal areas. Imagination is anchored in reality, and it is then adapted and reflected in the work in a personal way. Imagination is pragmatic, describes a known world, a world that is sometimes dark, sometimes bright, sometimes light, sometimes heavy, but that is made poetical by the use of appropriate words.

The role of imagination is to show the colour running through the band, to give it its 'genetic code'. But when it is modified, intentionally so, then it may create a lot of discontent among the fans. However, this 'new' identity is also a means of gaining new fans. The band therefore changes with the times and runs the risk of disappointing some people. U2 have used the times they have lived in as a springboard to show their different faces, deconstructing and reassembling them, and appropriating them very often in reverse. In the 1980s, they 'used' sincerity and authenticity as a shield against a superficial decade, whereas in the 1990s, they used simulacrum, that which only has the appearance of what it pretends to be, and irony against their own image, but also to transcend a postmodern era, while on the surface being completely submerged by it. Irony and simulacrum were the result of a radical musical and visual transformation which served to try and destroy the myth that had reared its ugly head in the 1980s.

U2 follow an ethics of aesthetics, as we have seen, which is part of a moral code set up by the band. There is no better example of this code applied to the community and especially to one of its members than that of Adam Clayton's difficulties during the Zoo TV tour. Here we have four individuals playing an instrument, being in probably the biggest band in the world. But we also have four young men whose friendship is the basis of everything. They are working towards the common good of the band and with a common goal. If one of them is in trouble, they react, they rally around and they find a solution because: 'pleasure has one common rule, that of giving the others what they expect and to receive as much in return, to make the common dream come true.'[67]

U2's philosophy of creating an album is best described by The Edge: 'We still feel that our records are as good as anything we've ever done, so our determination to make that be true means that we're not willing to take second best ever, and that means driving our engineers and producers completely mad.'[68]

U2 are a band truly on the creative side of rock, seeking to reinvent imagination, but also to be successful, to be heard.

4

SPIRITUALITY

If there exists a rock band that has used spirituality and faith as guiding princi-ples in its career without being branded a Christian band, it must be U2. It is obvious that these two principles are essential to the band's members. They are most obvious in the lyrics, but also in the many interviews that the band mem-bers have given over the years. Niall Stokes points to the fact that U2, being 'neither Protestant nor Catholic, neither working-class nor middle-class, [they] started out as a band who would have to forge an identity without much of the familiar ballast of Irish cultural life – or its baggage. As a result, they could wrap rock 'n' roll and religion up together in a way very few other bands would even have contemplated.'[1]

I feel almost ill at ease talking about U2's faith, as I am myself not religious (I use the adjective religious in the positive sense of the word.) However, spiri-tuality would be a more appropriate word to use when it comes to U2's world. Bono himself said that people tend to confuse religion and spirituality.[2] Religion is an organised, institutionalised set of beliefs concerning the existence of a deity. It is also the most divisive issue that one can think of, amongst believers and non-believers, or most often amongst people of different religions. Even pol-itics could never reach the level of disagreement that religion creates. Spirituality, on the other hand, is something we all share, whatever our beliefs. It is essential to our well-being as humans and is not necessarily religious. We are, amongst other things, spiritual beings and I believe that U2 appeal to that particular side of our humanity, because we all need to believe in something, whether it is God, nature, or something otherworldly. Spirituality deals with the side of human life which is called the spirit, as opposed to its material side. It allows mankind to ask questions about its existence and place in the universe. Spirituality is not necessarily religious, in that it is not organised, like a religion, and it has no dogma. There is a sense of freedom in the idea of spirituality that isn't found in that of religion. Spirituality is also a quest or a journey and it undoubtedly applies to U2.

What we will look at in this chapter is U2's faith and how it has affected their work and their outlook on life, but also the reasons why I was so drawn to their music and their sense of spirituality without ever sharing their religious beliefs.

U2 and Christian Rock

Let me first give a definition of Christian rock. According to Professor in Media Studies Roy Shuker, it is 'a rather loose musical style/genre, applied initially to those artists associated with the emergence of a Christian music industry established by American evangelicals (in the 1970s) as an alternative to the mainstream "secular" entertainment business.'[3] While the music doesn't sound different from its mainstream counterpart, the lyrics' main concern is God, God's love, sin, forgiveness and so on. 'The work of some mainstream performers has, at times, been influenced by their Christian beliefs, usually in terms of a more mystic Christian spirituality, such as Bob Dylan, Van Morrison, or U2.'[4] U2's way of dealing with spirituality and religion, and their relationship to others, has never been judgemental, even when they had joined Shalom and recorded *October*. It was always open-minded and that is exactly what people like about it. Steve Stockman, author and Presbyterian minister says: 'their faith isn't ridiculed.'[5] If you talk to people about it they don't seem to care that much about the faith of U2's members. If they don't share their beliefs, it generally leaves them cold and if they do, they possibly feel closer to U2 because of that.

Of course, over the years, the reactions have been diverse, from tolerance to intolerance when it comes to the members of U2 distancing themselves from the Church. However, I would say that U2 taking a step back was done in the public sphere. But, in the private sphere, and to the best of my knowledge, they still go to mass (albeit for Bono, it seldom happens[6]) and pray. Bono says: 'I try to take time out of every day, in prayer and meditation. I feel as at home in a Catholic cathedral as in a revival tent.'[7] The members of U2 just don't want to worship in public. After all, religious worship should be done in the private sphere and not displayed as a mark of the 'I go to Church therefore I am a good person' syndrome. That is the problem with some Christians who find it difficult to take criticism. 'A Christian's pleading for social justice without worshipping God regularly within the community of the church is little more than activism for its own sake,' says a Christian magazine about Bono's activism and criticism of the church for not doing enough.[8] Without any proof to the contrary, the magazine goes on saying: 'Bono's full-throated judgements on the Church prompt this question: Just how would he know? He has, after all, avoided the Church since breaking with Shalom, a Watchman Nee-inspired group in Ireland, in the early 1980s.'[9] However, they don't seem to understand where Bono is coming from. As far back as 1985, he was saying:

> We don't talk about our personal beliefs because there's too much to talk. You turn on the television (in America) and you have this guy who looks like a neo-nazi with a Bible in his hand and his fist is virtually coming out of the TV screen (...) The credits come up and the call for cash comes (...) For me, it's as much as I can do to restrain myself from throwing the television out of the top floor of the hotel. It's taught us to shut up.[10]

Larry observes:

> It was always a personal thing (...) On a personal level, I haven't lost my faith at all. I don't practise it in the same way I did when I was younger, but I haven't lost sight of the fundamentals of it. There are many people out there who would disagree and say, 'Well how can you do this and how can you consider yourself that?'
> There have never been any rules applied to my faith. My faith is a personal thing. I'm sure there are things you can get away with like anything else, and there's no doubt that we push it to the edge, to the very edge. And occasionally we fall off the other end. But I never felt that my job as a musician was to sing gospel or to proselytise. I've always felt that I'm a musician in a band and I've been given a gift. And I believe that gift is from God. I don't believe it's from anywhere else. And if at any stage I abuse that I think I'll know. That will be time to stop. I do think it's important.[11]

U2's faith is not defined by rigid rules and that's what gives it its free aspect. U2 were never a Christian rock band, indeed could never have been a Christian rock band and they didn't want to be known as such, contrary to what Susan Fast says in her paper about U2: 'In their earliest days, [U2] were known as a

Christian rock band.'[12] The album *October* may have been an overt way of expressing their beliefs, and was reviewed in Christian magazines, but U2 were never part of the Christian rock movement, despite that album and despite the fact that they appeared unannounced at the Greenbelt Arts Festival, in England, on 24 August 1981, the biggest Christian arts festival in Europe.

Had U2 been American, they may well have been sucked into the Christian rock music industry. As it is, saying that they were a Christian rock band doesn't make any sense. But that they were influenced by their Christian beliefs is a point that needs to be developed. Indeed, rock is very much linked to spirituality and U2 are not the first artists to deal with it.

U2 and the Blues

Rock is the child of jazz, blues, boogie, hillbilly, rhythm 'n' blues and soul, all largely influenced by religious beliefs and spirituality. Let me give you just one example of a largely unknown, yet most influential blues artist from the 1930s called Robert Johnson. The reason I chose him was that Bono talked about how he inspired him and there is a connection between U2 and the blues, not only on *Rattle and Hum* but elsewhere in their work. Robert Johnson was born on 8 May 1911 and his songs became standards of the genre and were later also sung by other musicians and bands, including the Rolling Stones and Eric Clapton. A legend accompanies the making of Johnson's myth. As a young black boy, living on a plantation in Mississippi, his dearest wish was to learn to play the guitar. He was told to go to a crossroads, near the plantation, with his guitar. There, he was met by a big black man (who was in fact the Devil) who tuned his guitar and gave it back to him. In less than a year and in exchange for his soul, Robert Johnson became the king of the Delta Blues, and played a 'prototypical rock' according to authors of *From Blues to Rock*, David Hatch and Stephen Millward.[13] The reality, of course, is 'slightly' different. What is interesting is that the blues, and Johnson's blues, talk about redemption, God, the Devil, sin, forgiveness and is therefore an earlier musical genre which deals with spiritual matters. It talks about the yearning for God, the sometimes difficult relationship between man and God.

Many of the songs written by U2 deal with spiritual matters. Some might even say that most of the band's songs are about the spirit. But they are not religious songs. Even at the height of irony, U2 still talked about such matters, albeit in a concealed way. Talking about fans having a hard time understanding the records made in the 1990s, and the seeming lack of spirituality, Bono says: 'They didn't see it. On *Pop*, I thought it was a tough relationship with God that was described there: Looking for to save my, save my soul / Looking for the places where no flowers grow / Looking for to fill that God-shaped hole. That's quite an interesting lyric, because that's the real blues – that comes from Robert Johnson, it happens through the machine age, through this techno din, but there it is: the same yearning (…) A lot of people didn't see it, because they wanted to feel it, not to think it'[14] It was indeed probably difficult for some people to see spirituality in such a confusion of sound and technology. The explanation may lie in the fact that when U2 took inspiration from the blues, they wrote 'When Love Comes to Town' for B.B. King, another famous bluesman, another song about redemption. It was as close to the blues as one could get. *Pop* was musically light years away. In spirit, it wasn't because spirituality can come in many guises. I don't think it must be packaged in one way for people to understand it. But maybe indeed people didn't want to think. It is no surprise that U2, given their background, should have been inspired by spirituality. Other examples of those inspired by it include Elvis Presley and Bob Dylan. Jann S. Wenner asked Bono if he ever 'saw rock & roll – the so-called devil's music – as incompatible with religion?', to which he replied:

> Look at the people who have formed my imagination. Bob Dylan. 1976 – he's going through similar stuff. You buy Patti Smith: *Horses* – 'Jesus died for somebody's sins / But not mine …' And she turns Van Morrison's 'Gloria' into liturgy. She's wrestling with these demons – Catholicism in her case. Right the way through to *Wave*, where she's talking to the pope. The music that really turns me on is either running toward God or away from God. Both recognise the pivot, that God is at the centre of the jaunt. So the blues, on one hand – running away; gospel, the Mighty Clouds of Joy – running towards. And later you came to analyse it and figure it out.[15]

It is not surprising that musicians of any genre should be inspired by spiritual matters. As I said before, this is part of our humanity and is as important as any other theme that could inspire those musicians. God is also linked to love and sex. Love is a spiritual experience, as sex can be. I have always thought that if God exists, he or she or it is first and foremost made of love. Why should we be afraid of God, if that is the case? God is supposed to be forgiveness and understanding. Bono goes further: 'If I could put it simply, I would say that I believe there's a force of love and logic in the world, a force of love and logic behind the universe.'[16]

Rock Band

..deed an Irish rock band who happens to have three Christian members
.. ..nd who writes songs about love, sex, politics, ambition, faith and God.
Anu we should not forget Adam Clayton, who never adhered to the fervent
beliefs of his fellow musicians. He was the grain of sand in the machinery and
may well have had more influence on the other three than we give him credit
for. He is sometimes caught in the flood. One would expect the three other
members of the band to answer positively to the following question by B.P.
Fallon: 'Do you believe in miracles?'[17] 'Yes! That U2 have got this far! I believe
in miracles and prayer and faith' is The Edge's answer. Larry said: 'I always
believe there's a chance through hope, faith or downright miracles,' while Bono
answered: 'Yes. Most people who make music see the spirit move in some way.'
Adam's answer may be surprising to some:

Yeah. We made *Achtung Baby*. I think it's a miracle that U2 are still together and alive and making records, considering the odds against us. Bit of a
miracle, that. I'm not saying it in a profound sense but certainly knowing
that we got this far convinces me that there must be things at work.
'Are you amazed at it?'
'By the success of the band? Yeah, I am. I'm generally in awe of it that four
people who really didn't know their arse from their elbows and were wet
behind their ears can actually travel the world and meet people.

Yet Adam Clayton is considered the least religious member of U2. But he can
also be transported by the spiritual side of U2 as can the fans. Bono said that
Adam, although not exactly in the same way as the others, is still a believer.[18]
However, the misunderstanding about U2 being a Christian band may come
from the fact that they spoke to Christian magazines at the beginning, and Steve
Stockman observes:

They were often misquoted and felt used and abused. The evangelical
Christian world seemed to claim U2 as its property, and therefore, U2's
members found their faith defined and explained by magazines rather than
by the members themselves. Aligning themselves with the Christian press
would have pigeonholed their faith and their art, squeezed them into the
mould of other people's expectations, and narrowed the focus of the band's
influence and scope.[19]

U2's sense of independence was again at play here. They never wanted to be put in a box. They may have been believers but didn't want to be part of one or more scenes. They wanted to conquer the world and become rock stars. That they could do it while keeping their spirituality a part of their music and larger way of life is a testament to their philosophy.

Henry VanderSpek, author, asks: 'U2. Who are they and what they are about? Something sacred? Profane? Neither? Or both? (...) Are they religious? Spiritual? Christian even?'[20] My answer would be all of that. They are sacred to their fans, yet profane in the kind of music they play. They are religious because they believe in God. They are spiritual because all human beings are. They are Christians because they are Catholic/Protestant and still practise their faith.

I can certainly understand why people with a Christian faith could have seen in U2 a different side, could have been drawn to the band because they shared the same Christian values. U2's achievement, however, lies elsewhere. They were never proselytisers. Even at the height of *October*, they celebrated their faith without trying to convert anybody. And they turned very quickly away from the sort of fervent display that could have been dangerous for them. The openness that they showed to anybody who was interested in listening to them was the key to their being accepted as a rock 'n' roll band and not a Christian rock band. One should never underestimate the fact that they didn't have a message to deliver, whether in the Christian or political spheres, despite what some people might think.

Faith and Spirituality

One of U2's traits is that they have incredible faith in what they do, in their mission as a rock band. But they also have faith in God. The whole thing goes hand in hand. Talking about his father, Bono said: 'In fact, it was what he liked best about the band: our faith.'[21] It is indeed a fascinating trait in U2, another essential part of the band's identity. To Bobby Hewson questioning his son about his relationship with God and how he could hear something in the silence, Bono answered:

> I hear it in some sort of instinctive way, I feel a response to a prayer, or I feel led in a direction. Or if I'm studying the scriptures, they become alive in an odd way, and they make sense to the moment I'm in, they're no longer a historical document.[22]

This response could have a different kind of explanation. For some people, it could be intuition leading them towards a certain path. It could have nothing to do with God. Bono describes it that way because he feels it, because he believes it to be that way. That's what faith is.

One of Bono's favourite subjects is faith versus luck. This is a difficult one. Do you get something you want because of a fluke or because you really believe in it so much that your faith can move mountains and you eventually get what you want (and maybe, if you believe enough, then you got a little help from above)? When Bono tells Michka Assayas about the episode in the late 1970s when he bet on a horse during the Grand National to pay for a friend's wedding and the horse won, he says it in a such way that you absolutely believe in the power of faith, at least in his case. In 1983, he already talked about it:

I'm frightened but I'm not cynical or pessimistic about the future and a lot of that must come down to my beliefs. It is my belief in God that enables me to get up in the morning and face the world. I believe that there is a logic and a reason for everything. If I didn't believe that and thought that every-thing was simply down to chance, then I'd really be afraid. I wouldn't cross the road for fear of being run over.[23]

However, Bono would not see himself as pious or indeed as a preacher. It probably is this flawed man that he describes himself as, this modesty that people find endearing, that brings him closer to the ordinary human beings that we are.

But he says that God is never far below the surface and that people pray even if they don't believe, for instance when they are sick.[24] But do people pray because they have nothing left except that? Does it necessarily mean that they believe in God or simply that our collective unconscious is still so steeped in reli-gious beliefs that even the most atheist of us would turn to prayer in a moment of crisis? That is what I mean when I say that U2 have appealed to our collec-tive unconscious in a spiritual way. Their belief in God is important to some of their fans who are believers, but most of the others, who are not, feel that what is important is not that they believe in God but that they follow the path of openness and spirituality without preaching, and that their music retains that spiritual quality without necessarily being openly religious.

The word that springs to my mind when I think of U2's music is 'uplifting.' I've already used it in the introduction. To me, the saddest and most bitter U2 song still possesses that particular quality. That is why a U2 song has always been a place where my heart, whatever its torment or peacefulness, feels at home, uplifted and serene, all at the same time. The oasis of peace that is sometimes created may also be a home for the spirit.

The Album October

This whole public idea of spirituality in U2 stems from the album *October*. Although Larry, The Edge and Bono have always had faith in God, who appears, albeit in a veiled way in their earlier work, *October* was offered up to the world as proof that they were actually true believers and weren't ashamed of it.

People know the story of Bono's lyrics being stolen in 1981 in Seattle and all the writing having to be done over again. The singer actually recovered them in 2005 and said: 'I'd love to say that they were genius – they're not. They're shorthand. But 24 years later, I can't remember what those word association games are!'[25] So the band had to write the whole album in the studio. Bono recalls the creative process and the thought process of the band: 'We can do this on the spot. The Spirit will inspire us. We will speak in tongues and words will form and songs will appear. And, y'know, they did! It's questionable how great all those songs are, but it is truly ecstatic music.'[26]

It was the Shalom period. Being involved in that charismatic sect, asking questions about the world and its injustices, where art fitted into all that, where rock 'n' roll fitted, all of this must have been very confusing in the end. Bono confesses: 'At that point we were so removed from the culture. Rock 'n' roll – that was the day job. We used to get together every single night, meeting in people's houses, reading, studying the scriptures. The band was what we did during the day.'[27] However, it could not last, as a decision had to be made either to stay with Shalom and leave U2 or leave Shalom and rescue the band. Larry talked about his leaving the charismatic group: 'I got out before anybody else. I'd just had enough, it was bullshit. It was like joining the Moonies.'[28] But The Edge was still in two minds. As for Adam, his reaction was one of dismay, and confusion. He simply couldn't understand how anyone would forego a rock 'n' roll band for a narrow-minded, religious sect, 'whereas up to that point I had always assumed that music and spirituality were on the same page – I didn't necessarily see the conflict.'[29] Paul McGuinness first and then Chris Blackwell saved the day.

October is a beautiful album, despite or because of its openly spiritual side. The songs reflect the band's state of mind at the time, the struggle between what should and should not be done, the decisions that needed to be made, more a crisis of self rather than a crisis of faith.

It was indeed unusual that a rock band should suddenly face spiritual doubt and jeopardise a promising career.

It was the first crisis of faith that U2 went through and there have been others. But spiritual doubt has, from then on, mostly been found in the songs.

Crisis of Faith

We all face a crisis at some stage of our lives, whether it is spiritual or a crisis of the self. No one can say that they are certain of everything all the time. And those who do are liars.

We live in a world full of doubt and U2 are no different. Can we make sense of illness or premature death? Can we accept the fact that what we thought would last forever is but a fleeting moment that cannot be regained? In this case, can we find comfort and perhaps an explanation in our spiritual beliefs, in our faith in God? Love may be the answer to that, and if we don't all believe in God, all of us believe in love and the power of salvation that love has.

I am thinking of the song 'Love Rescue Me', on *Rattle and Hum*. Bono had dreamt of Bob Dylan and of a song that he was singing. The next day, he started writing a song that Dylan could sing or that he thought Dylan was singing in his dream. Shortly afterwards, Bono was asked if he would pay a visit to the legendary singer. The pair met and finished the song together. Dylan even recorded it but asked for it to be withdrawn because he feared it might conflict with his Travelling Wilbury commitments. The song itself is about a man who is playing the role of saviour to many but whose own life is in a mess and who is in need of help himself. This man is seeking salvation through love, the love of God, especially. Bono sings: 'Love rescue me / Come forth and speak to me / Raise me up and don't let me fall / No man is my enemy / My own hands imprison me / Love rescue me.' In this song again, Bono uses the psalms as inspiration. 'Yea though I walk through the valley of the shadow / Yet I will fear no evil / I have cursed thy rod and staff / They no longer comfort me / Love rescue me' is inspired by Psalm 23, 'The Lord is My Shepherd'.[30] The whole of the Bible is an inspiration to Bono who says: 'It sustains me.'[31]

This song illustrates the crisis of faith that any believer must face at times and U2 are well able to convey that struggle in words. An example now of U2 experiencing a crisis of faith within the band is the recording of *Achtung Baby*. The record is seeped in an aura of palpable crisis, 'probably the heaviest record we've ever made' says Bono.[32] Here the idea of faith versus luck may apply. Were U2 lucky that they actually made it back to Dublin after the Berlin sessions and found inspiration or was it their faith in the band that prevailed? Bono would probably answer the latter. He says that he never had fear of failure, a belief that obviously allowed him and the band to go as far as they are now. That's what blind faith is. And faith can be found in U2 in a spiritual sense but also, in this case, in a sense of self, a belief in oneself. U2 function as a unit and have faith not only as a unit but in each other. It may seem obvious but one doesn't go without the other. They share a sense of faith and spirituality. It would not work without all members of the band being included though. That they should have been functioning like this for years, despite the ups and downs, is quite extraordinary. That they should still believe in themselves after so much time together is even more remarkable. Even the toughest times of the band, such as the *Achtung Baby* recording, have not broken that unity and have undoubtedly strengthened the partnership.

Other examples of crisis of faith are found in two songs which appear on the album *Pop* and which are 'If God Will send His Angels' and 'Wake Up Dead Man'.

'If God Will Send His Angels' is a very bitter song dealing with the crisis of faith through a story of domestic violence, more precisely of a man who is beating his partner. It isn't a religious song as such, yet it is a call to God to act: 'Hey, if God will send His angels/ And if God will send a sign/ And if God would send his angels/ Would everything be alright?' God is however not listening: 'God has got His phone off the hook babe, would He even pick up if he could ?/ It's been a while since we saw that child hanging 'round this neighbourhood/ See His mother dealing in the doorway, see Father Christmas with a begging bowl/ Jesus sister's eyes are a blister...the high street never looked so low.' God is pretending to be deaf. The child is the symbol of Christ who hasn't been seen around in a long time while the mother is not the Virgin Mary but a woman he loves like his own mother (that's why the 'h' of His is a capital letter) and his heart bleeds for her. Santa Claus, the symbol of hope and joy is begging while Jesus' sister is any woman who is addicted to drugs. The singer links all the people in that street to Jesus, and Jesus is present in their desperation. Everything is distorted and perverted: the police are corrupted, the lack of love and faith is screaming at everybody, violence is present at every turn and the innocence of children is shattered when 'the cartoon network turns into the news.' Bitterness is seeping through the song as faith in Christ is replaced by faith in a consumer society and even Jesus is up for sale.

Niall Stokes describes the song 'Wake Up Dead Man' as an 'end of the millennium psychosis blues-song'.[33] It begins with: 'Jesus, Jesus help me / I'm alone in this world, and a fucked-up world it is too / Tell me, tell me the story / the one about eternity, and the way it's all gonna be.' The song is about hopelessness and helplessness. The world is described as a place where values are lost and where hope has faded. The world has no meaning any more and therefore making sense of it is an impossible task. That's why Bono is having this one-way conversation with Jesus/God and asking him to explain the meaning of life. 'This is the end of the century when God is supposed to be dead,' says Bono. 'People want to believe but they're angry. If God isn't dead, there's some questions we want to ask him.'[34] 'Wake Up Dead Man' is full of questions indeed, one of which is: 'If there's an order in all of this disorder / Is it like a tape recorder / Can we rewind it just once more?' The song, of course, doesn't give any answers, as that would be rather presumptuous and very unlike U2. But it asks very real questions about the reasons for the kind of world we live in and about whether God is still here or just a mirage. Crisis of faith at its worst. Of course, one could say that man is responsible for the disorder of the world and that God, if He exists, is not supposed to intervene in the chaos as it is man's responsibility to sort it out. But that's another debate. U2 are starting from a different perspective, namely that God does exist and that He eventually may intervene, but that people must firstly help themselves: 'I've never believed that this is God's world anyway. I always thought that this was our world, and that we are the ones to hold to account, not religion. There's enough food to go around, we don't share it. There's enough medicine around, but it's too expensive. We could turn every desert into fertile land, but we don't. It is human beings that need to be held to account, not God' said Bono to Niall Stokes at the end of 2001.[35] It may be surprising in some ways for U2 to write so bitterly. But it makes sense. Instead of celebrating God, they berate human beings for believing that God is doing nothing, whereas human beings are responsible for the state of the planet.

Inspiration

So if this is our world, then art is also a human activity generated by our wish to go beyond the mundane, by our wish to transcend the ordinary human sides. But for some, it is not only that. When talking about their songs and the way they are created, the members of U2 sometimes talk about something other than themselves helping them in that process. That, for them, God is present during moments of creativity is doubtless.

Art and God have often been intertwined, although some people would argue that God has nothing to do with art. But the members of U2 seem to believe that art, and therefore their music, is somehow affected by a divine presence. It is understandable that they should believe that, if their faith is strong. There may also be an amount of modesty involved. When it becomes difficult to explain the reasons why an album or a song is so good, then choosing God as an explanation becomes obvious. And that U2 should lean on that choice is a logical step. Bono believes that 'music is the language of the spirit'.[36] Journalist Sean O'Hagan is adamant that 'in the post-punk wastelands of the '70s/early

'80s, U2 were impossibly idealistic, striving for deliverance through the healing power of music – rock 'n' roll as nothing short of spiritual transcendence'.[37] U2 as individuals have indeed become tied to their spirituality, but their music has also become inseparable from it. They have evolved though in their approach and understanding of faith and art. That comes from the discovery of the blues. Around the time of *The Joshua Tree*, Bono talked about the 'healing power of music'.[38] He also saw things differently and started understanding 'the paradoxes, contradictions and oppositions that forge both the creative and the spiritual impulse.'[39] Indeed, a sometimes one-dimensional view of things was replaced by something more profound and also more difficult to pin down. From the 1990s onwards, spirituality was still alive within the band but it was well hidden behind irony and image. Bono is adamant that 'We've found different ways of expressing [our faith], and recognised the power of the media to manipulate such signs. Maybe we just have to sort of draw our fish in the sand. It's there for people who are interested. It shouldn't be there for people who aren't.'[40] That their songs could all be read as spiritual is a point of view. However, I don't think it is actually the case. The biblical references abound indeed but some that are submitted to websites as spiritual are rather dubious. It is all a question of interpretation.

Let's take two examples. In 'I will Follow', Bono sings 'If you walk away walk away / I will follow', which is not a religious line but possibly about a boy who will follow his mother if she leaves. Some however see in the song more than is intended and suggest that the line is inspired from Ruth 1:16: 'But Ruth said, "Entreat me not to leave you or to return from following you; for where you go I will go, and where you lodge I will lodge; your people shall be my people, and your God my God."'[41] 'Stranger in a Strange Land' is not a religious song despite the fact that it appeared on the *October* album. Angela Pancella believes that: 'The entire song makes allusion to the Emmaus story from Luke 24, where the risen Jesus appears as a stranger, but miraculously cannot be recognised until he offers bread to the two disciples who have invited him in. The song paraphrases their exclamation when they realise who they have been with – "They asked each other, "Were not our hearts burning within us while he talked with us on the road and opened the Scriptures to us?" She refers here to the lines in the song: 'I watched as he watched us get back on the bus/ I watched the way it was/The way it was when he was with us.'[42] Bono recalled:

We were going to Berlin. We were all in the back of the van in our sleeping bags and we had to travel through the corridor between East Germany and West Germany. And we were stopped by this border guard. The song was just a little portrait of him. He was our own age, with short hair, in a uniform and his life was pretty grim and he was seeing these guys in a rock 'n' roll band passing through. I had a feeling that he realised how much we had in common, and yet it was all over so quickly.[43]

However, even if people don't perceive those songs as eminently spiritual, what I would call the 'collective unconscious' at a U2 concert becomes much more than a mere celebration according to Bono, especially when it comes to 'Where the Streets have No Name'. 'We can be in the middle of the worst gig in our lives, but when we go into that song, everything changes,' he says. 'The audience is on its feet, singing along with every word. It's like God suddenly walks through the room. It's the point where craft ends and spirit begins. How else do you explain it?'[44] One thing is certain: Bono wants to be born again every day and that notion is close to his heart. U2's career bears an uncanny resemblance to that notion, as the reinvention process they have periodically undertaken bears the marks of art born again through periods of renewal and actual rebirth for U2.

Spirituality (a)live

Nowhere is spirituality more present than at a U2 show. Several things are at play here: the band, the songs and the crowd, and the interaction between those three elements.

First, let me share my experience of the very first U2 gig I saw and my memories of it. I was a student and living in Paris with my parents and brother. Five of us ended up going together to the concert of 10 February 1985 in the Palais Omnisport Paris Bercy. What I saw and felt that evening has stayed with me to this day. More than the songs, U2's wonderful performance and the fun that we had being there, it is the atmosphere that struck me at the time – it was unlike any other concert I had attended. I have seen many talented artists and bands on stage since then but not many are capable of producing the atmosphere at a U2 gig. Seeing U2 on that cold Parisian night, I remember a unity of spirit in the band and in the audience unlike any other. What was just a rock 'n' roll show became something magical, something spiritual. The last song U2 played was '40'. Everyone sang along and even after the show had ended, leaving the arena, we were all still singing it. That night, we couldn't go home straightaway, so we ended up in a late-night café. We talked about the concert and we were just too excited to go to bed. We had all had a revelation. Although some of us were not much into God, or completely rejected the notion, we had had, if not a religious experience, certainly a very spiritual one. It was the sharing between the band and the audience that made it possible, the songs being the vital link. It was as if the songs, through Bono's voice, Larry's drums, Adam's bass and The Edge's guitar, became alive and transcended everything that was going on in that place, focusing all our attention on those moments of communion.

It is difficult to explain what really happens during a U2 show. Words sometimes are not strong enough to convey the sense of belonging, the strength, the sense of spirituality that comes from attending or having attended a U2 concert.

I have seen the band on stage many times since that day, and I always get a feeling of communion, and I feel that the people who are there feel the same. We all share in that moment. But somehow I wish I could recapture that first time.

Author Beth Maynard describes the first time she saw U2 on stage at the old Boston Garden during the Joshua Tree tour: 'I learned at that 1987 concert what many people learned during U2's Elevation tour: whatever flaws there may be in that band, they can deliver on religious ecstasy. And people love them for it – their cosmic joy in life and love and God.'[45]

People respect U2's faith because, despite the fact that the experience may be spiritual or even religious according to some, they still deliver a rock 'n' roll concert first and foremost. During a large part of the 1980s, U2 finished their gigs with '40'. For those who remember it, it wasn't so much the fact that that song was religiously inspired (after all, I'm sure many of us didn't have a clue about its genesis) but that it conveyed the spirit of community and participatory aspect of a U2 gig. The band have actually played it a few times during the 2005 Vertigo tour as well. It's not so much that '40' is symbolic of spirituality, but that it is symbolic of the link between the band and its fans, maybe a spiritual link.

U2 have a reputation as one of the best live acts in the world, if not the best, and it isn't usurped. There are flaws and mistakes, all isn't perfect but this is not opera. Perfection is not what matters in rock. A band could sound perfect on stage and be removed from its audience. 'I don't trust a performer who's content with the distance between him and the audience' says Bono.[46] It's this attempt at erasing that distance between U2 and their audience that creates this bond between the band and its fans. And this bond may be physical when Bono asks a fan to climb on stage, or when he touches hands during a show, signs autographs afterwards, talks to people. But this bond is also very spiritual in that people understand what the band are trying to do. They understand it most of the time in a non-intellectual way. They rather feel it than try to analyse it because music is something that is primarily felt.

Influence

U2 have influenced their fans and also others in more than one way. However, spirituality is one of the most interesting and unusual one, simply because, despite rock's relationship to spirituality, the concept isn't cool and doesn't really fit in the rock 'n 'roll lifestyle. U2 have proven that spirituality is acceptable and that it can be cool.

U2 have consequently been an inspiration for instance to presbyterian ministers. At least three books have been published which deal with U2's spiritual side, Steve Stockman's *Walk On: The Spiritual Journey of U2*, and Raewynne J. Whiteley's and Beth Maynard's *Get Up Off Your Knees: Preaching the U2 Catalog*. More recently, Margaret Benefiel, a best-selling religious author, takes a look at soul and spirituality in organisations in her book *Soul at Work: Spiritual Leadership in Organisations*, taking U2 as an example amongst others.

The first book I mention is Steve Stockman's. It was the first one of its kind. S. Stockman has been using U2 songs for his sermons for a long time. Apart from a couple of inaccuracies, he seems to know U2's career quite well and his anecdotes are very illuminating. He explains how U2 have been sustained by spirituality throughout their career and how they have been able to keep on being a rock band while at the same time having a very strong faith in God, thus responding to some believers who thought that U2 had abandoned their faith or didn't quite lead the lives of real Christians. Steve Stockman traces U2's career, in parallel with their spiritual journey and also gives examples of songs where biblical references can be found.

Preaching the U2 Catalog is composed of 26 sermons by Episcopalians who have used U2 songs to preach to a younger generation, the so-called Generation X. The sermons use popular culture and music to attract the young back to the church. Some are interesting and very revealing.

What bothers me however is the use of U2 songs in sermons as U2 have never tried to convert anyone and they have never preached to anyone. Using the songs is possibly distorting what they are trying to say or not to say. If Bono is writing about his own failings, doubts, uncertainties, his own crises of faith, he isn't telling anybody what they should do, he isn't preaching but just conveying his own thoughts and of course sharing them. 'Preaching the U2 Catalog' is like putting U2 where they don't belong, in the Christian rock ghetto. It's giving them a place that they shouldn't occupy. It's spreading the false idea that they have a message to deliver, which they don't. Bono has chosen to deliver his political and social message outside U2 and the framework of rock. It is a true message. He is appealing to everyone to get involved in the fight against poverty and Aids.

Using U2 songs that don't contain any message and preaching through them is fine in itself as long as the songs don't become bigger or are seen as more powerful than they're supposed to be.

Finally, Margaret Benefiel, in her book *Soul at Work: Spiritual Leadership in Organisations* examines organisations like U2 and looks at the way they do business and how their leaders have brought a spiritual dimension to their work, giving clues as to what others could do to improve their own organisation to bring a soul dimension into it. She has even dubbed U2 one of the finest examples of a spiritual organisation.

U2 and America

It is interesting to note that the three books mentioned above were published in America (although Steve Stockman is from Northern Ireland). That could be explained by the fact that America is much more open to any kind of preaching, even that which comes from popular culture, as we have seen. But as much as books like that can be illuminating, the dark side of America's preaching business is something Bono and U2 reject, which is in line with their openness and tolerance.

During *The Joshua Tree* period, Bono was fascinated by televangelists in America, 'knock-off salesmen for God,'[47] and he observes:

> What's always bothered me about the fundamentalists is that they seem pre-occupied with the most obvious of sins (...) I couldn't figure out why the same people were never questioning the deeper, slyer problems of the human spirit like self-righteousness, judgementalism, institutional greed, corporate greed (...). We thought that they were trampling all over the most precious thing of all: that God is love (...) They were putting people off God, especially young people who didn't want to admit to being Christians anymore (...) So it was very interesting to be in America at that time. We were fans and critics, getting ready to tell them the best and the worst on *The Joshua Tree*.[48]

Looking at the record, it is fascinating to see U2's relationship with America. And God is very present on it. But that relationship isn't surprising, as America is very open to spirituality. America is also very conservative, a trait that comes from that particular religious side. As much as America is open to different religious influences and allows the setting up of churches of any denomination, the fact is that it has also allowed the sort of preaching that Bono despises and the spreading of sects of all kinds. However, America is also a very conservative country despite its liberalism. It is this contradiction that is fascinating and sometimes difficult to understand for Europeans.

Bono's Relationship With the Late Pope John Paul II

Bono is open-minded and as much as he was fascinated by American televange-lists, he was also fascinated by a man whose influence was undeniable, despite the many controversies surrounding him. Bono's relationship with the late Pope is an ambiguous one. Indeed, it is sometimes difficult to understand Bono's fail-ure at challenging him on the issue of condoms and Aids, for instance. I may dis-agree with everything else that Ian O'Doherty wrote in his May/June 2005 *Magill* article, but I understand why the columnist is dismayed, not to say shocked, by Bono's attitude.

Bono and the rest of the band nearly met the late Pope in the 1987, when they were asked to set up an audience with him:

> We were told the Pope wants to meet U2. We thought, 'this is a good laugh, he must have heard "Gloria".' So we got this message and we said, 'Fair enough, we'll meet anyone'. So I thought, 'Yeah, I'll meet the Pope, impress the relatives.' In one way I'm attracted to him because he's Polish and I like Polish people and he has a tender heart but, on the other hand, he's very conservative and some would say he's put the Catholic Church back a few years. So in the end I said, 'Okay, we'll meet him privately'. Word came back from the Vatican, 'No press? No publicity?' I said 'Sorry, mate, join the queue with the rest of the punters'.[49]

The singer did meet John Paul II in 1999 to highlight the Drop the Debt campaign. In a gesture which was typically Bono-like, U2's singer gave the Pontiff his wrap-around glasses in return for the rosary beads he had received, and that he still wears everywhere, including on stage.[50]

Bono had a lot of respect for the pope. I have however asked myself why Bono failed to challenge the Pope on some issues concerning the use of condoms as a measure of protection against Aids, for instance. The explanation may lie in the fact that Bono respected the man too much and also saw all the good that he had done in other cases. The fact is that these are two people from different genera-tions, and from two different worlds. On the one hand, The late John Paul II was the highest representative of the Catholic Church, its symbol. On the other hand, Bono comes from the opposite direction, from a world as removed from the church as imaginable. The two men were able to meet and find a common ground in their shared faith and some of the work they are (or were) doing. The singer defended his position:

> I can be critical, especially on the topic of contraception. But when I meet someone like Sister Benedicta and see her work with Aids orphans in Addis Ababa, or Sister Ann doing the same in Malawi, or Father Jack Fenukan and his group Concern all over Africa, when I meet priests and nuns tending to the sick and the poor and giving up much easier lives to do so, I surrender a little easier.[51]

Bono is a man working on the inside. He has adopted a very challenging, a very courageous but a very innovative attitude when it comes to the struggle he is involved in. Meeting the Pope was another way forward, as has been meeting politicians from every side. I don't know how many people would be able to do that. Bono knew better, I believe, than simply telling the Pope that his attitude was wrong.

Bono's spirituality and faith are strong, and he obviously doesn't share the position of the Catholic Church on condoms for instance. U2 indeed helped the Irish Family Planning Association in the past, a gesture that showed that they were critical of the Catholic Church on some topics. But Bono also paid homage to the late Pontiff during the 2 April 2005 Anaheim show in California, while the band played the intro to the song 'Miracle Drug', and said, setting the record straight: 'I met the Holy Father and I was so taken by this showman, even if I didn't agree with everything he said.'[52] Despite believing in God, he is no fool and like many Christians who are not extremists, has an open mind on topics that the Catholic Church doesn't like talking about or facing.

Experience

The last section will look at U2's spiritual appeal. Reading the answers to the questionnaires I sent the fans of the band, I came across a very homogenous response when it comes to U2's Christian beliefs. There is a consensus among Christian and non-Christian fans. They all accept that U2 are believers, but don't seem to be concerned by that. Some even embrace it.

What I have found fascinating about U2 is the actual music from a spiritual point of view, sometimes much more than what a song means. Its melodic qualities don't speak to the mind but to the heart. And that is where I find that U2's music is spiritual. It is not so much the lyrics as the way the music and the lyrics are intertwined together. Rock is a medium where music and words have their place and simply go together. There is a connection and that creates a unique blend. I admit that some of the religious and spiritual connotations went over my head before I started analysing the lyrics. But what I have always felt was that, despite my ignorance, there was something more profound at play here.

U2 have always wanted to share that part of their identity with their audience, whether they were believers or not. Spirituality, faith, is part of them, but the band's openness is what matters. They don't play their songs for one type of audience. They play their songs for everyone. They want an all-inclusive, all-encompassing way of living their music.

What is also striking is that U2's members have remained idealists. There is no cynicism in the songs. Their exacerbated spirituality has undoubtedly played a big part in the idealism U2 convey. They are, however, realistic and are not idealists just for the sake of it. They don't believe in utopia. If Bono is involved with Africa, it is proof enough that he is a 'realistic idealist'. The fact he is a rich rock star is neither here nor there. That he chose to use his celebrity to try and make this world a better place is more relevant. He talked about that particular side of things and how people see him: 'If I gave my money away, I'd just be a bigger star! We've already got a problem with genuflection. Then people would be finding a donkey for me to sit on,' he says.[53]

I believe he is fulfilling his role well and his idealism, whether born out of concern or guilt or both, is particularly appealing to people. U2's idealism in general is something that has converted even the most cynical.

U2's openness and tolerance vis-à-vis people of every creed and origin is what makes everyone comfortable.

Bono also talks about those who don't believe and has wondered how they deal with it. He believes it takes a lot of courage to do that.

U2 give moments of hope and joy to many and that's the power music has.

Conclusion

During their days in Shalom, U2 started with the idea of being born again by being concretely baptised in the sea. They got their band back and went on reinventing what it was to be U2. And the idea of reinvention also stems from their spiritual life. '[This] is at the heart of redemption: to begin again. This is at the heart of religious fundamentalism too: to be born again. I wish to begin again on a daily basis. To be born again every day is something that I try to do. And I'm deadly serious,' says Bono.

Spirituality is at the heart of U2's core values. It is a rock that the band has been able to lean on not to stray too far from a line that could have been dangerous for them. It has always been a guiding principle.

I believe U2 have indeed been on a spiritual journey but also on a spiritual quest, a quest that is not over. What is interesting is the lack of certainty and the doubt, played in front of millions of witnesses. That part of U2 makes them human. Showing their flaws is one of the band's wonderful qualities. It is brutal honesty. Being honest despite the costumes and the personas is something U2 have always been good at. And that's why so many people love them. Spirituality in U2 is healthy and open. Spirituality in U2 is pragmatic. It is not an empty word. That's why it works.

One of the reasons why Bono is fighting for Africa is that he dreams of heaven on earth. Answering a question by M. Assayas about the dark side of religion, the singer replied: 'Zealots have no love for the world. They're just getting through it to the next one. It's a favourite topic. It's the old cliché: "Eat shit now, pie in the sky when you die." But I take Christ at his word: "On Earth as it is in Heaven".' But he is also very adamant that: 'I'm not sure if it's Catholic guilt or what, but I genuinely believe that second only to personal redemption, the most important thing in the Scriptures – 2,103 passages in all – refers to taking care of the world's poor.'[54]

For Africa, the word justice is Bono's motto. But before he got involved in his fight against poverty and Aids, U2 dealt with politics in many of their songs.

5

SOCIAL CONSCIOUSNESS

In December 2005, U2 received the Amnesty International Ambassador of Conscience Award, the highest human rights accolade bestowed by the organisation. Amnesty International Secretary General, Irene Khan, said:

> From Live Aid in 1985 and Amnesty International's 1986 Conspiracy of Hope tour, through to Live 8, U2 has arguably done more than any other band to highlight the cause of global human rights in general and Amnesty International's work in particular. Their leadership in linking music to the struggle for human rights and human dignity worldwide has been ground-breaking and unwavering.

Art for Amnesty founder Bill Shipsey added: 'U2 have sung themselves to where great singing comes from, that place where art and ardency meet in the light of conscience.'

U2's social consciousness has been awakened over the years and seemed to have reached a peak by the end of the 1980s. This particular side of the U2 phenomenon appears to be a fundamental aspect of U2's appeal. I could not have written a book about the Irish foursome without taking into account a controversial question, that being that the band has always refused to be thought of as political and as of having a message. A political band or a political artist use music as a means to put forward political ideas and beliefs. The music acts as a springboard for politics and this aspect is focused on more than the music itself. The songs talk about political or social struggles and even love songs have a political edge, for instance. Musicians of political pop, such as the American folk singers Woodie Guthrie and Pete Seeger, the Englishman Ewan MacColl in the 1940s, 1950s and 1960s, the Chilean singer Victor Jara in the 1960s and 1970s (until his death in 1973 at the hands of the Chilean dictatorial authorities) or the Australian band Midnight Oil and the South-African Johnny Clegg in the 1980s act as an interface between music, politics and social change. 'At various historical points, popular music has translated political radicalism into a more accessible idiom, identifying social problems, alienation and oppression, and facilitating the sharing of a collective vision,'[1] says Roy Shuker.

The case of U2 is rather different from the definition above. U2 have never pretended to represent a political party or a political opinion in their music. They sing about social and political situations, relate events, talk often about surrender and non-violence but they are not proselytisers. However, they were regarded in the 1980s as being a political band, a band with a message.

Beyond the controversy or the truth of it, the question is to know whether a band like U2, despite its non-political stance, could have a political or social influence within the community of fans. Lawrence Grossberg argues that: 'the popularity of such politically motivated groups as U2, REM or Midnight Oil often depends upon a radical disassociation of the music's political content and the band's political position from their emotionally and affectively powerful appeals.'[2]

In other words, the political influence of those bands is ineffective and doesn't really exist. For Grossberg, to believe that political songs could influence people, shake their ideology, or involve them in a form of political resistance is a false idea.

It is indeed rather difficult to assess the political influence of such bands. It is undeniable that a lot of people enjoy listening to U2 songs without necessarily sharing their political beliefs, or even without being aware of the political or social content of some of the songs. But there are also fans whose political beliefs are reinforced by political rock. However, it is difficult to really know if rock can change the belief of even one person. Most of the fans I have interviewed tend to say that they shared U2's beliefs before they even discovered the band. They are generally adamant that their convictions were reinforced but not changed by U2's political songs or actions since they were already there. But a few people also admit that U2 may have had a greater influence on them than they could have thought. That may prove that there is an influence, even if it is small.

In U2's case, their social consciousness is partly responsible for their success.

And their music is inextricably linked to what the band is socially. Of course, the idea that U2 fans are also people for whom social and political questions have a real importance and that those fans can recognise themselves in the music has to be confirmed, but it could partly explain the loyalty of many of them as well as the interest that many have shown in organisations that U2 have supported throughout the years: Amnesty International, Greenpeace, War Child and more recently DATA and Make Poverty History. Some of the fans definitely share the ideas and ideals of U2 and go as far as liking the band's music because of those ideas. They cannot understand that some fans like U2 yet have conservative ideas. For them, liking U2's music is linked to sharing their ideas and ideals. However, those fans tend to forget that U2's music isn't only about political or social ideas, and as it is, the 1990s songs' contents were rather poor in political ideology, unlike the 1980s, which proves the point that U2 isn't solely a political band. They are truly a rock 'n' roll band with a leaning towards political and social ideas. What is, however, more interesting is the stance that Bono took towards the late 1990s when he became a spokesperson for social equality and Aids awareness, not as part of U2 but in his own right, as a rock star maybe, but mostly as a man, a citizen of the world, concerned with his fellow human beings. That was a bold move because he didn't have the band behind him or a song to sing. He went out on his own to fight for a cause he believes in.

So why was the band seen as a political band and a band with a message?; how did they fight against that image?; how have they fared in the 1990s to the present?

U2's Place in Political Rock

Unlike the musicians of America, Great Britain or other countries, U2 don't seem to belong to any real tradition of political popular music in Ireland.

The popular music tradition on both sides of the Irish border has, however, seen a few interesting cases of protest singers.

In the North, the punk movement saw the birth of three bands – the Protestant Stiff Little Fingers and Ruefrex, and the Catholic The Undertones – whose lyrics, if not completely political, gave the army, the police and the repressive legislation a rough ride.

In the South, two 'cases' of political pop are striking: The Wolfe Tones and Christy Moore. The former are still popular and sing rebel songs: 'They were the commercial end of a political folk tradition that had flourished during the civil war, and provided regular music reports and comment on IRA activity.'[3] The latter has become the best-known supporter of the Republican cause in the Irish musical world. His first political song, '90 Miles from Dublin Town', was written in 1979 and talked about the blanket-men, IRA or INLA (Irish National Liberation Army) prisoners who had been deprived of their political prisoner status in 1978 and refused to wear prison clothes, wrapping themselves instead in blankets, but who also refused to cooperate with the prison authorities. This protest, which also had its roots in the deplorable conditions the prisoners lived in, led to a hunger strike and the eventual death of the most famous of the blanket-men and their leader, Bobby Sands in May 1981. The song was, however, censored. The follow-up album, the *H-Block Album*, was also regarded as a provocative stance because it highlighted the Northern Ireland situation but was also used to collect funds for families of the hunger strikers who had started their campaign straight after the release of the album. The Irish authorities were not pleased with the move and sent the Special Branch of the police to the launch, who named all the people present at the party. This move pushed Christy Moore to observe: 'In Ireland these days, it's easier to be a heroin dealer than a Republican.'[4] Christy continued to support the Republican cause throughout the 1980s. It seems he was the only singer who publicly showed his support. The rocky path taken by the artist brings with it concomitant risks, which include being called a terrorist or a even murderer, but also being censored and becoming the target of the authorities. That is probably why so few voices were heard. As in many places, being a political singer in Ireland is a high-risk business.

Seen in this light, the U2 song 'Sunday Bloody Sunday' can easily be interpreted as a political song. It is therefore not surprising that it was misinterpreted by Sinn Féin and literally hijacked by the extremist movement, with the poster for the album *War* displayed on one of the walls of its offices and the album *War* played continuously. Bono told Robin Denselow: '[Sunday Bloody Sunday] was obviously seen as a Republican anthem, a call to man the barricades. I think the real point of the song went over their heads.'[5]

U2 belong to a rather timid tradition of political singers. Only in traditional music can one find a movement that had an impact. In popular music, it is rather difficult. In that sense, U2 have more in common with bands like Stiff Little Fingers or Ruefrex, who advocated the surrender of violence and the bringing together of the Catholic and Protestant communities: that is how U2 must be seen in Ireland. The band have followed a path where it might meet politics without itself becoming a purely political band. The commitment of its members is at the crossroads between the political, the social and the humanitarian. But its place remains ambiguous. The members of U2 support organisations like Amnesty International and Greenpeace. They have put their point forward many times but remain untouched by censorship. They are seen as 'good boys', whose social consciousness is often praised because their behaviour is rarely provocative, despite criticism from the press.

It is therefore difficult to place U2 in the political category and Bono himself stressed that point a few years ago: 'We are not a political band, but politics does come into it.'[6] It is, however, this political ambiguity that gave the Irish foursome a particular image, that of a band who is committed to different causes because they believe in them and not because they seek publicity.

In the 1980s, the members of U2 played the role of spokesmen of a generation and represented a rock consciousness that was close to the heart of 1960s' rock.

U2's Christian beliefs also played a part in that representation. The committed pacifist band who cares about other human beings and must therefore take action to support the needy is part of an eminently religious philosophy. This role of representatives of a larger pacifist movement, however well played, exhausted the band. They felt very exposed because they aired their views so publicly, and they decided to change their path in the 1990s.

U2 hold a particular place in rock, because of their huge success but also because of U2's members' social and religious backgrounds. This is a crucial aspect that could help explain the band's political views. Their own religious mix could explain their open mindedness, a more conciliatory view of their country and of the situation in Northern Ireland. But it could also explain why they advocate moderation and that they don't hold a firmer stance when it comes to the situation in Northern Ireland. The pacifism and defence of non-violence they represent put them in a place occupied by legendary figures such as Martin Luther King or Ghandi, figures who did not see themselves as political, at least in the public eye. U2 have therefore been allowed to advocate peace and remain neutral.

This quest for peace and justice would reveal itself through the songs, of course, but also through very concrete actions by Larry, The Edge, Adam, and especially Bono. Let's first take a look at the main organisations that U2 have supported and the events that they took part in as a band. As they grew as a band, and as human beings, the members of U2 had to also broaden their horizon and look beyond the borders of Ireland. And that is what they did. Peace and justice were not only meant for their fellow countrymen and women but also for the oppressed and poor of the world.

The Chicago Peace Museum

As far back as 1983, U2 became involved in an exhibit called 'Give Peace a Chance' at the Chicago Peace Museum, a venue set up by peace activists whose idea was to raise awareness and educate people about non-violence through the arts. 'Give Peace a Chance' was, of course, based on John Lennon's songs. Yoko Ono had agreed to contribute several items of memorabilia recalling hers and John's fight for peace. U2 were then approached and, amongst exhibits from Woodie Guthrie, Pete Seeger, Bob Dylan, Stevie Wonder and others, U2 donated the concert backdrop which pictured the cover of the album *War*, a white flag that Bono used on stage, the original handwritten manuscript of 'New Year's Day', and a poem written by Bono called 'Dreams in a Box'. If U2 weren't overtly a political band, they were very close to that notion in people's minds, and *War* undoubtedly played a part in giving them that reputation. The 'Give Peace a Chance' exhibit was one of U2's first public displays of their commitment to world issues.

Ethiopia and Live Aid

Live Aid's line-up in 1985 was prestigious and extremely crammed. Organised by Bob Geldof and former Ultravox singer Midge Ure, it all started with a single called 'Do They Know It's Christmas?' released in December 1984.[7] It was a charity single, the proceeds of which were to go to the people of Ethiopia who were suffering from appalling starvation, too often leading to death after years of drought. Many big names from the rock world at the time took part in the recording, amongst them were Paul Young, Boy George, Sting, George Michael and Bono and the name used for the group of musicians was Band Aid. Another single was released later, in the USA. 'We Are the World' could be seen as the American counterpart of Band Aid and was also sung by famous artists. A concert was organised for 13 July 1985, taking place simultaneously in Wembley Stadium, London and in Philadelphia. It was beamed all over the world. That event is where U2 not only became a stadium band but started building a reputation as champions of human rights and humanists, the event acting as a springboard for both. They literally stole the show.

Two months after it, Bono and his wife Alison went to work in Ethiopia for a month as helpers, through the American organisation World Aid. Very few people knew about it and the couple went to Africa anonymously. The experience seems to have touched them deeply and the singer only spoke about it in 1987 when the photographs he had taken there were put on display in the Hendricks Gallery in Dublin, later to be sold and the proceeds to go to the charities World Vision and Concern.

Amnesty International

U2 were the first band contacted in 1986 by one of Amnesty International's founders, the lawyer-politician-former-head-of-the-IRA-turned-human-rights-activist, Sean MacBride. The organisation's goal was to celebrate the twenty-fifth anniversary of its foundation and to promote itself in the USA through a series of concerts gathering famous names: Sting (with whom U2 had already been involved in The Caravan For Human Rights that same year), Bryan Adams, Joan Baez, Peter Gabriel, The Neville Brothers and Lou Reed. The Conspiracy of Hope tour took place from 4-15 June 1986 in San Francisco, Los Angeles, Denver, Atlanta, Chicago, New York and East Rutherford. Apart from giving money to the organisation, people were asked to sign petitions to free prisoners of conscience and were recruited as volunteers to write to the prisoners. People were also urged to write postcards to be put in letter boxes with the inscription 'Set them free'. Those postcards were addressed to heads of state, asking for the liberation of six political prisoners. The tour was a great success. 130,000 people attended the concerts, $3 to $5 million were collected and 60 per cent of Americans heard about the tour.

What is interesting in U2's case is that from *The Joshua Tree* album on, the inside sleeve contained the details of Amnesty International contacts (and Greenpeace contacts, from *Achtung Baby* on), as well as names of political prisoners, inviting people to join the organisation. It was and still is an extraordinary advertising opportunity for those organisations, but it was also a means for U2 to put forward their social consciousness. The then director of Amnesty International, Pat Duffy, stated that U2's involvement in the Conspiracy of Hope tour had a very important role to play in the doubling of members of Amnesty in America in a short period of time. The Republican trend favoured by young Americans would also have been reversed.[8] In other words, young Americans could have started to vote for Democrats. It is probable that the tour had a very positive impact on the view Americans had of Amnesty International. If I hypothesise a little, this newfound involvement in the organisation by young Americans was a way of imitating their idols. By taking part in a political struggle, a fan will feel that he or she is part of something worthwhile because the singer or band he or she admires is also involved in that struggle.

Apartheid

Around the same time as Live Aid, U2 got involved in the fight against apartheid by first of all 'playing to hundreds of thousands of people, and every night we'd attack apartheid'.[9] The band were thanked by the South African

Bishop, Desmond Tutu, for their continued support. Bono took part in the single 'Sun City', written and co-produced by Steve Van Zandt, the E-Street Band's guitar player, a condensed political lesson on the plight of black South Africans. Taking part were Bruce Springsteen, Bob Dylan, Jackson Browne, Jimmy Cliff, Lou Reed, Pete Townshend, Bob Geldof, Run DMC and Afrika Bambaataa, amongst others. The record was also a reminder for other musicians who would have been tempted to go out and play in South Africa despite the December 1980 UN resolution which advised all artists, academics, and sportsmen and women to culturally boycott the country. The proceeds of the single went to the Africa fund, a charity which helped South African political prisoners and their families and which educated the people who were in exile. Bono wrote the song 'Silver and Gold' for the *Sun City* album.

Nicaragua and Salvador

Bono's involvement with the Conspiracy of Hope tour spawned a wider interest, and he visited two South American countries in a private capacity, Nicaragua and Salvador, where dictators had their opponents tortured and murdered. There, the singer met people fighting for their freedom. In Salvador Bono and his wife encountered a place where a war was waged between the rebel forces and the government forces, supported by the USA. Two songs that were recorded for *The Joshua Tree* album came out of that South American experience. The first one is 'Mothers of the Disappeared', which describes the unbearable wait of mothers whose children have vanished, generally they have been abducted by government forces for airing political views and fighting against the regime, and were then murdered and buried in unmarked graves. The second song is 'Bullet the Blue Sky'. Bono was witness to the fighter planes flying overhead and U2 tried to render that sound and feeling in the music. The musical result is impressive, as are the lyrics, notably the improvised rap the singer came up with during the recording:

Suit and tie comes up to me / His face red like a rose on a thorn bush / Like all the colours of a royal flush / And he's peeling off those dollar bills / Slappin' 'em down, 100, 200 / And I can see those fighter planes / I can see those fighter planes / Across the mud huts as the children sleep / Through the alleys of a quiet city street / Up the staircase to the first floor / We turn the key and slowly unlock the door / A man breathes into a saxophone / And through the walls we hear the city groan / Outside it's America / Outside it's America / Across the view / See the sky ripped open / See the rain coming down through a gaping wound / Pelting the women and children / Run into the arms of America.

In the movie *Rattle and Hum*, during the concert played in Arizona on 20 December 1987, at the Sun Devil Stadium, the American flag appears at the beginning of the song, lit up with hundreds of lightbulbs, and disappears with the Jimi Hendrix version of the 'Star Spangled Banner' that he played at the 1969 Woodstock festival. This, of course, adds to the feeling of irony since the song is about the unacceptable face of America. Bono adds at the end:

Back in a hotel room, with John Coltrane and 'The Love Supreme'; in the next room, I hear some woman scream out, her lover's turning off, turning on the television. And I can't tell the difference between ABC News, Hill Street Blues, and the preacher in the 'Gospel Hour', stealing money from the sick and the old. For the God I believe in isn't short of cash, Mister. I feel a long way from the hills of San Salvador (where the rain pours through a gaping wound ...).

A few years later, on 5 February 1998, the band played three concerts in Argentina and invited a group of women who called themselves the 'Madre de Plaza de Mayo' to join him on stage during the song 'One'. Those women who were fighting for human rights all had a son or husband who disappeared during the military dictatorship and demonstrated daily on the Plaza de Mayo. Most came to the microphone to name the loved one who disappeared. U2 took advantage of the place to make a political gesture.

U2 come across as a band trying to gather people together and preaching non-violence, following a philosophy shared by the greatest peace-makers of the world. However, U2 clearly took issue with US foreign policies by their use of the American flag or national anthem, and have done so in Ireland too.

Flags Used as Symbols

Bono will admit he doesn't like flags very much. He seems to find it hard to accept they symbolise a nation. A flag's use on stage can cause confusion. Early in U2's career, Bono started using the white flag as a symbol of peace and renunciation, which is classical and rather simplistic. When a roadie gives him a white flag during 'Sunday Bloody Sunday', in the film *Under a Blood Red Sky*, the message is clear. However, he flirted with controversy when, in 1985, during the American leg of the Unforgettable Fire tour, he denounced national flags and told the crowd that he had enough of the Union Jack, the hammer and sickle and of the Star Spangled Banner. During that same tour, he tore the Irish flag, on one side the green and on the other the orange, to keep the symbolic white of peace: 'I think it was an offence to have done that and I don't know if these symbolic gestures come off, but I believe in them.'[10] he told Robin Denslow in 1988. These rebellious acts became rarer in the 1990s and the singer's maturity is undoubtedly one of the reasons for the change in behaviour. However, during the 2001 Elevation tour, he wore a leather jacket whose lining represented the American flag. The symbol was more discreet but still there. Eight years earlier, in 1993, he was less reserved; for example on 2 June 1993, during a concert in Frankfurt in Germany, where he again tore the Irish flag in three. If some saw in that a rejection of his Irish nationality, according to John Waters, Bono was simply trying to reclaim his 'Irishness'.[11] The singer explained how he performed a spontaneous gesture that he repeated if the reaction of the audience is positive. When the flag is thrown on stage by a fan, he must do something with it, so instead of wrapping himself in it, he tears it:

> Are you going to show everyone that you're Irish? No! You hate that flag. Why do you? You hate the flag because of the stuff that has gone on with it. Because it has betrayed us. Because nationalism has betrayed the nation.[12]

This behaviour may seem extreme but is part of the band's thought process, the expression of a violent Republican past that the members of U2 reject. They have, however, always felt close to their fellow countrymen and women.

Self Aid

The aim of the Self Aid single, 'Let's Make It Work', and the subsequent concert was to help raise funds for unemployed Irish people. Many stars of the Irish music scene gathered for that occasion; amongst them were Van Morrison, Clannad, Chris de Burgh, Christy Moore and U2. Inspired by the Live Aid experience, the event which was a protest against unemployment was heavily criticised by the press and by some political groups belonging to the opposition. They believed that the government, and not musicians, was responsible for creating jobs. Therefore the Self-Aid event had no reason to exist, and was basically useless. *In Dublin* magazine probably had the most virulent headlines such as 'The great Self Aid farce' and 'Rock against the people' with a photograph of Bono, as U2 headlined that day. Bono hit back on the evening of the concert during the song 'Bad' by replying, with a slightly altered quote from a famous Elton John song: 'They crawl out of the woodwork onto the pages of cheap Dublin magazines.' The criticism was understandable since unemployment isn't a question of charity but of political will. It seems that Self Aid drew the attention of politicians to that problem though and to the fact that too many people had to emigrate to find work elsewhere. But it also stirred controversy by its charitable aspect. During the concert, people were asked to phone in and pledge money which would help create jobs. Employers were also asked to offer jobs. Treating unemployed people as charity cases was considered an insult and U2 found themselves directly in the line of fire.

U2's relationship with their hometown, their country and its inhabitants is very special. They have always said how proud they are to be Dubliners and how much they love the city and the country.

Dubliners can be very critical of U2 too. U2 represent and express 'their hopes and aspirations, fears and frustrations'.[13] U2's success is an example to be followed and in 1986, U2 were already international stars. But their ties with their country are very strong and to this day, they still live in Ireland. The veiled suggestion that U2 should not have taken part in Self Aid (and that the whole event should not have been organised in the first place) because it is governments who create jobs, not charities, is understandable if one accepts that way of thinking. However, U2 had no choice but to take part in the concert from a humanist more than from a political point of view, to give some hope, to entertain and give some joy. For U2 not to play in front of their compatriots would have been considered an insult towards them, especially since so many other Irish musicians were taking part.

These controversies indicate the larger issue of the political inclinations of the band, which lean towards the left, even if the members of U2 have always refused to officially wear the colours of a political party. When in 1982 Bono met the Irish Fine Gael Prime Minister, Garret Fitzgerald, at Heathrow Airport, and then went to him to challenge him on political issues, he wasn't endorsing the party but was interested in the man. After Fitzgerald was photographed in Windmill Lane studios during the recording of *War*, and conveniently before a general election, he was also trying to show a more modern face to the young electorate of Ireland. Bono was subsequently offered to sit on a committee for unemployment and other issues, which he attended once, to never return. Even with this first attempt at some concrete action, the singer was ill at ease and didn't want to be labelled. One can understand Bono's reluctance.

However, the paradox lies in the fact that U2 succeeded in a capitalist world when they had a tendency in the 1980s to apologise for the money they made.

U2 are in Ireland a symbol of professional and financial success. That success tends to reinforce the idea of capitalism as the only system capable of giving birth to it. Consequently, the belief is that the same success can be repeated by others. The symbol is very strong but the other side of capitalism is that everybody doesn't reach that level of success, however hard they try. U2 may have inadvertently given two contradictory messages to the unemployed during the Self Aid concert. The first one was a message of hope that told them their situation could improve; the second said that Bono could not understand what it feels like to be unemployed but that they had to keep on hoping. There is a sense that the singer didn't want to judge the situation (which would have been in keeping with the whole U2 philosophy) and some of the songs written about Ireland are only a mere description of the situation the country was facing at the time. This lack of judgement has definitely had an effect on the fans who tend to agree with that approach. U2 owe a lot to the Irish fans who have supported them throughout their career and helped them pursue an international course. The members of the band are very much aware of that and want to thank them at every opportunity.

It is difficult to establish a link between Self Aid and an improvement in the job situation in Ireland and it is doubtful that the concert had a huge impact. However, 1,300 jobs were created after Self Aid and IR£500,000 were collected. The event was therefore a small success, despite the criticism.

Greenpeace

Another organisation U2 have supported over the years is Greenpeace. Again, they gave their time for free but they also gave Greenpeace free publicity. Since the end of the 1980s, U2 have given their songs to albums that support Greenpeace, for instance 'Pride (In the Name of Love)' for the *Rainbow Warriors* album in 1989, and 'Until the End of the World' for *Alternative NRG* in 1994.

However, Greenpeace received the most media attention during an action which took place on 20 June 1992. The target was the Sellafield nuclear reprocessing plant in the north of England, geographically very close to Ireland. U2 firstly agreed to support the 'Stop Sellafield' campaign by playing a free concert outside the plant, which would be followed by a demonstration. However, a court order taken by British Nuclear Fuels Limited (BNFL), the company in charge of Sellafield, prevented it from taking place there. The concert was then held in Manchester, as close to Sellafield as possible. What happened after the concert was interesting. Early the following morning, the four U2 musicians and some members of Greenpeace, with journalists in tow, disembarked from a small boat on the beach near Sellafield, behind the high water line, so as not to be arrested for trespassing. They had brought with them barrels of contaminated Irish soil that they deposited literally right at the plant's door. The photographs adorning the newspapers showed the members of U2 in white protection suits, with masks and gloves. Bono attacked BNFL, as well as the Irish government, for its apathy over the Sellafield issue and asked the Irish Prime Minister to change his position. He also observed: 'Greenpeace have got more publicity in the last week than they probably got in the whole of the previous year.'

U2's support of Greenpeace should not come as a surprise, even if one remembers the incidents of a violent nature paving the history of the organisation, which contradicts U2's philosophy of non-violence. However, Greenpeace is considered as one of the most powerful environmental pressure groups in the world and is probably the most well-known.

In the 1980s U2 are considered one of the most politically committed bands, fighting with their limited means for human rights, poverty and the environment. Their involvement in major charity events in the music industry puts them in the position of leaders of 'conscience rock'[14] of that era. But the band didn't succeed in that by chance. The voice of a generation that they expected was different to many of its contemporaries. The 1980s were the era of synthesised rock, when many successful bands didn't play live and quickly became obsolete. It is not surprising that U2 received the title of 'band with a message' when others kept their mouths shut. U2's support for Greenpeace and Amnesty International can also be found in their magazine *Propaganda*.

U2 showed a high level of idealism and humanism and that was part of the reason people were attracted to the band. They were admired on the one hand for the political positions they were taking, but they could also annoy because they were seen almost as proselytisers. The 1990s brought great changes for the band, in their music and also in their image. Socially, the band's role then became more complex. Was their image in line with reality? Should they be themselves and go against the flow or should they follow others who were less concerned?

Zooropa *and the War in Former Yugoslavia*

The change that came about in the 1990s stems from a conscious desire to escape from the saintly image carried by Bono, without abandoning the fight against inequality and injustice.

This strategy seems to have succeeded when the band started using irony as a weapon and they began using the music system for their own ends.

Europe was in focus again during the European leg of the Zoo TV tour, nicknamed Zooropa. If the songs on *Achtung Baby* and *Zooropa* were not as openly political as on other albums, the members of U2 had not suddenly become indifferent to the causes they had always defended. Indeed, the contacts for Amnesty International and Greenpeace were on the inside sleeves of their albums. But the members of the band seemed to have focused their attention elsewhere: on appearance, on fun, on seduction. The past caught up with them, however, when they met an American journalist and film maker named Bill Carter. He lived in Sarajevo, in Bosnia, during the siege of the town by the Serb forces and was filming the daily lives of its inhabitants. In July 1993, he met Bono, The Edge, Adam and Larry in the Italian city of Verona. He represented Bosnian TV and wanted to tell them about the situation in the war-torn country. Bono decided to help and suggested that U2 should go to Sarajevo. That was, of course, impossible for many reasons: logistics, insurance, and the safety of the band and crew. Bill Carter was also against it, but suggested instead a satellite link between U2 and Sarajevo during the concerts. Since the band had the necessary equipment on stage, it would give the Sarajevans an opportunity to explain the situation to the audience as the world seemed to have forgotten about them. U2 agreed because it was a question of humanity. However, this involvement would cause them grief, especially through the media who didn't understand where U2 were coming from. Indeed this public display put into question the cool and detached image that U2 had been building for themselves for a couple of years, an image that tried to erase that of good samaritan since the 1980s.

Historically, the problem that rock music has is that it is political but doesn't get on well with politics. The 1980s press found it hard to come to terms with this return of rock music to moral values, a music that refused to be only a source of entertainment. According to the press, rock 'n' roll has to remain in the realm of music, must belong to the world of cool, must have its scandals but cannot be political. Some rock musicians, however, regard rock 'n' roll as an instrument for change, envisaging a wider view of society.

As far as the opinion of the press about U2 was concerned, Bono had a clear idea of it in 1993 that he shared with Bill Flanagan:

So far all the press has been great, the best of our career. You could get the impression that everybody loves what we're doing. But you watch what happens next. Watch what happens when we get to England. And wait for Dublin. Come home with us and get another perspective. Come home for our beheading.[15]

The singer was very conscious of the stakes in this case: to break away from

U2's new image for the sake of another political cause would have been a new opportunity for the English but also for the Irish press to vilify the band again.

The satellite link took place about twelve times between July and August 1993. The last four times were in London, at Wembley Stadium, and the *New Musical Express* took another chance at reviling U2. Bono's prediction became reality. On 21 August 1993, the last Wembley concert saw Bono dressed up as MacPhisto phoning the English writer Salman Rushdie, still under the fatwa decided against him by the Ayatollah Khomeini for his book *The Satanic Verses*. The writer actually appeared on stage in person and the next day, the *Independent on Sunday* was extremely critical.

What the newspapers reproached U2 with was not to have been able to keep quiet, suggesting that the Sarajevo link had been in bad taste and that the Irish band had never had any credibility anyway. This last criticism was unjustified as credibility is exactly what U2 built their career on (both musically and from a human aspect). The presence on stage of an author ostracised by Muslims was not suitable at a rock concert though and could have offended some sensibilities.

The real stumbling block lies in the world of art. The press was asking in a roundabout way a crucial question: how far can an artist go and where are the limits of art? The answer was obvious for them. An artist cannot go further than his/her own art. If he/she is a singer, all he/she is allowed to do is sing. If he/she is a writer of fiction, he/she is only supposed to write fiction. It is obvious that one of the biggest rock bands in the world, who had turned their image upside down, who had finally joined the system, could not again step out of it. That particular aspect bothered the English press who didn't know what to do with U2 once they had finally displayed the expected image, only to revert back to type. This is indeed a contradictory message but the members of U2 believed in what they were doing. And more importantly, they believed that what they were doing was right. There is no doubt that beaming images of unbearable suffering, through the voices of a few first-hand witnesses, to a rock concert must have hampered the mood of the party. But it is also that particular event that made those concerts memorable and made U2 into human beings again, as well as sending a very powerful message that said that a rock concert could also be more than mere entertainment. The juxtaposition of contradictory cultural messages (rock 'n' roll vs Rushdie) obviously confused and mystified the press, and provoked an insurmountable incompatibility. This whole event was a glimmer of hope, however, in the eyes of the people of Sarajevo and a Bosnian Muslim said that: 'U2 have given Sarajevo a window into the world, and we pray that some light shines through'.[16]

U2 also took part in the War Child organisation, a charity helping the children living in war zones. They recorded the single 'Miss Sarajevo' in 1995 with the Italian tenor Luciano Pavarotti and took part in the yearly concerts given in Modena to support the organisation.

George Bush's and Bill Clinton's America

The question can be asked as to why, apart from their leftist tendencies, U2 embarked in 1992 on a campaign against George Bush and in favour of Bill Clinton, during the US presidential campaign of that same year. According to the book *U2: A Conspiracy of Hope*, 'U2 played a small but significant part in the campaign to remove George Bush from the White House',[17] which at first glance seems completely absurd. If Bono's shenanigans during the Zoo TV tour in America might have brought a smile to many faces, a deeper involvement in American politics seems incompatible with the band's philosophy of 'non-alignment'.

During the 1992 American leg of the tour, Bono tried in vain to phone the White House to speak to George Bush. This 'publicity stunt', which undoubtedly served U2's interests, belonged to the spirit of Zoo TV, which lay in the idea of creating publicity around it, of belonging to the system in general, and to the star-system, a system, originally created with movie stars in mind, which exploits the image of a star, on and off screen, to sell movies or in this case records. This, of course, included the press, which delighted in Bono's antics.

On 28 August 1992, Bill Clinton, the then Governor of Arkansas and presidential candidate, answered an ironic invitation by the members of U2 to phone an American radio show called Rockline to talk to them. This was by all standards an usual event. The fact that Bill Clinton was interested in one of the most famous rock bands in the world, the fact that other American musicians supported him, and that he was interested in the young whom he targeted as potential voters, seems to have weighed in the balance more convincingly that Bono's attempts to contact George Bush, or a sentence repeated in concert over and over again during 'I Still Haven't Found What I'm Looking For': 'I hope you get the president that you're looking for or we're all in trouble.'[18] It is surprising that U2 lent Bill Clinton their support, when they are known not to interfere. However, their political inclinations are clear. It is more likely that Bill Clinton's general use of the popular culture platform though, through MTV for instance, yielded more results than the actual support of rock stars. U2 also took part in the 'Rock the Vote' campaign on MTV to encourage young Americans to go to the polls. Their slogan 'We're not telling you who to vote for, but we're asking you to use your vote', however neutral, is still a call to vote for the right candidate. One can only surmise the reasons for this ultra-political participation but it could be that it was a sort of challenge for the band and a desire to control their image.

In the first half of the 1990s, U2 looked as if they wanted to get away from the political and humanitarian debate. *Achtung Baby* was a far more personal album and probably the least political of all. For the musical press, the band had finally entered a new era. It had entered the star-system and behaved like a rock band. U2 had finally entered the world of cool.

But this was only the outer shell that lay at the heart of appearances. The follow-up album, *Zooropa,* was subtly political, with photographs of dictators on the sleeve. The satellite link with Bosnia was only another way for U2 to show that they were still interested in political and social issues. The longevity of the band is partly due to this awakening to political and social consciousness, which was developed over time, and that the fans of the band embraced as being an intrinsic part of it.

It is therefore not surprising that the members of U2 have continued that policy even in the 1990s, despite the radical overhaul of their image. The primary concerns of the band were never hidden from view though.

The Good Friday Agreement

One of the most openly political acts of U2's career was when they took part in the concert of 19 May 1998, for the 'Yes' vote in the Good Friday Agreement campaign in Northern Ireland. It took place at the Waterfront Hall, in Belfast, with the Northern Irish band Ash playing as well. U2's involvement was part of the logic followed by the band, that of peace and an end to violence. It is not in fact surprising that U2 decided to get involved: it reinforced their position as far as Ireland as a whole was concerned, but it also sent a message to those who had not yet understood that particular aspect in their homeland. It was a message of reconciliation that U2 sent. It was also an unambiguous political gesture. The image of Bono holding David Trimble's and John Hume's joined hands above his head was a symbol of the bringing together of two divided communities but also of the bringing together of Bono with the political world, with which he would build closer ties for humanitarian reasons later on. Incidentally, this gesture was similar to an episode in 1978, when the singer Bob Marley took part in a concert for peace in Jamaica in an attempt to bring together the rival political gangs of the island, but also to raise funds to provide sanitary installations in the ghettos. Michael Manley, the Prime Minister and leader of the People's National Party, and Edward Seaga, the leader of the Jamaican Labour Party, got on stage with Marley who sang the song 'Jamming', while holding both politician's hands above his head. The parallel is striking.

Bono looked more at ease on that particular occasion than he had in the past with former Irish Prime Ministers Garret Fitzgerald and Charles Haughey, due to the cause he was supporting: peace on the Island of Ireland. He was not supporting a politician but an idea, a dream that could come true. In 1998, Ireland was therefore back on the agenda for U2 who, like many, believed in the agreement. The Omagh bombing that same year was a stark and tragic reminder that peace is fragile and difficult to achieve.

Change of Plans

If U2, as a band, have supported a number of causes throughout their career, there was a difference between what they could accomplish as a band with their music to fight injustice, and what each of them could accomplish as an individual, by using their status as celebrities.

From 1999, Bono decided he would play another role outside the band, a role that is still developing, whilst Adam, Larry and The Edge may have remained discreet, the singer started making his voice heard beyond the stage. His association with the most powerful politicians of the world was to defend one cause: the poor of the world, and especially the African continent and its fight against Aids. The ease with which the singer can today express himself on a political rather than a musical agenda is astounding. He learned to speak the politicians' language and met them on their own ground rather than asking them to meet him on his. It is obvious that he had to rise to the challenge if he wanted to make a difference. The saintly image that stuck to him in the 1980s and that seems to pursue him wherever he goes doesn't seem to bother him any longer. He has turned it to his own advantage and from good samaritan, he has become a sort of secular saint, using his fame to fight for what he believes in, and able to forget his rock star status to become a political activist.

Bono and Africa

'I first went to Africa, to Ethiopia, to work in a feeding station following Live Aid in 1985 – one summer that stayed with me for a lifetime,' said Bono in an interview to the World Association of Newspapers for World Press Freedom Day in May 2004. He subsequently decided to take on that cause, about which he says in the same interview: 'But I don't see Africa as a cause. To me, this whole thing is about justice. The fact that 6,300 people die in Africa every day of Aids, a preventable, treatable disease, for lack of drugs that we take for granted in Europe and America – that's about justice, not charity.' One can see Bono feels strongly about the whole issue and that his first African trip touched him so deeply that he could not but get involved.

In 1999, he first started supporting the Jubilee 2000 'Drop the Debt' campaign, which fought for the unpayable foreign debts of the poorest countries to be dropped at the end of the year 2000. Jubilee 2000 also advocated foreign help as well as larger international trade agreements. Bono was one of Jubilee 2000's ambassadors and most ardent supporters, and visited the United Nations, the White House, Downing Street and the Vatican. He also took part in demonstrations (at the G8 summit – a yearly gathering of the 8 wealthiest nations in the world consisting of Canada, the USA, Germany, Italy, the United-Kingdom, the Russian Federation, France – in Genoa, for instance) and in meetings. He talked about it for the first time at the Brit Awards, in February 1999. The movement is still active and although the debt of the 52 countries in question was reduced by $100 billion, the work is not over yet.

The U2 singer also got involved in the fight against poverty and Aids in Africa. Along with Bob Geldof, the computer tycoon Bill Gates and the billionaire businessman and philanthropist George Soros, he set up DATA (Debt Aids Trade Africa), a non-profit-making organisation which argues in favour of debt relief for the African states, but also in favour of more aid for the development of Africa and the development of commerce on the black continent. Bono is the organisation's spokesperson and its main benefactor. DATA also argues for help in the health sector, as 'Aids is the worst pandemic in 600 years', as Bono put it. He has made the Aids issue his main concern.

Bono, a Secular Saint

Bono has become the epitome of the political activist rock star, mixing with politicians and business people to make his ideas heard. He has also become a secular saint, ready to give time to improve things for Africa.

The singer seems to be set apart in the rock world. There is a general wariness towards rock or movie stars who fight for a cause. The question is to know whether they are doing it out of goodness, or if they are seeking publicity. Another concern could be their lack of knowledge about the issue they are defending. Bono's case is different and he has the reverse reputation: Aids and other issues facing Africa seem to have no secrets for him and he says himself that he learned to talk to the politicians with the economic and not the emotional vocabulary. To convince the world's most powerful leaders that his fight was the right fight, he had to take part in political, financial and economic discussions. That's why he was taken seriously by many very powerful people. His presence and hands-on action undoubtedly gave this struggle a more sophisticated image, but more importantly a more public image, which is what was obviously needed. In the 1980s, Bono's and U2's political involvement took place within the rock world, through concerts and records, but they also took place in private. The end of the 1990s saw the emergence of a new form of public commitment by Bono. The other three members of U2 were not with him and he was working in a private and personal capacity. And now he is ready to use his fame to try to change things. By doing so though, he is excluding U2 from political action and is putting the band back in its own sphere, that of music and art. In that sense, he has abandoned the idea that music could be a political force:

I'm tired of dreaming. I'm into doing at the moment (…) U2 is about the impossible. Politics is the art of the possible. They're very different and I'm resigned to it now (…) When you sing, you make people vulnerable to change in their lives. You make yourself vulnerable to change in your life. But in the end, you've got to become the change you want to see in the world.[19]

In that sense, the singer has become highly politicised, without being a politician himself, but he has also built a wall between politics and the band, between politics and music. The power of change in music cannot be used without real action, and using his fame as a tool allows Bono to act in a concrete way. Through his meetings with Bill Clinton, Tony Blair, the Pope, Kofi Annan, Paul O'Neill, George W. Bush or Jacques Chirac, he has placed himself in the political arena and communicates with these men on an equal footing.

However, there are other reasons for Bono to be where he is, and they can be found in his religious upbringing and beliefs.

He confesses that his Catholic guilt is at the basis of his struggle. His faith is based on the Bible, which preaches generosity towards the poor. The roots of his commitment can undoubtedly be found there. In that context, he becomes a secular saint because he is drawing lessons from the Bible. He is, however, both worshipped and criticised at the same time, which puts him in a peculiar place. Although it is expected that an artist should be talked about and criticised, U2's situation is more complex. The band were criticised not for their music but for their political commitments.

Bono's and even U2's 'sainthood' since the 1980s stems from their political and humanitarian actions. Indeed, at the root of that phenomenon, we find deeply religious men. The members of U2 would not see that in negative terms because they reject the notion of fundamentalism. Bono has the reputation of knowing the Bible very well (a fact which can be verified in some of the songs) and takes from it some of his life principles. He observes about himself: 'Everyone knows that I'm a "need to practice more" Catholic/Protestant. But I grew up with the sense that if my faith meant anything, it must be tackling inequality.'[20]

Bono's image of a secular saint and his image as a dispenser of justice work together. Bono's dream of heaven on earth and the idea of justice also work together. The singer dreams of heaven on earth becoming a reality but of course, heaven on earth appears as a totally utopian ideal. But Bono is obviously no fool and well aware of it. That's why he takes concrete action, knowing that only by acting can one get closer to that goal.

The singer's political and humanitarian actions are marked with religious beliefs which have become a sort of guide. As a wealthy man, Bono must therefore regain some humility by giving his time to the needy, not his money.

But the question, outside any religious context, is to know whether his views contain the classical idea of the star who has a lot to give because he has received so much. It is hard to question Bono's sincerity in a struggle that is quite obviously close to his heart. He went back to Africa in May 2002 with Paul O'Neill, to try and convince the then American Minister of Finance that the African continent 'can and does put Western aid to good use',[21] despite the fact that O'Neill openly criticised the aid programmes that were set up against poverty in Africa, saying it was a waste of money because it didn't generate a long-term economic development. The two men went on a ten-day tour of Africa, visiting Ghana, Uganda, South Africa and Ethiopia. Moreover, according to the *Irish Independent*, when young South Africans were asked if they knew U2, they all looked puzzled, which says a lot about U2's lack of fame in the black ghetto. Most articles in the press praised Bono for his actions. However, Vincent Browne and Kevin Myers, both from *The Irish Times*, launched a scathing attack on the singer, inferring that he was only seeking publicity and a photo opportunity when he appeared at the side of politicians. Bono's response was that the two journalists were 'naughty boys',[22] and that they were well aware that the singer's commitment doesn't come down to just a couple of photo opportunities.

In the name of DATA, the U2 singer also went on a tour of America in December 2002 with actors Chris Tucker, and Ashley and Wynonna Judd, dubbed the 'Heart of America tour, Africa's Future and Ours', to raise awareness about Africa in the USA through speeches and conferences. They went to Lincoln, Nebraska, to the University of Iowa, to Chicago, Indianapolis, Cincinnati, Nashville and Louisville, accompanied by Agnes Nyamayarwo, an HIV positive Ugandan woman, as well as the group of singers and dancers from

Ghana, the Gateway Ambassadors. Bono also appeared on American television in the Oprah Winfrey Show and on Larry King Live. It is obvious that the singer isn't simply waiting for a photo opportunity. Bono was also seen in Berlin in May 2004, at the Global Business Coalition on HIV/Aids awards. He was at the Labour conference in the UK in September 2004. In the middle of the Vertigo tour and before the Brussels concert on 10 June 2005, the singer met with the president of the European Commission, José Manuel Barroso. He was also invited to lunch with George W. Bush on 19 October 2005, while in Washington, for a concert. Earlier in the year, he contributed a foreword in the book by American economist Jeffrey Sachs, *The End of Poverty: Economic Possibilities for Our Time*. These are just some of the list – it is impressive.

A Politically Aware Rock Star

Bono no longer appears as simply a rock star but as an extremely famous man who is also taken seriously in political and economic circles. By separating the emotional from the rational, he created a new identity for himself which renews his image. He is aware of the problems inherent to Africa and he has made the necessary efforts to understand them. He cannot, however, leave behind his rock persona, without which he would not be the guy everybody knows as Bono. It is a help and a hindrance in some ways, in that some may still wonder what the reasons for his involvement are. However, the most important aspect of it all is that he has become a man of influence for the cause he is defending. We must realise that Paul O'Neill would not have gone on a tour of Africa if he did not take the singer seriously.

Bono has become a sort of political figure in America. One could wonder if Bono is a bit naive when he said on Larry King Live in December 2002:

> The work I'm talking to you about on World AIDS Day and trying to get a historic initiative led by the US with a president who, I believe, has a feel for this and a Congress that has a bipartisan interest in this, that is part of this discussion. I really want to convince the Americans of that. This is important. The way the world sees the US is important.

That could be the speech of a politician. The diplomatic manner in which he includes George W. Bush and the American Congress in the fight against poverty and Aids in Africa and shows them as having an essential role to play in that fight are very political and put both at the forefront of it, while giving them a good image. But Bono wants to show a certain image of America, the good side, a nation which is humane and generous. This interest in the USA may seem excessive at times, but could be explained by the fact that the Irish have a special relationship with America. Maybe too Bono simply wants to open up the American social consciousness a bit more and encourage that side. Apart from anything else, America is the wealthiest country in the world and, as such, should give more to poor countries than any other. This is not the case, however, although efforts are being made.

In the context of his action in Africa, Bono gives three juxtaposed images of himself: that of a rock star, that of a concerned citizen of the world, and that of a saint. If he somehow came to terms with being a rock star, he rejects the idea of sainthood, which must sound ludicrous to him, but some continue to compare him to Mother Teresa. He rejects that strange blend, but he is also very hesitant when it comes to political actions and confesses to Larry King that he is first and foremost a singer: 'I don't want to be doing this other job is the truth. It is just – it's an accident of fate that I ended up in this place. I think I'm much better being in a band.' This confession may seem like a contradiction in view of his actions, but goes back to his refusal of being thought of as a saint when it comes to his involvement with Africa. He can only strengthen an already positive image of himself by doing that. He is refusing the role of politician because he is a singer and is adhering to the philosophy of rock, which is first and foremost entertainment. And by rejecting that role, he is back where he belongs, in the star-system. Therefore, he becomes a human being who modestly refuses all the compliments because he isn't worthy of them. But all this puts him in a special place in the world of rock, but also in the world of humanitarian action.

He is admired because he recognises his weaknesses, calls himself a spoiled rock star, and accepts that people sometimes cringe when he asks for more money for Aids when he himself is a millionaire. All these contradictions allow Bono to do his mea culpa, in other words, he recognises that he is just a very rich rock star and that he may at times feel guilty about it. He is defending the weak and the poor but can and must continue behaving like a rock star despite or maybe thanks to the critics. Whatever his reasons for doing this, Bono is ready for action and in Dublin in 2003, during the launch of the United Nations Report on Human Development, accompanied by the Irish Prime Minister, Bertie Ahern, he desperately wanted to defend the poor of this world, and was ready to play the political activist: 'I am ready to march with my activist friends, to begin campaigns of civil disobedience. We are about to get very noisy, we are about to bang a lot of dustbin-lids.'[23] Through those words, Bono becomes a member of that group and finds his place amongst them. But he is still also a rock star and thanks to that, people listen to him. If he acts, his credibility not only as a rock star but also as an activist is reinforced. But there is no doubt in his mind that Ireland has a role to play in this struggle and can be used as 'a special interface'[24] between western countries and the third world, thanks to its history and because Ireland has been a developed country for a relatively short time.

Bono doesn't want to talk about the left and right in politics. His ideas are more leftist but he refuses to get drawn in the debate. The singer also goes against the received wisdom, notably after March 2003 and the war in Iraq. He is pro-American. He believes that if America abandons its protectionist ways and opens up to the world, it can change the world in a positive way. U2 have both praised and criticised America openly. The band's image as a socially conscious act in the 1980s was reflected by and in America rather than by and in Europe. That image was international and reflected the band's openness to the world, through international rock.

U2: a Band with a Message?

U2 have always refused to be seen as a band with a message. Their political reputation though originates in the topics found in certain songs, where the lyrics tend to be of a political or social nature.

During a 1987 press conference in Madrid, Spain, Bono replied to the following question:

> 'Your music is music with a message – do you see yourselves as the inheritors of Dylan's title of Music with a Message?'
> 'As the writer of the words, I write about things the way I see them. I never set out to change the world, more to change my own world. Rock 'n' roll is a noise that has woken me up and it's good that, if along the way, it wakes other people up. But I feel that we mustn't fall asleep in the comfort of what you call our messages.'[25]

It is indeed difficult to compare U2 with Bob Dylan, Pete Seeger or Ewan MacColl. U2 songs merely tell of dramatic human situations but don't attempt to give solutions. For instance, 'Bullet the Blue Sky' describes Bono's experience in Salvador, though the rap at the end is more politicised. The song questions American policy in South America but doesn't offer solutions to the problem. The band may express political opinions in speeches and their actions. It is very doubtful that any can be found in the songs.

A simplistic analysis may indicate that any song mentioning a political or social problem automatically has a message. As we have seen, political pop or rock is only a means to an end; those musicians use the music to a political end. The situation is rendered more complex because so many artists write about those issues without automatically being branded with the burdensome title of musician with a message. A particular view of the world, an artistic approach to a problem is only one side of the story.

After a long process of deconstruction, whereby U2 tried to reinvent the band and tried to change the image of band with a message, when Bono talks about Africa, he is sending a message that something needs to be done urgently. But he is also reconstructing his own image. In this way, he puts a distance between himself and U2 and offers the band a different role, in which it can develop musically, while he takes on the role of activist. He is dissociating himself from the band on that level when he talks about the issues he feels passionate about. If critics voice their discontent, the criticism is pointed at him rather than at U2. The band is therefore protected. Bono's commitment is personal. His message is also personal, even if he often talks in the name of DATA for example. He took the initiative to join Jubilee 2000 and to create DATA, without the help of the other members of U2. This kind of commitment is not often seen in the rock world, and if Bono visited Nicaragua, Salvador or Ethiopia without alerting the media, he needs the media so that others can become aware of the plight of Africans, for example. Bono is aware of the power of the media, being constantly in the public eye, and he gave an interview to the World Association of Newspapers for World Press Freedom Day in May 2004, saying how crucial their role is in the fight against the Aids pandemic, but also pointed out how the freedom of the press is essential when talking about such issues:

> Aids is the worst pandemic in 600 years. People need to know about it to avoid becoming one of the statistics. Even in the poorest places I've been to, someone, somewhere has access to a radio. The media is our messenger, a modern-day town crier. China is an example of what happens when there is a conspiracy of silence through censorship. HIV spread like wildfire through certain regions because no one knew about it. A million people with HIV and only now it gets in the national newspapers. The media need to be telling the truth about what's going on, exposing the myths – like the one in South Africa where men believe that sex with virgins will cure them of HIV.[26]

A Controversial Commitment

Despite Bono succeeding in inventing a new form of resistance in the rock world, the episodes of charitable fervour that U2 displayed have often put the band in the line of fire and raised much criticism. That trend became apparent throughout the years and the press, whether musical or general, took advantage of the situation.

Some, like Michael Ross, didn't agree with Jubilee 2000 and the dropping the debt of the world's poorest countries. According to him, if the debt was dropped, those countries could use the money to finance corrupt political regimes or even starting wars.[27] Others also reproached Bono with having used the Brit Awards ceremony in 1999 to talk about Jubilee 2000 when there were so many other causes to defend.

The problem between the British press and U2 seem to remain the same and a reconciliation is not easy. The British media seem to disapprove of the way U2 do not follow the party line of the music industry as far as charitable actions are concerned. Why does the industry not support U2 openly? Does it need more publicity? Is it that it does not approve of its members doing something other than just play music? Is it out of fear to commit to a worthwhile political struggle that so few people in the music industry understand or want to support? 'The consensus seems to be that supporting a cause is a waste of time,'[28] writes Michael Ross. However, U2 have a power that few bands have. Although industry insiders didn't like the fact that they invited Muhammad Ali to the Brit Awards to lend his support and promote the Jubilee 2000 campaign, rumour has it that they forced the General Manager of Universal Music UK, John Kennedy, to accept the deal and that he could not refuse because he didn't want to offend his biggest act. Whatever the truth is, the industry is certainly powerful but is only as powerful as its biggest acts will allow.

The relationship between the Irish press and U2 is also interesting. There is still a love-hate relationship between the band and the Irish. Some like them while others will write scathing attacks just because they are called U2.

The issue is obviously that rock does not mix well with politics. The two go together but don't get on well and critics are on the prowl. One could argue that if rock music is an art, it has the right to tackle any topic; romantic, philosophical or political. Rock music continues to hold a political meaning, whether on a collective or individual basis amongst performers. However, it seems that the collective side has been forgotten and if it was very much alive from the 1960s to the 1980s, no major charitable event has marked the 1990s, despite the stage being a classical place for the 'proselytising' of rock musicians. Bono seems to have opened up the way for another kind of commitment, on an individual basis, which may prove more efficient in the long term. The danger is that the star who is committed to that role of ambassador of good will could easily overshadow the actual struggle at hand.

Here lies the deep contradiction between the rejection of rock music as a form of resistance against the establishment and the system, whereas one of its roles (albeit not originally, for it was created as an entertainment form) in the beginning was as a form of resistance. When U2 embrace a cause, the musical press and the press in general should surely support them in their action. From the British *New Musical Express*, to the Irish *In Dublin*, journalists have attacked the band, and particularly Bono. The Self Aid debacle, the satellite links with Sarajevo during the Zoo TV or the attacks against Bono for his Jubilee 2000 are examples. When Bono is photographed in the company of heads of state though, one may see why he is criticised. The message can be misinterpreted. A rock star seen with a politician tramples underfoot the idea of rock 'n' roll as street opposition. Nevertheless, the nature of the media in general is also put into question as their goal is commercial. Publishing a controversial photograph will help sell a newspaper. That is, however, another debate.

Two things can trigger a negative reaction in the media: what is shown and what is said. Images and text can trigger a negative reaction in the media. The problem of images is extremely complex because images can contain different messages. A photographer can wait for an opportunity to take a picture that will not reflect the reality of the moment. The perfect example is the photograph of Bono with the Russian president Vladimir Putin and British Prime Minister Tony Blair, during the G8 summit of 2001 in Genoa, when the anti-globalisation demonstration turned to blood. The three are seen laughing and Vincent Browne of *The Irish Times* vilifies Bono and Bob Geldof (who was also present) for having amicable relations with the two heads of state, for being on the other side of the demonstration (in other words, for not being on the right side), and for wanting to be friendly with men responsible for the tyranny of today's world.[29] Bono replied to this by explaining that it was a very short moment which didn't reflect what really happened. The reason the singer was laughing was that Putin had told him that after he solves the problem of third-world debt, he should look at that of Russia. A photographer was present at that moment and the image was inevitably sent around the world. Bono admitted that their behaviour sent a confusing message. But he also explained that he had to reach some compromise for the cause that he is defending: 'I've met people the band would rather I didn't meet and there are some people I have to talk to, or appear in a photograph with, that in other circumstances I'd rather not.'[30]

The heart of the issue lies in the place that a rock star such as Bono is supposed to hold. To be credible amongst ordinary people, he should demonstrate with the ordinary people in the street. A rock star must keep his/her place on a stage, where he/she is merely supposed to sing while he/she can criticise whoever he/she wants. However, rock stars are not supposed to talk to political leaders, who represent authority, the establishment, in other words everything that rock music is not supposed to be. The image of rock stars is in question. They are not politicians or activists, except if they belong to the political side of rock; they are only supposed to get angry on stage and not delve in politics. They can write political songs and talk about politics but are not supposed to act. Putting people in boxes, however, is a very easy option, showing a one-dimensional attitude. 'There was a time when our pop singers – Bridie Gallagher, Larry Cunningham and their like – knew their place,' claims Vincent Browne.[31] According to the journalist, a rock star isn't supposed to take a definite position on any political matter and must not, under any circumstance, leave the group he/she belongs to.

Perhaps the difficulty lies in Ireland and in the way U2 are regarded. The biggest stumbling block is probably the size of the country, for a band that has become one of the biggest in the world. In the US or in the UK, the problem might not create such controversy. In Ireland, U2 are not only the biggest rock stars in the country but they are also the biggest celebrities. There always seems to be a sort of embarrassment evident when Bono expresses an opinion, as if he was talking for the whole Irish nation, whereas he is only speaking for himself. For their compatriots, Larry, Adam, The Edge and Bono stand for a fundamental aspect of Ireland, which is music. They also represent Ireland abroad in many ways. U2 have become the modern symbolic cultural link that ties Ireland to the rest of the world. If Bono finds himself in a position that can trigger controversy (not only on a humanitarian front but also in the use of bad language, for instance), all the Irish seem to be affected. The members of U2 are role models. They are almost intruders in the music industry because they have always refused to surrender to the system and to compromise even if they belong to it, and their refusal to compromise has always been admired. They are part of Ireland in the same way that other artists, like writers, are; that is why they are expected to be and to do a lot more than ordinary citizens.

The attacks of the press are also a way to bring U2 down from the pedestal they are put on by fans and by that same press, to make them human again. These comings and goings between praise and criticism are the symptoms of a some-time chaotic relationship between U2 and their country of origin. According to the *Irish Independent*, Bono's activism seems destined to conquer even the most cynical of journalists.[32] Derek O'Connor says: 'Some may question [Bono's] sincerity, a few may occasionally question his integrity, plenty will diss his music, but a quarter-century down the line, it's getting harder to find people who really, really have a problem with U2. They're an institution.'[33]

A New Form of Resistance

Through his social and political commitment, Bono has created a new form of resistance to the system. He has also given rock music a new protest image, even if he is considered as a 'traitor' by some when he is courting politicians and giving them a new role to play. This (new) form of opposition is generally taken on by younger musicians; Bono gives that resistance a more mature form. Two images are juxtaposed. On the one hand, the rock star in his mid-forties stands for an aging but dynamic side of rock music, fighting against a cynical world. And it is exactly that lack of cynicism in U2, that unrepentant idealism, that is still obvious and makes the band what it is. On the other hand, there is Bono the man, the citizen, the husband, the father who refuses to compromise. He is still resisting the pressure, this time not through his music but through political activism. The rock world and political activism can be regarded anti-establishment, and Bono feels at ease in both.

I am not suggesting that rock music doesn't belong to a system, to the structure of the music industry, or even to capitalism. The link between rock 'n' roll and commerce has always been all obvious. These inevitable commercial ties don't mean, however, that all music recorded is just a product destined for immediate consumption. Resistance to a system comes from the fact that precisely the system didn't suit the spirit of rock and that it had be fought. Rock resistance to the system stems from the spirit of rock rejecting the system and fighting against it. But fighting a so-called perverse system with music coming from an opposing side is undoubtedly a romantic vision of rock and its power. The dominant culture may have felt threatened at the beginning but didn't wait for long to take over rock music, which in the end was born from capitalism. Bono learned to use the system, and embraced capitalism to use the system better. He is seen with politicians, themselves eager to be seen with a rock star to appeal to the younger voters. Bono uses people in power to argue for those in poor countries. The music press didn't find this unnatural friendship to its taste.

What Kind of Impact?

The last point I want to examine is the kind of impact someone like Bono can have on social and political struggles such as the 'Drop the Debt' campaign and the HIV/Aids issue, and what the tangible effects, if any, are on those causes.

When the U2 singer got involved in the fight against poverty and HIV/Aids in Africa, he first of all had to convince politicians of the validity of his approach. He must act as a politician would, by putting forward solid economic and political arguments. He must know his subject and he must be able to convince. His fame allows a very important media coverage, which in itself is a victory for his side. At the end of the G8 summit in Gleneagles, during the 8 July 2005 press conference, the French president, Jacques Chirac, was adamant that: 'The campaign that was led by non-political personalities like Mr Bob Geldof and Bono has undoubtedly had an influence on the decisions taken during the G8 summit of Gleneagles.' Indeed $50 billion in aid were pledged, half of which is to go to Africa.

Through his involvement, Bono tried to prove that he isn't merely a rock star but a man who cares about other human beings. He is a socially conscious man who doesn't spare his time to go around the world, literally haranguing politicians to stop and listen to him. His campaign in the name of DATA and other organisations has already yielded results, but he knows that there is a long way to go before anything of great impact is done.

The U2 phenomenon is partly based on this socially conscious aspect. But Bono also represents a new trend in rock 'n' roll by sitting on the edge of politics. He seems to consider a complete politicisation of U2 a danger for its music. Music in the end can only be used as a backdrop for political struggle. If it can help to raise funds and create a social consciousness, it can only touch upon some of the political problems and cannot resolve conflicts.

It is true that Bono's place is a difficult one. Rock music is there primarily to entertain. In that context, political and social involvement is only optional. Most rock songs don't seem to contain any message, preferring the romantic to the political theme, and no musician is forced to support a cause. When musicians embrace a political, social or humanitarian cause, three scenarios are possible. Musicians will fight for a cause because they believe in it, to bolster their image or out of a guilty conscience. However, their position is difficult since their political involvement can be suspected of having ulterior motives, even when there are none. If the political commitment of musicians in the 1960s is historical, the 1980s commitment doesn't seem to have been followed in the 1990s, and in the new millennium, individual commitment may start a new trend, set by Bono. But to allow Bono to do that, U2 had to separate their music from Bono's commitment. It seems that this situation has not created conflict within the band in the long-term. Bono admitted at the end of December 2005 in an interview with BBC 4's Today Programme, however, that his activism created a lot of tension and might even have forced him out of U2 at one stage.[34] Other comments previously made by Bono as to The Edge's, Larry's and Adam's opinions show a tacit agreement though and he says that the rest of the band are very aware of the positive effect of Bono's actions on U2's audience: 'Our audience feels like they have a better voice through me and the band can see that.'[35] The Edge said of Bono in 2004:

> We've grown up being a political band. We never saw a need to separate religion and politics from everything we write about and care about. We have always been well aware that steaming in on any issue was liable to get us into trouble, or just come off as uncool. My own real fear was that Bono was going to lead us into doing things that were desperately uncool and we would regret. But even though I have winced on his behalf, I've had more times when I've just been so proud of him and blown away with the success of what he's done. Who would know that someone who stopped his formal education at sixteen, and had been writing songs and touring the world as a singer, can get stuck into the body politics and be listened to on the highest levels?[36]

Conclusion

Bono has undoubtedly an important role to play in the political arena when it comes to supporting Africa. But what about the rest of U2? Are they willing to openly embrace other worthy causes through their actions or their music?

After much debate, Bob Geldof organised Live 8 and thought that U2 as a band still had something to say. Live 8 took place on 2 July 2005 in London, Philadelphia, Tokyo, Berlin, Paris, Rome, Moscow, and Toronto (as well as Edinburgh on Wednesday 6 July) to highlight the plight of the world's poor, ahead of the G8 summit in Gleneagles which took place between 6 and 9 July. Raising awareness of the issue was the concerts' main concern. U2, amongst others, headlined the London concert. The aim was 'to call for complete debt cancellation, more and better aid and trade justice for the world's poorest people.' Live 8 was the biggest 'mega-event' – a term coined by sociologist Reebee Garofalo to designate musical events taking place on a massive scale and gathering several famous acts to support a social or political cause – ever staged. It was only the starting point for the Long Walk to Justice which is calling on world leaders to act after the G8 summit. Despite their Vertigo tour commitments, U2 agreed to take part, as they and Bob Geldof have led parallel struggles when it comes to the poor of this world.

During the Vertigo tour, which Bono said was partly a political rally, the song 'Sunday Bloody Sunday' was illustrated by the giant screen lighting up with the word 'coexist' – Bono explained in Dallas, at the American Airlines Arena on 30 October 2005, that it is a piece of graffiti by Piotr Mlodozeniec found written somewhere in the midwest – in red, the C in the shape of a crescent moon, symbolising Islam, the X in the shape of the Star of David, symbolising Judaism, and the T in the shape of a cross, symbolising Christianity. This was a message of peace and reconciliation, a very strong reminder that U2 may not be a political band, but that they are a band committed to social ideals, whose social consciousness has developed over the years and who have reached a place where politics can coexist with its outlook on life.

6

AMBITION AND STRATEGY

To believe that the members of U2 were not ambitious would be naive. And to believe that they did not have a proper strategy to conquer the world would be even more so. Paul McGuinness is adamant about it: 'It could never have been accidental and the idea that it might have happened that way is ludicrous. We had a plan and we had to work at it. Even though the plan changes all the time, we have always felt we knew what we were doing.'[1]

Of course, there is always an amount of luck in any type of adventure, and the fact is that it was pure chance that U2 met when and where they did. That they should be so successful is also down to chance. But the fact is that they didn't leave their business strategy to chance. Their career is paved with decisions that were thought through carefully. Paul McGuinness said about U2 in 1986: 'What's always impressive to me about the way they conduct their affairs is they have never lost interest in the business that surrounds them and they've never forgotten that unless their business is under control, doing the work of being U2 is not possible.'[2]

So what drives U2 and how has their ambition to be the biggest band in the world never failed?

U2's relationship with the Record Industry
Paul McGuinness observed in an interview with *Propaganda* magazine in 1987:

150

I have always felt that our interests and the record company's were quite different. The record company is a source of finance for a baby band but by attempting to have hit singles, you become hostage to your next record. The touring base that we built up was really a means of defending ourselves from that. It would not be possible too for the record company to say, 'this band has no support, we'd better drop them and not spend any more money on them.' Clearly, we did have support, large support and that's very impressive.[3]

What is most impressive about U2 is the way they have kept the record company and the record industry at arms length, while simultaneously being part of it. They would not have made it on such a big scale without the system that, despite themselves, they belong to. They were clever in their approach and knew from the very beginning what they wanted to achieve. However, they didn't want to achieve it at any cost. The fact that they decided to base their operation in Ireland was an indication of what they were made of. Paul McGuinness talks about a conservative approach because they were 'not prepared to risk what we had on the chances of having a hit single next time out and the time after that'.[4]

It is also obvious that U2 did not want to be part of the record industry as it was and is. This is not an easy business to be in and Paul McGuinness has proved himself to be a tough negotiator on the part of his band. U2 wanted something more than hit singles. They wanted to make a lasting impact and they ended up making hit albums: 'We never had hit singles and now we are described as the band who was so smart that they didn't have hit singles: they made albums and had hit albums,' said Paul McGuinness in 1986. Indeed, in the first half of the 1980s, U2 produced two hit albums, *War* and *The Unforgettable Fire*. By 1985, the band was already successful and had all of its production, including *Under a Blood Red Sky* and *Wide Awake in America*, in the British charts; a unique achievement for an Irish band. The following table shows what position each album achieved in 1985:[5]

	July 1985	August 1985
Boy (1980)	77	
October (1981)	76	
War (1983)		29
Under a Blood Red Sky (1983)		11
The Unforgettable Fire (1985)		9
Wide Awake in America (1985)		11

The most unusual aspect about U2 is that they achieved their first UK number one single only in 1988 with 'Desire', the second one being 'The Fly' in October 1991 and the third being 'Beautiful Day' in 2000. However, almost all their albums reached the number one position.

Between September 1979 and November 2004, U2 released eleven studio albums, two live albums, two 'Best of' albums, 41 singles taken from those albums, seven singles from movie soundtracks, with other artists, B-sides and 'orphan' songs. The band sold over 100 million albums and played 1185 concerts until December 2005, in front of over fifteen million people. The figures are impressive and give the extent of U2's success and the power that they achieved over the years. An example of the building of that power is the 'release rate' of the albums. The first four albums were released between 1980 and 1984, at a rate of approximately one a year. There then was an almost three-year gap before the release of *The Joshua Tree*. U2 had finally some space to breathe. *The Unforgettable Fire* had sold well and their performance at the Live Aid concert had helped them achieve the status of stadium band. Then *Rattle and Hum* was released in 1988, riding on the wave of success of *The Joshua Tree*. In the 1990s, the rate of release slowed down, with on average two to three year gaps between each album. In other words, U2 released more albums in the 1980s than they did in the 1990s, which fits in a strategy of conquest based primarily on building an audience through live performance. By the early 1990s, U2 was still at the top, and although it is a challenge to conquer a younger audience, they achieved the same level of success. Another example of their power and strategy is to conquer an audience, the number of concerts played for each of their tours until 2005

The analysis of the activity rate of the band, taken from 984 concerts and nine tours over a 25-year period shows that the largest number of concerts was played in the early part of the band's career, between 1980 and 1986. (see Table 1 in Appendix) The chosen strategy was simple: the larger the number of people who saw the band live, the more likely they were to become known. During those crucial years, U2 played 561 concerts in four tours, compared to 622 in six tours, between 1987 and 2005. The first tours were long and difficult, and between 1 September 1980 with the beginning of the *Boy* Tour and 18 December 1983, which spelt the end of the *War* Tour, U2 did not stop touring, except for recording purposes, and they played 369 concerts. Only from *The Unforgettable Fire* album on did things start to 'ease up', when the band started making a name for themselves. One also notices that six of the nine U2 tours took place in the 1980s with 685 dates, compared to 440 between 1992 and 2005.

This leads to two important conclusions. Firstly, U2 conquered their

audience on stage, based on a classical model of rock 'n' roll touring. They quickly started touring the US after practising in Ireland and in the UK. Their success
could only come from that classical model, according to their philosophy, a
model tried and tested by other bands before them, notably in the 1960s.
Secondly, once a band like U2 achieves that level of success and stays on top, it
also acquires a level of artistic freedom, in the eyes of its record company and the
record industry in general. This leads to a freedom of movement to do what it
wants, which allows for a much larger choice when it comes to albums and touring. However, there are also risks involved and two dangers can face a band like
U2. If they release an album too often, it may lack in quality. If they release an
album too rarely, they may run the risk of being forgotten. That is the reason
why, when a U2 album is released, the industry's machinery is used. The promotion of a new single, for instance, followed by the album is extremely important.
An interesting example is the release of the very first single from the album
Achtung Baby, 'The Fly'. It was the first single and first album of the 1990s. The
change of musical and visual direction was drastic. U2 was almost like a new
band, entering the 1990s with a new sound and a new look. 'The Fly' had to have
an impact. It was therefore on release for only three weeks, which ensured its sale
and a number one spot in the charts. Bono says of it: 'That wasn't our idea, it was
the record company's idea (…) I don't know, I just think this is a cool thing to
get away with … and that's our job, to abuse our position to get stuff on the radio
that wouldn't normally get on the radio.'[6]

A second example of the music industry's machinery is the release of the single
'Vertigo', along with an endorsement by the band of a special edition of the i-Pod,
and a 400-song pack, downloadable from the Internet. As much as it may have
shocked some people that U2 would finally endorse a commercial product, this was
a very clever strategy which ensured that they could be seen and heard everywhere.

Another example of U2's pulling power is the number of people who attended the concerts, which must be considered in comparison with the details of the
number of concerts played. (see Table 2 in Appendix)

Over 21 million people saw U2 live between 1980 and 2005. The audience
number has steadily increased throughout the years to reach a peak at the end of
the Zoo TV tour, and has since then slightly declined. There are several reasons
for that. U2's first official tour, The Boy tour, attracted around 122,000 people
and the gigs were played in small venues. Even the *War* tour only managed an
attendance of around 453,000. Only from the Unforgettable Fire tour did we see
a real increase and the million mark was reached. The attendance trebled for the
Joshua Tree tour, but declined sharply for the Lovetown tour (approximately

748,500). The reason was that U2 only played 47 dates, mainly in Australia, New Zealand, Japan and Europe. They also played small arenas, hence the low attendance number.

The attendance for the Zoo TV and PopMart tours was the highest, with the attendance at the Zoo TV tour reaching 5.3 million. PopMart was seen by 4 million people. But what is more interesting is that the Boy tour and the Zoo TV tour are the tours with the most dates, the first being a birth and the latter a rebirth for U2. Boy had 158 dates while Zoo TV had 156. However, the Boy tour took place over one year, while Zoo TV took place over the course of two years, with a long break to record *Zooropa*. For the Elevation tour, the band had decided to play mostly arenas, which meant less attendance and an overall audience of about two million. It was a strategic choice. U2 had decided to abandon the stadium environment for a while. They wanted to play smaller places to feel closer to their audience with less special effects. As for the Vertigo tour, the choice was to play stadia in Europe, while playing arenas in America. That automatically boosted the numbers. But what is more interesting in the strategy employed for their latest tour is that dates were added as whole shows got sold out. In Dublin, for instance, there was originally one date, 24 June 2005. Then the band added another and both shows were sold out in record time. Then a third show was added for 27 June. It was again sold out in minutes. The same happened in Paris with one extra show. Were U2 being overly cautious, wanting to see how ticket sales would go, considering that tickets were expensive and it was their first tour in four years?

That the first tour of the 1980s and the first tour of the 1990s had the most dates and both were the start of a new phase for the band reveals a strategy of conquest or reconquest of the audience. The first was an introduction to U2, a strategy meant to woo people, to show them that U2 were first and foremost a live act. The latter was on a much bigger scale and possibly with more at stake, because U2 had to conquer their old audience again while wooing a new one.

Another noticeable trend in the tour strategies is the marketing. For example, the 31 December 1989 gig in Dublin was broadcast live in over twenty countries (including Poland, Yugoslavia, Hungary, and the USSR – others chose to defer the broadcasting). The audience was therefore over 300 million. Some fans without tickets were even allowed into the Point Depot, shortly before midnight.

As for the Zoo TV and PopMart tours, the use of the latest technology allowed for some impressive moments. But the tours almost bankrupted the band, notably Zoo TV, which cost $250,000 a day to run. However, the tours reflect U2's image in the 1990s: a bit distorted, over the top and fabricated. Going back to basics was therefore a necessity and was to prove successful.

Control

The fact that U2 conceded only what was necessary to the record industry undoubtedly comes from their fierce sense of independence and control. Bono says:

> Yeah, we have had to deal with some bullies at a corporate level in the music business, but in the end, I don't have 'slave' written on my face, like Prince did in the early nineties. U2 is in charge of its own destiny. We own our master tapes, we own our copyrights, we run our show, the music business does not own us.[7]

To own their own stuff, U2 had to take a lower royalty rate and were paid less on big-selling albums, but they were prepared to wait for the big money and hit the jackpot. Bono adds: 'There's no excuse in the twentieth century for intelligent people signing a deal they don't understand.'[8]

This is a rather rare trait within the music industry. Indeed, the majority of bands don't have as much control over every aspect of what they do as U2. Paul McGuinness commented in 1987 in *Propaganda*: 'We've always controlled our own graphics and packaging and timing, and, for a long time, we thought that every group did that.'[9] Indeed from the very start, they didn't want the record company poking its nose in the creative side of things. Even on the live side, the control is as tight as it can be.

> More than most bands, we take control of the circumstances in which we perform. It's part of a process we apply to most things, of not letting luck, or indeed other people's judgements, control us. We do not hand over control to the promoters, we do not hand over control of the T-shirt business to a T-shirt company, we tend to do those things ourselves. We tend to produce our own videos.[10]

One example of U2's will to control every aspect of the band is the image they want to portray. Steve Averill has been in charge of that aspect since U2's beginnings. Michael Ross says that the designer of the band 'subjugated himself to the will of U2'.[11] There is no doubt that U2 have always wanted to control the band's image. They even went against the advice of the record company when it came to the sleeve of the album *October* (they admit that it was a mistake). Their image is their own creation though, even that of the 1980s, despite the fact that they pretended they didn't have an image. This is a difficult aspect for U2, one that has created more controversy than you could imagine. The fact is that rock music has always been intertwined with the image. The visual is very important, in some cases sadly even more so than the music itself. But that is what sells!

Another example of their need for control is the video for the single 'One'. I have already mentioned that they didn't want to release the first version of the video because they didn't want to be seen putting back Aids in the realm of homosexuality. So they made another video and then another. But it had to be to the band's liking. In the commercial DVD, *U2: The Best of 1990-2000*, The Edge said:

> I'm at a stage now I think that's the future for U2. I'm sick of sitting around and editing suites, getting really hands on with all these kinds of things. I think the way forward is just to find people who we trust and just let them do and see what happens … and then fire them and start all over again!

This observation is important in that U2 have found people that they trust and they tend to work with those same people all the time. If they can trust those people, then they are in control of everything. The decisions they make are a reflection of that aspect. And if the record company puts an idea forward that they don't agree with, they would not yield to Universal.

Paul McGuinness also says that 'in the end, I suppose you have to admit that a rock 'n' roll band does things for its own selfish reasons – not necessarily, or not only, to supply demand and satisfy customers'. Indeed, in that case, rock 'n' roll is also seen as an art form, rock as art expression rather than just music to be sold in any shape or form.

U2's Impact on the Irish Music Industry
Some might say that bands like Them, Taste, Thin Lizzy or Horslips were the pioneers of the Irish music industry. And I would not disagree with them. Those bands were essential in the history of Irish rock and the Irish music industry. However, they didn't play an essential part in shaping the industry, as they almost all went to England to further their career, due to the dismal lack of infrastructure in Ireland. Thus they became an integral part of the British music industry.

U2 were born almost at the same time as the magazine *Hot Press* and Windmill Lane recording studios (the first Irish studio with international standards), as well as 2FM radio. As it happens, the magazine was to champion them from very early on and the studios were used many times by the band.

U2 were an incredible catalyst for the Irish music industry. They took a risk. They stayed in Ireland and developed from there. Ireland was their home and they wanted to participate in the evolution of Irish music. What amazes me is the confidence they had in themselves to make it. What amazes me even more is that the lack of infrastructure didn't seem to be a deterrent for U2 to stay in Dublin. As a matter of fact, it was almost a blessing, as U2 didn't want to be a one or two-hit wonder. They wanted longevity, they wanted international recognition, they wanted to make an impact.

The music industry is interested in discovering, developing and selling new talent and in keeping on their books the artists already signed. An array of creative and business people is needed to make it work. From managers to producers to engineers, to accountants and lawyers, they all have a role to play.

In the 1970s, the pool of talent in Ireland was already obvious but the showbands were still popular. Former showband member, Keith Donald told me:

Showbands were a unique phenomenon in Ireland. They were unique to Ireland because in most parts of the world in the early '60s, people were beginning to play original music, especially in the UK and in the USA. In Ireland, showbands weren't allowed to play original music ... They had to play cover versions of UK and USA-generated hit records, because in the early '60s, you couldn't hear those records unless you imported them personally from the UK and the USA. Some of them would finally get distributed here but not a lot so the only way the audience could hear them was by showbands doing their very imperfect renderings of these hits.

I moved to Dublin in September 1963 to go to Trinity College and I needed money so I started playing with the showbands (...) The first one was in Belfast and I used to commute twice a week. The next one was called the Greenbeats Showband which was a development from the Greenbeats group and we played all over Ireland four or five or six nights a week. And I completed my degree by studying from the back of a Volkswagen van.

Socially, the showbands were an important phenomenon, allowing couples to meet. Ireland was an extremely conservative country and this was a way for boys and girls to meet to escape a stifling environment, to have fun, to dance, and for some couples to even marry as a result of those meetings. However, culturally and musically, the showbands had no impact on what happened later. But they were extremely successful, and there are several reasons for their success. Firstly, there were hardly any international band or artist that would play in

Ireland in the 1960s. The Beatles played Dublin only twice, in November 1963 at the Adelphi cinema, and the Rolling Stones played their first gig in the country in 1965. Secondly, the lack of original records and of original musicians, as Keith Donald pointed out, allowed for the development of the showbands. Thirdly, there was no adequate venue where a big international band or artist could play. Fourthly, and most importantly, the showbands and their managers created a real music industry and controlled the dissemination of pop music. They therefore dominated the market.

It is understandable in this context that the showbands should be so big. And young people, bored with life at home, preferred to go and see a showband on Saturday night than watch TV at home or listen to the radio. They wanted to be entertained, they wanted to socialise, and the showbands fulfilled that role.

The showbands became idols, stars of 1960s Ireland. They had names like The Clipper Carlton, The Royal Showband, Capitol, Miami, The Drifters, The Dixies, The Freshmen, The Plattermen, The Cadets or The Mighty Avons.

The main aim of the showbands was to make money. With their managers and promoters, they controlled record distribution in Ireland, but the concerts were the most lucrative activity and so they toured incessantly. They played in venues purposely built by ambitious promoters such as Jim and Albert Reynolds (the latter was Prime Minister of Ireland between 1993 and 1995 and also a member of the Irish Parliament), and which could hold up to 3,000 people. There were 450 venues of the kind in the Ireland of the 1960s. The promoters would let the venues to the bands and decide which was likely to fill it. If the band was popular, it received 60 per cent of the price of tickets. The remainder would go to the promoter. The lesser-known bands received a salary. The showbands were also a source of employment as there were approximately 10,000 people making a living out of them.[12]

It is obvious that only a handful of them made a good living. But Ireland's youth, especially rural youth, found in them the type of entertainment they were denied elsewhere.

Urban youth, however, was often more discerning and more demanding. They did not merely want an ersatz of a rock band. They wanted the real thing. They wanted originality and the beat groups provided that. The groups were in a way rivals to the showbands. They were the response to a movement that was bound to peter out eventually when genuine rock bands were formed.

Mark Prendergast sums up the era and the rise of rock 'n' roll in Ireland in a simple way:

The genesis of Irish rock is in no way logical. There was no simple linear development from one type of music to another. More a reaction to circumstances and the effect of the expanded awareness of the sixties when some of the youth decided enough was enough.[13]

Some young people needed originality. They wanted the Swinging '60s with stars who created their own material. They wanted that spirit to become real. They wanted all that came with it: freedom of thought and freedom of taste. The Irish youth was stifled by rigid conventions and morals brought about by the power of the Catholic Church over its flock. Rock 'n' roll could loosen those conventions. However, there was not much in terms of such music on Irish television and radio. So, young people listened to Radio Luxemburg, Radio Caroline or the BBC, in order to hear that type of music. Obviously, rock had an effect on Irish youth even if one could not buy the records there.

The beat groups were therefore the closest thing young Irish people had to 'real' rock 'n' roll. Directly imported from Great Britain, theirs was a world closed to the adults, with its own rules, its own behaviour, its own ideology. The beat groups in Ireland made rock 'n' roll real for young people, and mainly Dubliners. They were playing in clubs and were the antidote to the showbands, creating a real underground circuit, a mainly urban phenomenon.

However, the beat groups developed in Ireland in a chaotic way since the showbands had created a unique music industry, therefore preventing the development of an Irish form of rock music. Irish record companies were not interested in beat groups. The showbands were a far greater source of income. The Irish market was also small and diversity was difficult to achieve. It was difficult at the time to find a niche market. Because beat was an urban phenomenon, problems also arose:

In Ireland difficulties arose because of the rural nature of the country. Country folk, unused to the complexities of the city, really enjoyed the showbands. It was a business, a dance band business, where music as such was the last priority. An important aspect of their presence was the lack of developed sensibility in listening to music in rural Ireland. The radio was popular, but stereo systems were not in great demand outside the cities. A showband playing locally was much preferred to the weirder strains of music emanating from across the water. Rural people could identify with the showbands. The very young who were mostly disenchanted with that scene favoured the beat groups.[14]

Mass culture therefore had not reached Ireland yet. The first rock band recognised in Ireland was born in 1964 and was called Bluesville. Ian Whitcomb who, in an ironic twist, turned out to be English, was studying in Trinity College, Dublin, and founded the band. He and Barry Richardson (bass player), Deke O'Brien (guitarist), Mick Molloy (guitarist), Ian McGarry (drummer) and Peter Adler (saxophone) toured the country within the underground circuit and acquired an excellent reputation as a live band. Their first single, 'You Turn Me On', widely considered as the very first Irish rock single, was released in 1964 and even reached the American Top Ten in 1965.

From then on, Irish rock started developing. However, the Irish music industry was still in a dismal state.

In the 1970s, professions directly connected to the music industry were almost literally non-existent. During my research, I compiled a table with the data available from the *Hot Press* yearbooks between 1980 and 2002, and the result was a steady and major upward trend in the main areas of the music industry spanning those 22 years. But in 1980, everything remained to be done: from the number of artists (only 147 professional or semi-professional musicians and solo artists compared to the 1767 registered in 2001), to the number of record companies (at the time, even the majors had small operations in Ireland), to the number of recording studios (only nine in 1980 compared to 113 in 2001), to the number of music publishers, to the number of promoters, to the number of venues (the number of venues increased from 126 in 1980 to 323 in 2002 – including pub and hotel venues). The only area that remained steady was that of record shops (interestingly, however, until 1997, the Irish were among the lowest consumers of records in Europe. Then the trend changed upwards with the Celtic Tiger.[15]) In short, the music industry in Ireland was underdeveloped and underexploited. So much so that when U2 arrived on the scene, it was a rather bare landscape, ready to be harvested.

U2 were there at the right place and at the right time, and were ready to take a risk. Staying in Ireland always sounds like it was an easy decision for them to make. And it is understandable in view of their attachment to their home land. But it took them longer than some to make it. That, however, didn't seem to bother them too much.

Although they focused on playing live, Paul McGuinness' job was to try and find a recording contract for the band. As any band seeking a contract with a record company, U2 recorded another demo tape in August 1979, in Windmill Lane studios in Dublin, with Chas de Walley, from CBS London. Three songs came out of that session, 'Boy/Girl', 'Stories For Boys' and 'Out Of

Control'. Jackie Hayden then persuaded CBS London to release those songs on a single. This was the first U2 single, entitled 'U2-3', which was released in September 1979 in Ireland. It would also become their first number one in the country. The marketing of the record is actually interesting because it shows that, even at the time, U2 were astute and very ambitious. Firstly, the listeners to the Dave Fanning show on Irish radio could vote for what would be the A-side of the single. It turned out to be 'Out of Control'. Secondly the single was available in seven-inch and twelve-inch formats (unusual for that time). And the first 1,000 copies of the latter format were numbered by hand by Jackie Hayden. It was an original strategy which paid off.

But the unusual thing was that at that point, U2 didn't have a recording contract. They simply had an agreement which led to one last recording session with Chas de Walley in December 1979 in the CBS studios in London, at the time of their first London gigs. Although they were not very successful, a few articles about them appeared in the London newspapers. The single which came out of that session was 'Another Day', released only in Ireland in February 1980, with 'Twilight' on the B-side. It also reached the number one position in the charts. But there were other reasons for releasing a new single. Paul McGuinness explained:

We had to do that because we had a large and growing Irish audience which wanted a record. We didn't have the resources to put out as good a record as we subsequently put out, but at the time, it was necessary to put something out. It was also a time when it was comparatively unknown to put out a single without a record deal.[16]

Paul could now look for a deal again on the strength of that small success. One of the reasons why U2 were happy to sign a deal with Island Records was that they shared the same philosophy and the band could therefore develop at their own pace, without undue pressure. In 1981, after the release of the first single on the label, '11 o'clock Tick Tock', and the release of the album *Boy*, the following remark by Bono tells of the band's ambition and drive: 'I don't mean to sound arrogant ... but at this stage I do feel that we are meant to be one of the great groups.'[17]

It took U2 a while, however, to become famous; it actually took seven years and five albums to make it to the top with *The Joshua Tree*. Before that, they were the best-known underground band, as a French music magazine put it.

But U2 had already contributed greatly to the Irish music industry at that stage. The industry would actually grow with them, and with Paul McGuinness, who has become a major player in the field.

By remaining in Ireland, U2 gave others the idea that it was possible to make it without necessarily leaving the country. The truth is that the music industry is only viable if there are musicians to make it live. It has to nurture its artists, give them the means to develop and survive. But it also needs to nurture talent that will be successful and that will carry a reputation. That is what U2 did.

U2 and Business

The band and their manager have become a source of employment in Ireland; world representatives of Irish rock who lobby not only for the poor of this world but also for their own interests and those of the arts and record industry.

Basing themselves in Ireland meant employing people not only in the music industry but in other professions from accountants, to insurers, bankers, lawyers and so on.

It is, however, difficult to get a clear picture of the companies owned by U2 and of their finances. In 1995, journalist Graham Walsh, of *Business and Finance*, called their financial affairs 'complex and opaque'.[18] Ten years later, it doesn't look like it has changed much. Journalist Paul T. Colgan talks of 'a myriad of subsidiaries'.[19] In 1998, the magazine *Forbes* estimated U2's profit at $200 million.[20] Since then, that estimation has increased and probably tripled, as one has to take into account the profits on the sales of the *Best of 1980-1990* album, the profits of the Elevation tour, of the *Best of 1990-2000*, of *How to Dismantle an Atomic Bomb*, and on top of everything, the profits of the Vertigo tour. The band would therefore be worth $630 million, according to the *Forbes* magazine music rich list.

We can get a picture of what those companies are and in which areas they operate by briefly talking about them. The first company set up by U2 and Paul McGuinness was Principle Management, with its New York twin, which mainly takes care of the U2 affairs. Anne-Louise Kelly was for a long time second in command before becoming manager to Irish singers Gavin Friday and Paul Brady in 1997. She also took part in 1996, in the name of Principle Management, in the report commissioned by the then Minister for Arts, Heritage and Culture, Michael D. Higgins, on the state of the Irish music industry, 'Access All Areas: Irish Music, an International Industry'.

Principle Management has invested in other areas, notably Ardmore Studios and TV3, the third Irish television channel. A consortium of Irish companies, including Principle Management, also has owned a licence since 2002 for a radio station based in Waterford, Beat 101, and whose target is the fifteen to 24-year-old age group.

But beyond the most well-known U2 company, the band and their manager have set up other companies over the years, some more successful than others.

Mother Records was founded in 1984 and gave young bands a chance to record one or two singles before moving on to a bigger label. However, Mother Records closed its operation at the beginning of the 1990s, finding that its pivotal role had been fulfilled. Other labels were created by U2 and Paul McGuinness, for instance Celtic Heartbeat, part of Universal and founded in 1995 by Paul McGuinness, Dave Kavanagh and Barbara Galavan, which has on its catalogue Bill Whelan, Frances Black and Anuna. It tries to promote traditional and Celtic music. The label is actually one of the largest of its kind. Kitchen Records, set up in 1998, is trying to promote dance music.

In the field of music publishing, Paul McGuinness and Bill Whelan set up McGuinness/Whelan Publishing in the late 1980s, while the members of U2 created Mother Publishing, which no longer exists.

Not Us Limited is the best-known company set up by U2, outside of Principle Management. It is a holding company and deals with the promotion of musical events, as well as having ancillary activities, through companies like Straypass (concert presentation), Upfront EGS (concert staging) and U2 Limited (master tapes).

But the members of U2 have also made business ventures outside the music industry. In 1992, Bono and The Edge purchased the Clarence Hotel in Temple Bar, Dublin. They renovated it and the pair also opened a night club there called the Kitchen, which has become popular. The accounts are filed under the name of Brushfield, a holding company.

However, according to *Magill* and *Business & Finance*, not all those companies are necessarily making a profit and some would even have lost money. More recently, 'a cursory glance at U2's accounts might lead hasty observers to conclude that the band is in a spot of financial bother. Accounts for Not Us (...) for the year ending December 31, 2003, show the firm with debts of more than €18.5 million. A deeper inspection of the band's finances – a myriad of subsidiaries, inter-company loans and trusts – reveals that much of the money owed by Not Us is owed to other companies under the control of U2'.[21] But it doesn't prevent U2 from having a very healthy bank account. 'It is thought that the majority of U2's money is stored in trusts and partnerships.'[22]

As well as that, the members of U2 are named as directors or company secretaries of one or other of the companies:

The Edge (Dave Evans) and Bono (Paul Hewson) both sit on the boards of the following companies: Kitchen Recordings, Lakehaven, Lorijudd Investments, Mother Records, Mother Music, Not Us, Ravencrest, Remond, Straypass, the Fair City Trust and Thengel.

The Edge is recorded as a director of the ill-fated Media Lab Europe and a former director of Salmeen Enterprises Ltd, while Bono is listed as a former director of Media Lab Europe.

Larry Mullen Jnr is named as a director of Mother, Not Us, Parlade, Remond, Restwell, Straypass, Fair City and Thengel.[23]

Bono talked to Michka Assayas about the U2 business, and some bad investments that were made by the band and this was the first time I read about a member of U2 talking of some business mistakes that they made. Bono remembers that they gave money to invest to some people they liked, who were not as honest as they pretended to be. However, that experience made them aware of the need to take charge of their money and business affairs.[24]

The band has definitely diversified. Could what they own be termed an empire? Not strictly speaking. It is relatively modest and U2's chief interest remains music. But U2 are a huge source of income and employment in Ireland. Their philosophy is clear when it comes to their home country: business should be done by people who are Irish.

The members of U2 are aware of what is happening in their companies. But they first and foremost trust Paul McGuinness when it comes to that end of things. As for their share in the business, they each get twenty per cent, an unusually democratic agreement. That is also possibly one of the reasons why they get on well. Money is not an issue since they are all getting the same amount, including the manager. And they say that Paul McGuinness may just be U2's fifth member? In my eyes, he definitely is.

U2 have been compared to the Swedish band ABBA when it comes to what they brought financially to the country. Considering the size of Ireland, it may well be true.

U2 and album sales

U2 have naturally affected the sales of Irish albums abroad, notably in the UK. 'The music industry in the Republic of Ireland was boosted throughout the 1980s and 1990s by the international sales generated by U2, and perhaps more significantly by the band's commitment to remain located in the Dublin area.'[25] Indeed, everything Irish had become fashionable around the world by the mid-1990s. There was a phenomenon of globalisation of Irish music, in other words

Irish music became known all over the world at that time, but its roots can be found earlier in the decade. However, the phenomenon that accelerated this globalisation of music was boy bands. These were exports that put Ireland on the global map. In fact, music was the item that had the highest rate of export, ahead of tourism and alcohol.[26]

What is interesting is the penetration rate of Irish albums in the UK in other words, the sales impact that Irish albums have on the UK music market is quite impressive. The British market is, along with the American market, the most important in the western world when it comes to sales but it is also one of the most important in terms of music production. One must remember that the music market tends to fluctuate. Figures change rapidly from one year to the next, especially nowadays with the easy downloading of music from the Internet, whether legally or illegally. Ireland, however, produces a lot of artists and the release of a U2 album can very easily tip the scales of sales in favour of Ireland when it comes to countries other than Britain or America.

In 1987 and 1988, U2 released two albums: *The Joshua Tree* sold 15 million copies, while *Rattle and Hum* sold around 10 million. Those sales have undoubtedly contributed to an increase in the market share of Irish albums. This trend persisted in 1989, helped along by the success of the albums. Then, there was a lull in 1990 and 1991. In 1992, there was another increase when *Achtung Baby* was topping the charts and the Zoo TV tour was underway. In 1993, the figures were similar, also undoubtedly due to the fact that the Zoo TV tour was continuing (U2 were playing in Europe) and because *Zooropa* was released. The sales were not as high as for the previous album but helped maintain the figure. In 1995, there was another increase, probably due to the success of the Cranberries' second album, *No Need to Argue*, which was a worldwide success. As for boy bands, they had not yet appeared on the scene by this time. So, here we have a small country competing with the giants of music, and holding third place after the UK and the US. The average penetration rate in the UK was 5 per cent in the early 1990s; in Holland it was 3 per cent, while in Germany it was 4 per cent.[28] It is therefore obvious here that U2 played a concrete role in establishing the Irish music industry as an important player on the world stage.

U2 and Artists' Rights

U2 have also fought for artists rights in the Republic of Ireland. Several organisations take care of copyright. The first is the Irish Music Rights Organisation (IMRO). It is in charge of collecting and managing the rights for its members, who may be authors, composers or publishers, as well as over 60 affiliated foreign counterparts. IMRO was created in 1989 with the sole objective of collecting those rights, as its parent company, the British Performing Rights Society (PRS) took care of all other aspects of the business. IMRO finally became independent in 1995, an important step in making the Irish music industry independent from its British counterpart. IMRO also grants licenses for those who wish to make public use of music (pubs, cinemas, discos, hotels, etc.). It fulfils another role; that of music sponsor in Ireland, through festivals, competitions, seminars, workshops, research projects and concerts. It helped the Irish government to draft new legislation on copyright, the Copyright and Related Rights Act, which was accepted in 2000. In 1999, there were 3,500 members and IMRO's director of services has said about the size of the membership that:

> It contrasts with about 900 when we split [from the PRS] in 1995 and the reason for that phenomenal growth was because membership criteria was defined by the PRS for the UK market which, of course, is a much more vibrant market. They have about 20 or 30,000 members. Their idea is to keep as many out of it as they can because the more you put in, the more expensive it is at that level. So we changed the criteria from three published or recorded works to one, to let people in, and that has made it much more friendly for members, so if you were going to ask me how many more are out there, I would suggest there probably are several thousand still out there, but people who are like shooting stars.

IMRO's independence has therefore been a great chance for Irish musicians, who have been able to benefit from the organisation's help, unlike what the PRS could offer.

The Phonographic Performance (Ireland) Limited (PPI) is the second organisation, which actually collects the monies owed to record companies. Since 2000 and the new copyright law, they are also in charge of collecting monies due to performers, when their records are used for public performance on radio or television. They are subsequently redistributed by an association called Recorded Artists And Performers Limited (RAAP). U2 took part in its creation and have supported it. It is independent and controlled by the performers themselves. It can negotiate with the PPI about the sharing of royalties between record companies and performers, and ensures that the collection and distribution information are transparent and fair, so that the biggest number of performers avail of it.

U2 and Arts in Ireland

U2 and Paul McGuinness also play an active role in the arts in Ireland and in the promotion of popular music because promotion of popular music is part of an overall arts strategy. Paul McGuinness became a member of the Arts Council on 1 January 1988 and was to be part of it for twelve years. He was nominated by the then Prime Minister, Charles J. Haughey. The Arts Council was set up in 1951 to promote the arts in Ireland. It is the State's representative and its consultative body. Its role is to distribute the funds allocated to the arts by the government. But some areas of the arts were always more funded than others and, curiously, the first music officer was nominated only in 1975. And until 1976, only classical music received funding. From that date, traditional music and jazz started receiving money, which by 1983 was 2 per cent of the total spending.[29] However, popular music remained completely unfunded until 1988; that is when the first popular music officer, Keith Donald, was nominated. This nomination came about in the words of Keith Donald himself in the following way:

> How it happened was that seven people who were 'captains' of the music industry, including Paul McGuinness, got together in 1987 and decided that the Irish music industry needed some kind of a focal point. So they approached the Arts Council and there were numerous discussions and the seven people said that they would get the music industry to fund the position if the Arts Council put the person there. The Arts Council advertised and received 279 applications for the post and after a rigorous series of interviews and written submissions, they gave it to me. The reason I suspect is that I have an Arts degree, a background in social work and sociology and a wide experience of the industry.

However, Keith's role was not a funding role:

> My job in there was quite different from any other officers of the Arts Council for two reasons. One: I didn't have a budget, and two: I was funded by an external source. I was not funded by the tax payer. So I started a lot of initiatives while I was there, including educational workshops, seminars, sponsorships in the music industry. I organised regional seminars for young musicians who needed help. What made me different from all the other officers was that they got applications for money and they had to make recommendations to the Arts Council as to how those applications could be responded to. In my case, after a while nobody applied for money because

everybody knew that I didn't have any. So people came to me with ideas and I tried to help those ideas progress.

Through his connections to the Arts Council, Paul McGuinness was therefore instrumental in promoting popular music as an essential part of Irish music and culture.

However, the creation of another post in 1992 for Keith as head of Music Base, an organisation which was an information centre for young musicians who needed advice on the many aspects of the music industry,[30] this time funded by the Arts Council, was not to last for long, as in 1997, the Arts Council decided not to fund it any more, a move that could be interpreted as seeing popular music as music that was not important or influential enough in Ireland.

Paul McGuinness and some of his colleagues resigned from the Council on 18 February 2000. The official reason was that he was overworked, whereas his decision was due to the inefficient functioning of the Council

Paul McGuinness and U2 have given Ireland and Dublin something to be proud of and in a gesture that reflects that pride, they were given the Freedom of the City of Dublin in 2000 by the then Lord Mayor, Mary Freehill, who said: 'You contributed to Dublin's change of image abroad but more importantly you helped change the way we saw ourselves. Dublin's current success has many fathers but I am talking today to five of them.'

Bono commented on the honour as something incredible, while the others were equally thrilled. The fact that Aung San Suu Kyi, the Burmese leader, was also honoured on the same day, was not lost on anybody, I am sure as U2 were very much aware of her struggle for freedom in her native country, her emprisonment and even wrote a song paying homage to all she has done, which is 'Walk On', on the album *All That You Can't Leave Behind.*

The members of U2 were more proud of this than any other award they received in their career. And they have received many, from the Brit Awards to the Grammys, (22 so far), to the Irish Meteor Awards, the French NRJ Awards, and more. And these awards are important in that they grant them a special status in the world of music.

International success

At the end of the 1980s, U2 was granted the title of band of the decade by several magazines (*Melody Maker*, the French music magazine *Best*, and *Hot Press*, to name but a few). Later, they were even called the biggest band in the world. To try and understand why a band gets that title is not as easy as you may think. The

Rolling Stones were the biggest band in the world at one stage. Does it mean that they are not considered as such any more? Can there be two or more 'biggest bands in the world'? It is difficult to be certain. The concrete reasons for the selection that spring to mind are the sales of albums and concert tickets, the number of awards received, the quality of live performances, as well as a reputation built around a vision of rock. U2 have undeniably all of those qualities and more.

But more importantly, they represent the Irish music industry in that they are the most successful act to have emerged from Ireland so far and they have helped put Ireland on the music industry map, and they also represent the international music industry because they are called the biggest band in the world and have held on to that title for many years now. They are therefore definitely on a par with all the more famous bands that have existed in the past 40 years, if not more so. The crucial difference is that their line-up has remained the same since their foundation, which is an exceptional achievement.

On 26 February 2001, at the Brit Awards ceremony, U2 received the 'Outstanding Contribution to British Music' award. This was the first time such an award was given to a foreign band. And the fact is that U2 have always competed in the international band category. The president of the awards committee justified his position by saying: 'The band signed their record deal in Britain and they have always been an integral part of the British music scene.'[31] It may have seemed strange to many that suddenly U2 were part of the British music industry. It looked like a form of hijacking. After twenty years of their career, U2 were suddenly being described as a British group. However, we need to realise that U2 cannot be part of the international music industry if it is not endorsed by the British music industry. The relationship between the British media and U2 was not always smooth though. In his acceptance speech, Bono thanked the Beatles, the *New Musical Express* and the BBC. In that way, he recognised British popular culture as having played an extremely important role in Irish popular culture, and he recognised its influence. In the 1960s, those three entities played a crucial role in the Irish awakening to mass culture and to rock 'n' roll. The Beatles were the first rock band in the world. The *New Musical Express*, in spite of its sectarian and sometimes overcritical attitude towards everything Irish, including U2, was a vital element in awakening the Irish to rock music. As for the BBC, it also played a major role, with Radio 1, and showed nothing but utter respect for Ireland. Therefore, Bono recognised that British rock played a crucial part in U2's own existence, whilst the British rock establishment recognised that U2 created something special which could only have been born in Ireland. U2's influence and values, which had been disparaged by the British, were now embraced as part of the British and international rock scene. This outstretched hand was a symbolic reconciliation and formally placed the Irish band on the international rock platform.

Another dimension to U2 on the international rock scene is their relationship with America. It is an important relationship and U2 are almost considered as an American rock band over there. Their American audience is one of the most faithful, after the Irish. It may be because of so many Americans of Irish descent. It may also be because U2 remain a rock band, in the most classical sense of the word. U2's music is rock music, with something more. But U2's music has three essential elements of classical rock: respect of their elders – those artists and bands who have inspired U2 and who were around before them, communication and respect between the band and its audience, and live performance as the anchorage point of communication. U2 are still aware of the roots of rock, of this particular mixture of jazz, blues and rhythm 'n' blues which created rock 'n' roll. On 16 December 1988, during 'The Late Late Show', Bono told Gay Byrne: 'The Irish have soul and the blacks in America have soul and that's just what sets them apart.' This comparative feeling in Black Americans and the Irish that Bono observes justifies the relationship U2 have with American rock 'n' roll. Despite their Irish roots, U2 could not but acknowledge the American influence, particularly in the second half of the 1980s. U2's link with America falls within the larger scope of the Irish historical link with it. Beyond that, however, the band sees both sides of America, the positive and the negative. And despite the fact that they have written songs that denounced that negative side, Bono still loves America and believes in it. Music belongs to the bright side of America though. Looking at Irish music, we can see that it was first exported to America mainly by nineteenth-century emigrants, that it was transformed by the years and the people who played that music and subsequently reimported in an altered form to Ireland. In the Irish tradition, U2 exported their music to America, although it had already been influenced by rock 'n 'roll, and then reimported it, its form influenced by many other types of music, with its Irish spirit still intact.

U2's influence on the Irish and international music industries is very important. Universal has been their record company for some time. They have so much power that in France, for instance, promoting U2 doesn't seem to be a very difficult job. According to inside sources, U2 promotes itself. U2 are the only Irish rock band with such power and their success has turned the Irish music industry upside down. However, not everything is rosy and it is still difficult for young musicians to make it in the music business. Reports on the music industry commissioned since 1994 have pointed to the lack of major record companies, the lack of distribution power, the lack of managers, etc. As a consequence, many young bands must produce and release their records independently.

U2 are at the crossroads between the national and the international. They are first and foremost Irish. But they are also an 'English-singing' rock band and as such, have the power to touch the whole world. However, their being Irish gives them an aura that may fascinate foreigners. Ireland has a reputation of being a musical nation. As already stated, 48 per cent of foreign visitors who came to Ireland in 2001 did so partly because of music.[32] U2 wiggled their way into this opening and conquered the world.

Conclusion

U2 are a powerful force in the Irish music industry and their ambition, not to mention their talent (one rarely goes without the other), have led them to become one of the biggest bands in the world. Their success has in turn made the Irish music industry aware of its potential. The members of U2 have turned into lobbyists for the Irish music industry and its development, including when it comes to venues. A perfect example of their involvement is the refurbishment of the Point Depot, in Dublin. Before it was made into a venue and was still a derelict locomotive warehouse, U2 used it to record some songs for the 1988 album *Rattle and Hum* and some of the interview scenes for the film took place there. The place was subsequently renovated and turned into the biggest arena in Ireland, with a 7,500 seat capacity.

There is evidence of a parallel development between U2 and the music industry in Ireland. The band are part of the development and the industry is supporting them. U2 are investing money in Ireland, in the music industry and elsewhere. The tax exemption scheme for artists may have played a part.[33] People often tell me about the fact that U2 stayed in Ireland because of that reason. However, my reply is always the same: were they absolutely sure that they were going to be huge, that they were going to become rich? Did they not struggle at the beginning just like any young rock band? Did they know what the future held? They couldn't have, therefore tax exemption must have played a minor role.

However, some musicians have accused U2 of running a sort of a mafia, and of not giving young bands the chance they pretended to give them. This belief may sound ludicrous but may be explained firstly by the fact that U2 are so huge that they actually overshadow everybody else, and secondly by the fact that their affairs are rather opaque, which may have been another reason for gossip and misinformation. But there is a consensus as to the positive influence the band has had on the music industry.

The relationship U2 have with its industry of origin and the State can be illustrated by an event that took place in June 2001. U2 had taken an injunction against the demolition of their Hanover Quay studios in Dublin, which they lost. The studio will, however, be rebuilt in one of the buildings that is part of a redevelopment project for that part of the city. Adam Clayton was actually part of the panel who decided which architect would draw the plans. The Hanover Quay or Windmill Studios are important to U2's career. They have used them for almost all their albums.

The relationship between the music industry, the State, the local authorities and U2 is crucial. The fact that Adam Clayton participated in the choice of architect for the new studios shows how important U2 have become, even in the eyes of the local authorities and the State. That relationship is therefore crucial. The local authorities came to U2's rescue several times when the organisation of U2 gigs flirted with controversy. For instance, in 1997, the Lansdowne Road residents took an injunction against U2 playing there on 30 and 31 August. The residents nearly succeeded, but the band and their supporters are powerful when it comes to playing concerts in their hometown and the concerts went ahead.

U2 were always ambitious but have known that only hard work could make them succeed. U2 have chosen a long haul strategy, of working hard and of reinventing the band on a periodical basis. Paul McGuinness shares their work philosophy and said in 1997:

The plan is to keep doing it as long as they are good at it. And I would hope to stop when they start repeating themselves. They are creatively stronger than ever, they're doing their best work and constantly surpassing themselves artistically. That's why they stay together and that's why it's fun to manage them because it's very challenging.

Eight years later, they are still able to sell millions of records and sell-out concerts.

The fact is that few things happened by accident in U2's career. The band have always had precise plans, a vision of what the band is supposed to be, and the capability to be relevant.

U2's contribution to the music industry must not only be seen in terms of record or ticket sales, or in terms of marketing plans. These are four individuals, four men, who make music together. As such they form a very unique entity looking in the same direction.

And in the end, the marketing strategy must yield results. U2 have achieved artistic and commercial success, the latter due to Paul McGuinness' highly astute commercial sense. In 1997, for the PopMart tour, they decided that they would only use one promoter for the American leg. The reason was financial efficiency for a tour that required a huge initial investment on the part of the band. This particular tour and the previous one nearly bankrupted them. But the fact remains that they made money for the 2001 Elevation tour, and the 73 concerts would have grossed them $62.2 million, according to *Rolling Stone* magazine,[34] which also claimed that U2 were the biggest earners in its category for 2001, earning $109.7 million.[35] In 2002, according to French television channel M6, U2 were still ahead of all the others with $70 million, without an album or a tour that year.[36] At the end of 2005, the Vertigo tour was the highest grossing tour of the year with $260 million (€216 million).[37]

Nowadays, the band are turning their attention to new technologies, like the Apple deal. It is important to note that since the early 1990s, U2 have integrated new technologies in their records and tours. The band see the possibilities that Internet downloading can bring the artist as well as the fan and the music industry. The idea is basically to adapt to new trends, and even to foretell what is going to happen so as not to be left behind. Bono revealed:

> For the first time, U2 is considering technology partners. We have to understand the way our music is going to be bought and sold, and the sort of systems of distribution. So now we're on to meet phone companies. We want to meet the people in Vodafone. We like the people at Apple. Jonathan Ive, the genius who designs for Apple, if he had a fan club, I'd be in it (…) Steve Jobs made the downloading of music sexy with iTunes, while the music business argued amongst themselves. He has created those beautiful objects that are Apple Macs. Even their commercials are great. We want to be in them, turn them into music videos.[38]

Bono goes on: 'We want to work with someone if they give us creative control. We can collaborate if you let us into your company with your scientists.'[39]

What is clear is that U2 have never actually sold out, despite what some may think. They would have sold out had they just sold songs to companies solely for commercial purposes. But they have turned down millions of dollars because it was not what they wanted. These new technological ventures, if they happen, may bring more surprises than expected, from the musical and iconographic points of view.

7

MYTH, IMAGE AND THE NEXT U2

The focus of this chapter is on the struggle U2 have faced when it comes to their image as a rock band and as rock stars, and the reasons why, in the 1980s, a myth emerged, triggered by the image and the songs.

But this chapter also tries to answer a question asked in many newspapers and magazines: who will be the next U2? The question at first glance seems astonishing and indeed, how could another band of U2's stature come out of as small a country as Ireland? But it is not so when one looks at the success of Irish music around the world. Bands such as the Cranberries, the Corrs, the Divine Comedy, artists like Enya and David Gray are all part of a growing number of Irish pop stars known all over the world. However, they have not reached the level of U2's success, and Irish people would still like to see another U2 on the world stage. It may also be due to the fact that Ireland as a small country produced four Nobel Prize winners for literature. Why not another biggest band in the world? The recurring question of the 'next U2' may also find an explanation in the way U2's career evolved, in their constant reinvention, and in the mythical construction of the band.

But first, let's focus on what a myth is today. In the nineteenth century, a myth was seen as an imaginary event, a fictitious event, something invented. More recently, specialists of the modern myth (sociologists, ethnologists and religious historians) tend to believe that the notion of myth originates in archaic or traditional societies, societies without a state or a social division, societies which no longer exist.

174

According to those societies, a myth is a true story 'of a creation'.[1] The story is true because 'it tells how something has been created'.[2] If that something exists today, it is therefore there to prove that the story is real.[3] The story would be about a birth, a new situation, a beginning. It is a founding story.

It is also a sacred story, showing heroes whose examples are to be followed, heroes who are offered as role models, who show how to behave, who set norms and tell what should be done.

The myth represents rites, traditions and social norms. Through its narration, the myth is relived. It is a story where the exploits of the mythical beings are re-enacted, where the narrator becomes the hero himself, by re-enacting those exploits.

A myth can also be a communication system, a message, according to Roland Barthes, who also says that anything can become a myth when we talk about it.[4]

According to religious historian Mircea Eliade, myths are found everywhere in our society, although they are 'secularised, weakened, concealed',[5] in other words they are not religious anymore, they have lost some of their power over us and they are often not visible. We also cannot rid ourselves of them. In this way, everything can become mythical. Things are mythical (cars, toys, clothes, etc.). People are mythical, most notably celebrities. Because people or objects are turned into myths, nowadays the idea of the sacred, of the religious within the myth is therefore replaced by the profane, although the sacred is still visible.

What about movie stars or rock stars, then? The social critic Edgar Morin talks of movie stars and says that their mythology lies between the aesthetic (we find them beautiful), the magical (they may sometimes appear as having mysterious powers) and religion (we worship them).[6] They are not however completely one or the other because we still see through them at times. Movie stars, rock stars, sports stars are all the most modern incarnations of the myth. They have that mythical potential but become 'mythically complete' after their demise, because they then become imaginary in some ways; what they did or what they said is changed, distorted and we have a new image of them, which is different from what it was when they were alive.

Who is therefore responsible for the creation of a myth? It is actually a mixture of the celebrities and their behaviour, of the media, of the biographers and of the fans. Thus, 'music stars are deified, made sacred by facts, the media, the biographies which make them into a kind of personalisation of the sacred'.[7]

Image
The concept of image is essential, as it constitutes the basis upon which the U2 myth was created.

What is an image? Celebrities are charismatic figures. They have an inexplicable power over us. They dress in one way and we will follow that fashion. They believe in something and we will believe in it. And when celebrities are photographed without make-up and looking dishevelled, we delight in it because we catch a glimpse of their human side, we have a complicated relationship with them. We admire them and yet, somewhere deep inside, we wonder what makes them exceptional. That's what I mean by the word 'image'. An image is projected but never shows what the reality is. The consequence of that image is that legends, beliefs and myths are created and surround those stars in magazines, in films, on television, in interviews, in songs. Stars must have an image so as not to reveal too much, and to be able to change, to fit an ideal desired by the fans, to conform to a certain image. And if they don't fit, the fall can be fatal, because the image given to the public can sometimes be quite different to the real one. This is the gap between reality and image. Although it may be obvious, the fact remains that what you see is not necessarily what you get. The perception that each of us has of that image can also be very different. We do live, as screenwriter, author and professor Enricho Fulchignoni put it, in the 'civilisation of the image'.[8]

Throughout the 1980s, U2 gave their audience an image closer to their own reality than most bands. It was a very simple, straightforward and serious image. The many photographs taken then testify to that. But this image did the reverse of what it was supposed to do. It was meant to free U2 of the image, even of the idea of an image, that they might have had. However, it actually made them prisoners of it.

For the Zoo TV tour, U2, and especially Bono, were influenced by Daniel J. Boorstin's book, *The Image: A Guide to Pseudo-Events in America*, written in 1962. It is interesting to understand the thought process at work in creating that new U2 image. The book is fascinating and is as relevant now as it was 40 years ago. The author talks about people who are famous for being famous, and also about pseudo-events, which are events created only for media purposes: press-conferences, for instance. But he also talks about image and its definition. He says that image is 'synthetic, believable, passive, vivid, simplified, and ambiguous'.[9]

An image is synthetic because it is planned. It is created with a purpose. It also must be believable since people must believe in it, must identify with it, otherwise it doesn't serve its purpose. It is passive because its bearer must be part of it without becoming it. It is vivid in that it appeals to the senses. It must be simplified because it 'must be simpler than the object it represents',[10] an image which is accessible and remembered easily but which is not simplistic because it must not become 'the natural symbol of the whole class of objects it describes'.[11]

Finally, it is ambiguous, floating 'somewhere between the imagination and the senses, between expectation and reality'.[12] In other words, an image is what we make of it. It is sometimes real and sometimes we make up a whole story about it.

An image is also a social link, in that it creates a visual link that can spread within society. An image can influence how people see things in society. It tells them how to behave, what to wear, how to talk. For instance, an image can create fashion trends, for example if a model is seen wearing an outfit in the street. It also creates emotions, whether they are positive or negative since it is a communication tool. It is symbolic of the person or institution it represents. And it is an emblem of the here and now, it must be relevant, of its time, active and changing. Do U2 fit this criteria?

Spanning 25 years or more, U2's image has changed. But at the beginning of their career, it is difficult to ascertain if U2 really knew what their image meant. Adam Clayton told Bill Flanagan in 1992:

We've been lucky to have been a young band. I'm the eldest and I'm 32. A lot of our contemporaries were still struggling at this age. By the time they're in their forties maybe it's just a little bit too late for them to be able to go back to the drawing board. The early mistakes we made – not understanding cool, not understanding attitude, clothes and haircuts – were because we were seventeen and eighteen and our idols like the Clash and the Jam and the Police who had all that shit down were making their first records at 27 or 28. We were making our first record when we were twenty! So yeah, they had their image together. It's taken us fifteen years to get an image together, or indeed to realise that image is important. And not important.

I don't believe that it was because of their young age that U2 did not get their image together. Indeed, many young artists have been conscious of their image, and manipulated it at will. Youth is only an excuse and U2 simply did not want to comply. They did not want to be like everybody else. And, most of all, they did not seem to care about their image. Adam uses the words 'important' and 'not important' when he talks about image. The music they played in the 1980s did not need a sophisticated image, because it was good enough to stand on its own. What happens often is that image is enhanced because the music is weak. That is the case with most manufactured bands, bands which are created artificially for instance the Spice Girls (producers put a call out to form a girl band or a boy band; the people who are interested sing and dance and the band is formed with the ones the producers think are suitable to their idea of what a band like that should be. In other words, it isn't a natural process of young people getting together and starting a band for reasons of friendship or love of the same music for instance.) They need the pretty boy or girl look, the sexy clothes and the choreography to make it look interesting because the music is not enough. The image becomes more important than the music and the latter supports the image. However, U2's image has always represented the band and what it is, just like a manufactured band's image has always stood for what that sort of band is.

U2's image has been believable throughout their career, albeit a little too serious at times. In simple words, people believe in what U2 are. Even during the early 1990s and the Zoo TV extravaganza, it was clear that their image fitted the music during that phase.

The complexity of U2's image reached its peak in the 1990s. It was rather simple earlier on. Basically, what you saw was what you got, the classical image of a rock band. The problem was that U2 did not want to admit that they had an image. However, we all live with an image, whether we want it or not. That is why U2's 'non-image' in their early years was still an image. And because they denied its existence, it was far more complex than it actually was. It was multi-dimensional and ambiguous, and became the subject of many articles in newspapers and magazines.

Their image remains the symbol of their music, the here and now constantly in need of reinvention. However, their image was less relevant than their music.

Their image also became original but it was never shocking or exploitative. Even the picture of Adam Clayton in his birthday suit was not shocking, possibly because it was not shown in that manner.

The image of an artist becomes more important, than the reality it stems from. It is, however, part of a fragmented identity. The real identity of a band is in their music so the image must reflect the music. But it also must go beyond the music so that the audience can recognise the band's image instantly. The real identity of the person or persons in the band, not as musicians but as individuals, becomes blurred and the adopted stage persona emerges. The latter is invented and presented as such. The identity is fragmented into three pieces: the person, the musician and the persona. All are bound into one but the audience may perceive things differently. We create an image of Bono or The Edge, for example, but we don't know if it is true. And often, a rock star will protect his/her true identity by becoming someone else in order to protect him/herself. There is therefore a real contradiction between celebrity and the protection of one's personal life. The private and the public spheres collide constantly. However, as John Waters says: 'Celebrity comes, by and large, to those who want it. And this desire can be detected in even the most vehement and heartfelt protests against the invasion which ensues.'[13]

The members of U2 have protested against the invasion of their privacy. It may be due to the fact that, in the 1980s, they presented a less fragmented identity than others. The music reflected, as it always has, the different personalities in the band and the real people. They were definitely more exposed than other bands because they were themselves. They did not wear a mask, which may have been detrimental to their music and their philosophy.

In the early 1990s though, U2 had to appear as fabricated characters. Bono turned into the megalomaniac star that he was supposed to be; The Fly, the Mirrorball Man, MacPhisto, they were all an answer to the myth that surrounded U2. They were one way of deconstructing it, in other words of changing it, making it smaller, less intrusive, of dismantling it. But why create such characters? Why select such an iconographic revolution? To escape the grip of the media, the four members of the band decided to play the media game by becoming megalomaniacs, particularly Bono, of course. The critics said that U2 were too serious, did not have a sense of humour. The new image completely negated that. And it is at that point that the image began to fragment. In the 1980s, Bono, as the singer and charismatic figure, was constantly catapulted to the front of the stage. However, the other members of the band were not constantly in his shadow and contrary to many other bands, Bono on his own is not U2. He told Michka Assayas: 'Maybe the reason why the band hasn't split up is that people might get this: that even though they're one quarter of U2, they are more than they would be if they were one whole of something else. I certainly feel that way.'[14] In the 1990s, this homogeneous image was divided into fragments and put Bono even more at the forefront. He carried the image of the band through his shiny leather suits and Fly shades. He was the preferred target of the media and had to find some kind of protection. The Fly gave him just that.

U2's Place within the Concepts of Image and Myth

What are the origins of U2's image and how was that image created? What role did image play in the creation of the myth? Was it instrumental in the emergence of the myth and what role does music play in it? Was the image the primary reason for the myth's existence? and how did the members of U2 deal with it? How did U2 deconstruct the myth, and was the myth reconstructed in any way?

U2's image changed several times during the band's career and is now very different to what it was. It evolved with the music, the maturing process and was consciously changed. This image, which is not only visual but also moral, is partly responsible for the myth surrounding the band. Each decade shows a change in U2's image and that is what the media present. The media also suggest that U2 albums go in pairs, in other words *Boy* goes with *October*, *War* with *The Unforgettable Fire*, and so on. However, the process is far more complex than it appears and each album is a reinvention in itself.

U2 SAYS NO TO IMAGE

Throughout their career, U2 have had a problem with image, and the band's refusal to have an image is almost legendary. Bono insisted in 1992 that: 'We don't have any style (…) Swagger. No style.'[15] A few years later, in 1997, Larry observed: 'It's kind of weird that the way you look is about as important as the way you sound.'[16] This comment is not surprising in that it is totally in line with the band's well-known view on image and yet, it is surprising because U2 have used their image to their own end. The Edge said: 'Early on, we thought that we were making a non-statement, that our style was an "anti-style style". What we didn't realise is that that was a style anyway.'[17] This is definitely U2's paradox, the contradiction that permeates the whole of their career. It may appear very naive to pretend that the band has no image. If they reinvented their music, they also must renew their image. It is obvious when one looks at the videos, concert footage or record sleeves. If you look at their appearance since their careers began, their clothes are different, the haircuts are different. The real metamorphosis took place in 1991 with *Achtung Baby*.

Image is bound to rock 'n' roll. 'When you heard rock, you saw it as well, whether live, or in films, or on television, or on record sleeves,' says the sociologist Lawrence Grossberg.[18] You still hear and see it matched to a certain style of dress, to haircuts, to make-up, to images of the body as an object of desire, to a way of moving, of dancing. Rock 'n' roll cannot escape its image, whatever it is. Rock 'n' roll is a musical and visual culture. A band may decide against its image becoming a label or even may decide not to have an image, but it is there, whatever they do, and it will be used by the media.

Coincidentally, U2 began their career almost at the same time as MTV, which started broadcasting on 1 August 1981, at a time when rock's image was becoming even more visual. In typical fashion, U2 tried to turn their back on that and be 'ordinary'. It did not work.

The Genesis of the Image

U2 wanted to be without an image. Yet, they did create one. And it turned out that that image, while reflecting the band's music, was austere and serious. The trend appeared at the beginning but became more prominent with the album *War*. The members of U2 were on average 23 years old and had to reinvent themselves for the first time. The album was different from the previous two, harder, more rock 'n' roll. I remember coming across articles in French music magazines calling their music 'heroic rock.' This was the way U2 were perceived in France and although the expression may bring a smile to your face, it can possibly be explained by the mixture of their new music, their Irish origins, and a myth that was at an embryonic stage. The origin of the myth lies partly in this intangible idea of 'Irishness'. But 'heroic rock' was also a musical trend of the time that encompassed other bands with a Celtic background, like Simple Minds or Big Country. There was hero imagery in the expression, the hero being the one who fights and wins. The hero is authentic and in the world of rock, this image of U2 as having integrity and being authentic was already defined.

But U2 must have other qualities outside of their integrity and authenticity to become a myth and according to sociologist Gabriel Segré, there is a pattern of traits that define a rock star. He is talking here about Elvis Presley yet a rock star must be gifted, self-taught, must be successful very early on in his or her career, must be unselfish, unfit for social and economic life, must love to live in luxury, must be humane, humble, must be incapable of being happy, must have sex-appeal, must have a sense of sacrifice, must be sometimes isolated, immature and sometimes mad.[19]

This pattern was true of many rock stars of the 1960s and 1970s. It became rarer afterwards. U2 are far from fitting that image. They seem to have many of the positive traits without the negative ones. They are well-adjusted people with happy family lives. The number of children in the U2 camp is a testimony to that. Adam Clayton's problems were the closest one could get to the real rock lifestyle. However, even that has changed since.

It is true though that the members of U2 live in nice areas in Dublin and own several other homes elsewhere in the world. They live in luxury in beautiful areas, but they have to live behind high walls with security cameras. That is the price to pay for celebrity. However, in Ireland, they live more or less ordinary lives. It may be because it is a small place and people are not as obsessed with celebrity as elsewhere. Bono's house is nevertheless a tourist destination for foreign fans, who spend hours waiting and hoping for a glimpse of their hero.

U2 have their careers well in order, make their own decisions and always have a positive image of themselves, an image of self-control. The fans therefore receive a positive, probably slightly distorted image of the band, something that has served U2 well throughout their career.

The band's faith has probably played a vital role in their behaviour. Bono, Larry and The Edge are fervent believers but they are open-minded about their faith and ready to talk about it. They also follow certain principles, like being charitable. They have not rejected, like many, that aspect of their upbringing and it has not been an hindrance to their career.

U2's Image in the 1980s

If you lay any of the U2 record sleeves of the 1980s on a table, the photographs are all in black and white, except for *October*, which is bland. The second thing you might notice is that the band's photograph appears for the first time only on the *October* album. Peter Rowen, Derek Rowen's (or Guggi from the Lypton Village and Virgin Prunes) younger brother, is on the front cover of *Boy* and *War*. He represents innocence and childhood in the former, his lovely face and eyes open to the world; and he represents the loss of innocence and childhood in the latter, his eyes fearful and his lip bleeding. Bono said that Peter was chosen twice to represent the changes taking place in the world.[20] Peter reappeared on the cover of the *Best of 1980-1990*, released in 1998, this time wearing a soldier's helmet. It is interesting that U2 should have chosen a photograph from the 1983 session taken by Ian Finlay. In 1980, the picture was in harmony with the songs on *Boy*. It was also in harmony with Lypton Village's philosophy of not wanting to grow up, of innocence and childhood preserved. The same harmony goes for the album sleeve for *War*: the boy's split lip and fearful eyes, the name of the album in red letters, the songs, everything portraying of war. The cover of the *Best of 1980-1990* is slightly more problematic. U2 could have chosen photographs from *The Joshua Tree* sessions. They chose one of the *War* ones instead. This could be explained by the fact that that is when they started being known internationally, *War* being their first album to reach the top ten in many countries. *War* was the catalyst. Also, *The Joshua Tree* was so big that they might not have wanted to use it again. Whatever the reason, it was definitely the start of a process of going back to one's roots after the madness of the 1990s.

The cover of *October* is dull, and U2 themselves admit that the choice of picture was a mistake. The picture was taken on the Canal docks in Dublin, although it could have been taken anywhere similar. What is interesting is not so much the picture itself but the way the members of U2 are already starting to change from their beginnings.

The process of change will continue from then on. But back to *War* and especially to the 'New Year's Day' video. It was shot in Sweden in December 1982 by Meiert Avis. U2 are seen riding on horses and carrying white flags.

However, it could be considered ordinary, beautiful but not very imaginative, were it not for the archive footage of the Second World War in between images of the band. The concept of the album is represented there. The lyrics of the song though are slightly out of line with the images. The message is that of peace, the white flags and the snow symbolic of ceasefire and hope, whereas the black and white images of fighting soldiers represent the cruel nature of war. The images of soldiers reinforce the meaning of the song, which is not the case with U2's video. If you look at videos over the years, most of them are performance clips. Nevertheless, 'New Year's Day' can be put in the socially conscious category.[21]

The band's social consciousness is at the root of the myth. The white flag will be used from then on throughout the 1980s during concerts as a symbol of what U2 believe in: peace and reconciliation. The 'Sunday Bloody Sunday' extract, on the *Live at Red Rocks in Colorado* film, is a moment of communion with the crowd and the crowd share in that moment by singing.

The first noticeable thing around 1983 is that the image is starting to change. Haircuts are different although the clothes are the same. But Bono wore a hat during the *War* period and continued wearing one for some time.

Although the myth will start emerging around the time of Live Aid, there are already signs of it with *The Unforgettable Fire* album. The photograph in black and white shows the band in front of a ruined castle in Moydrum, County Westmeath. The four band members look small in front of this massive building, steeped in Irish history and mythology, Ireland being steeped in a deep mytho- logical past of invented creatures like banshees and leprechauns. The area looks ethereal and mysterious. One can imagine the castle haunted by ghosts. This is a somewhat stereotyped vision of Ireland, like other Celtic countries such as Scotland, where every castle is supposed to be haunted.

The video for 'Pride' is also simple. Just the band singing in Saint Francis Xavier's Hall in Dublin, the East-link bridge connecting the northside to the southside of Dublin symbolising U2's place of origin and of the Irish capital's divide. And this is what is striking. The theme of the song is not to do with Dublin. This song is about Martin Luther King. Why did U2 not put the politi- cal side of the song in the promotion video? The reason may lie in the fact that 'The Unforgettable Fire' was the first single from the album, and they wanted something socially neutral so the music could take centre-stage.

The video of 'The Unforgettable Fire', the second single from the album, released in April 1985, is different because it is closer to the song's theme. The outside footage was shot in Sweden and is reminiscent of 'New Year's Day'. War, violence, attempts at reconciliation are all themes found in both songs. In June

1985, 'The Unforgettable Fire and Martin Luther King' exhibition was shown at the Grapevine Arts Centre in Dublin, courtesy of U2. On the eve of their 25 June concert in Croke Park, Bono was at the opening and explained:

> [These pictures] were from six year olds to 60 year olds (…) to exorcise from themselves the fear that they felt about the bomb being dropped on the two cities. It's not just pictures. It's any medium.
>
> We've been trying to do this for about a year, a year and a half. The original's The Unforgettable Fire Exhibition, a national art treasure in Japan. We went through the Japanese Embassy. We went through our offices here in the Dáil. We had tried to get the originals here. They won't let them out of Japan. But this exhibition we picked up in Chicago, because U2 were doing a peace exhibition along with the Clash, Yoko Ono, Stevie Wonder, going right back to Woody Guthrie. That's how eventually we went through the Chicago Peace Museum. We brought them here. We just said that we'd pay for the package and the production and the whole deal. The Grapevine Arts Centre offered their place.
>
> [The people who painted these pictures] wanted to exorcise from themselves the fear they felt over the Holocaust and the bombs that had been dropped on Nagasaki and Hiroshima. They just painted. And that's what got me even more than the paintings, just the idea that people should use art if you like, paint on canvas to get something out of themselves. A bit like what we do with our music. That's the way we get it out of us. And it just stuck on me. It stuck in my memory and when I was writing the words for 'The Unforgettable Fire', it just came back.[22]

The video is bleak, the lights of the city reflected behind Bono being the only reprieve from an otherwise dark background. The symbolic merry-go-round at a funfair turning into a nuclear bomb spells the danger of nuclear power and the madness of man. The merry-go-round, a place where children are supposed to have fun, is symbolic of innocence shattered.

That same period saw U2 at Live Aid, a turning point for the band. Here, from arena band, they became an international stadium band. Midge Ure said of the Irish band ten years after the event: 'I think U2 seized the moment. They were just brilliant in that big stadium environment … Not many people make the transition into being the big stadium band. And U2 went for it and they won.'[23]

That very moment when they became a stadium band is also the moment when they were looking for something more intimate with the audience. They had intended to play three songs, 'Sunday Bloody Sunday', 'Bad' and 'Pride (In the Name of Love)'. 'Bad' lasted longer than its normal six minutes, and the band weren't able to play the last song of the short set. During the song 'Bad', Bono climbed down from the stage, and as was his habit, started looking for female fans to dance with. He hugged the girls and danced with them, and millions of people were witness to this extraordinary display of communion with his audience. It was participatory and communitarian. Suddenly, the physical distance between artist and audience was erased. When Bono hugged and danced with those girls, he hugged and danced with the whole audience and he made Wembley Stadium a small place, where everyone was included.

Two years later, *The Joshua Tree* was about to become U2's biggest-selling album. Again, the image had changed. The Edge's hair was long and Bono was hatless. This time, U2's focus was America and the music reflected that interest. The picture on the sleeve is of the four members of the band in the American desert. The by now famous Joshua tree is visible to the side. At this time the band was about to conquer the world and that aspect was shown in the video of 'Where the Streets Have No Name'. This clip carried the impression that U2 had conquered the world by being authentic and that could be why some people criticised the clip. The authentic approach was again used for the video for 'I Still Haven't Found What I'm Looking For', though in this case, the interaction with the crowd was possible and therefore very physical. Bono, Adam, The Edge and Larry were seen walking amongst the crowd in a shopping mall in Las Vegas, shaking hands and kissing girls.

The Joshua Tree tour was captured on film and on record with *Rattle and Hum*. The record sleeve is of The Edge playing the guitar while Bono is turning the attention of the crowd to his friend by holding a big projector towards him. This was the routine during the song 'Bullet the Blue Sky'. It shows U2 going back to the roots of rock 'n' roll. Bono is letting the guitar takes its rightful place as the symbol of rock 'n' roll. The sleeve is stereotyped because U2 wanted to be part of a tradition which they found difficult to integrate at the beginning. But the other reason is that it is partly a live album as well. The project was much more ambitious though as there was also a film to accompany the record. The single/album/single/tour cycle was broken and there was an unusual cycle of single/album/film/single/tour. Indeed, U2 released the single 'Desire' in September 1988. Then the album was released in October of that same year, followed by the film, plus three more singles ('Angel of Harlem' in December 1988, 'When Love Comes to Town' in April 1989 and 'All I Want Is You' in June 1989) before the *Lovetown* tour started in September 1989. The 'Desire' video uses the imagery of

America that U2 were inspired by in the 1980s, the idea of America having become definite, coherent. At the same time, the experience of doing Rattle and Hum brought about a feeling of release from that obsession. The iconographic message of that era borrowed many of its aspects from America and carried an impression of déjà-vu, a feeling of having already experienced something, when in reality, it is the first time it is experienced. Wim Wenders, the German film-maker said that America had 'colonised our unconscious'[24] (by that he means the European unconscious)and 'Desire' played on that imagery: the big cars, the avenues, the skyscrapers, the police, stars who have reached a status of being looked upon as exceptionally gifted and who are seen as having achieved a mythical status (B.B. King, Ella Fitzgerald) and politicians (Richard Nixon, Robert Kennedy).

Eight out of the eleven videos from The Joshua Tree and Rattle and Hum were filmed in America, six carrying a strong American imagery.

In the Rattle and Hum movie, the visit U2 paid to Graceland is depicted, this being Elvis Presley's house, now a museum. The band are seen visiting the house while 'Heartland' is playing; Larry is sitting on one of Elvis' Harley Davidsons. I can understand they were fascinated with Elvis Presley and his influence on rock music. They had found inspiration in him. But what was behind their symbolic visit, caught on camera? U2 may have wanted to get closer to the original rock 'n' roll myth, represented by Elvis Presley, in order to lessen their own fragments of myth, to make their own myth smaller, to perhaps try and destroy it. If the members of the band behaved like fans, they may have then been able to deny the myth they represented for others.

But it was not that easy to deny and destroy the myth. Their attempt to exorcise their fascination with America may have been successful, personally, artistically and even commercially. After all, 'Desire' became the first U2 single to reach number one in the British charts and the album was the fastest selling of all time in the UK. However, all was not wonderful. The British press was extremely critical, despite Paul McGuinness being adamant that 60 per cent of reviews by the American critics were excellent.[25] What happened then to explain this difference between the British and the American press? On the one hand, the UK always had difficulties with U2's uncool, less sophisticated image. On the other hand, U2 have always been the darlings of the American press. The UK was always America's rival regarding rock music. U2 were caught between the two, deciding that conquering America first was a better strategy. U2 did not belong to the British music industry and it may have irritated the latter that an Irish rock band could become so enormous. Britain hadn't seen that since the Beatles. But also, according to journalist Gavin Martin, 'there was some bemusement if not antipathy to U2 among the British rock press because [U2] were able to be a more successful band in Britain by staying based in Dublin than many groups on the mainland.'[26]

The Unforgettable Fire period may well have been the time when U2 found a visual style. The choice of black and white film for the video may be explained by the fact that they had refused the idea of an image. It is indeed frequent for rock 'n 'roll bands to reject the image and to just be content with playing music.

There are profound contradictions between what U2 said and what they did. If they agreed that music guides the visual, then they could not deny the very idea of image. A record sleeve, for instance, is fabricated. You have to choose the colour, the photograph and so on. U2 have always had the reputation of controlling everything they do. They therefore have always taken part in the creation of their image, and it was a conscious process. Videos are the same. If the band does not like a video, it will not be shown on television.[27] U2's influence on the image is thus as important as the music.

U2's Image in the 1990s

Many of us were witness to U2's music and image overhaul in the 1990s. This is another reinvention of the band, albeit a spectacular one. From black and white, the image of the band became colourful and fun, with smiling faces, mad clothes (U2 dressing as women was nothing short of mad, but there were also shiny suits) and top models hovering in the background. The whole new image was beautifully put together, with extensive media coverage. However, and despite the apparent transformation, the music was still the core of the band. Above all else, the Zoo TV tour proved once more that U2 were the greatest live rock act on the planet. That reputation had not changed.

The band wanted to dismantle the idea that people had of U2, of what they were or of what they were not. How did they do it? What tools did they use?

The image U2 had created gave them a musical and visual style that did not suit them any more. The myth was therefore impossible to deal with. U2 might not have been relevant for the younger generations. Although they were still young, they had been around for ten years and had to adapt to the times. They could not pretend to represent a generation anymore. U2 therefore had to appeal to a younger generation to stay relevant, while still retaining their original fan base.

Their choice was to break the mould, start afresh, become what a lot of people thought they were, notably Bono and his supposed megalomaniac streak. They had to seduce, cajole, pretend they were what they were not. Many people did not know what to make of this whole Bono-The Fly rock star that he had supposedly become. It was irony at its best; it was theatre on a grand scale. *Achtung Baby* and Zoo TV, followed by *Zooropa*, were the mirrors of that transformation.

If you look closely at the front sleeve of *Achtung Baby*, you see sixteen different photographs of the band, of its members, details of clothing, of animals, of places. It is confusing at first but is already an indication of what to expect. In other photographs, on the inside sleeve, we see Adam and The Edge wearing dresses. Bono is wearing lipstick. This is a hint of the video for 'One'. The *Achtung Baby* sleeve is symbolic of U2's desire to radically change their image and to start deconstructing the myth through their new image. Some of the photographs were taken in Morocco, where the video for 'Mysterious Ways' was filmed. Another detail is from the trousers The Edge is wearing during the shooting of 'The Fly' video. All are hints of what is in store. It is almost as if U2 had set up a treasure hunt for their fans. But that is obviously what the band wanted: to confuse everyone visually, to show only snippets in different parts of the globe. However, it has definitely a European feel to it.

This new image was very homogenous. The music was obviously the element that determined it. But it was in contrast with the actual themes of the songs. The title, *Achtung Baby*, is humorous but it is a bleak album, with blood on the tracks, the manner in which it was recorded and the difficulties U2 had to go through are evidence of it.

The first video from this album was 'The Fly' directed by video directors Richie Smyth and John Klein in 1991 in Dublin and London. It is a performance video, which is nothing new for U2. However, the imagery is different. Bono is in character as the Fly. He is wearing a shiny leather suit, his fly shades; his hair is black, cut rather short and waxed, a totally different style from the one he donned in the late 1980s. He described the Fly character as a disoriented megalomaniac who was trying to escape the madness of the world. The Fly is reciting aphorisms throughout the song. The video is showing some of those aphorisms, along with slogans and words that have apparently no connection between them. The clip made the Fly alive and some elements of the Zoo TV tour are already there: the slogans, the Zoo TV logo, the televisions, the remote control. The beginning of the clip shows Bono walking in the streets of London. He has a cigarette in his hand, puts a miniature bus on the ground, controls the flow of traffic so that pedestrians can cross the street, talks to them. He then comes out of a shop and stops in front of a television shop called Bobsboxes. The TVs are precariously piled on top of one another and the singer is holding a remote control. He sits in front of the shop in an armchair and starts flicking. The clip alternates between Bono impersonating the Fly (walking on a roof or flicking channels) and the band in performance. There are actually two slightly different versions of the video when, during the guitar solo, the Fly/Bono is in front of Bobsboxes and is watching The Edge playing the guitar. In both versions, however, slogans in red appear which say 'Everything you know is wrong' or 'Watch more TV'.

The Fly was, as we know, Bono's first alter ego. It allowed the singer to be someone else, but also, mostly for the press, to be this megalomaniac that they had described so many times in some acerbic articles. The character, taking its first steps in *Achtung Baby* and on 'The Fly' video, reached maturity during the Zoo TV tour. The postmodernist element was balanced by the theatrical aspect of the show, something rarely used in rock. However, that was nothing new for U2 as they had already used theatre to a certain extent alongside the Virgin Prunes. Music for the Prunes was an accessory for their shows. The Boy, the Fool and later the Fly were accessories for U2's music. However, the link between U2, the Virgin Prunes, Dada and the Cabaret Voltaire was not fortuitous. Where the Prunes became a cult band, U2 turned to the mainstream, and had only brushed against Dada. The Dada principle of destruction followed by rebirth is a principle though that U2 have applied liberally throughout their career.

In December 1989, changes are on the way and the deconstruction of the myth is on the cards. The reasons are obvious when one assesses the burden their image must have been for U2. Bono said they had 'to go away and dream it all up again'. To dream up the new U2 for Bono and his friends meant to use imagination to find something new not only musically but visually. It was the end of an era, the end of the U2 myth as it was in the 1980s. Accepting the image, being a star, searching for a lighter aspect to U2, being influenced by new music, are all aspects of this conscious deconstruction of the myth. The myth had been built along with the media and the fans. The same thing happened during its deconstruction. The media played an essential role. They followed the band in the labyrinth of their new approach, helped them. And U2 played the media game as well.

Bono explained why he had decided to follow the media, and why he had turned into someone else: 'I didn't recognise myself in the person I was supposed to be, as far as you could see in the media. There's a kind of rape that happens when you're in the spotlight and you accept it.'[28]

From the Fly to the Mirrorball Man to MacPhisto, the distance was just a hop. Within the concept of Zoo TV, Bono had to become a character, not entirely someone else, yet still Bono. Zoo TV was theatrical in a lot of ways, but it was mainly a rock concert. U2 are a rock band first and foremost and could only inte-grate theatrical aspects without losing sight of their main mission, which was to play songs and interact with the audience. Of course, the stage was the perfect place for Bono's alter egos to come to life.

What did this all mean? Did U2 feel removed from the world of rock despite being part of it and playing that part? The 1991 reinvention did not seem to go against the rock trend of the time, but embraced it. However, it is the subversive and ironic side which went against 1990s rock, which was supposed to be much warmer than in the cool 1980s. Rock had lost its rallying power. This mixture of theatre and rock was not often used and that is where humour and parody could be found, through stage props and characters.

What is also interesting is Zoo TV's postmodern side. Apart from the fact that the concept was inspired by science-fiction author William Gibson's cyber-world, television was a symbolic accessory of postmodernism. According to Bono, it was 'hyperactive' TV (TV which was restless, which played constantly without a break).[29] During the Zooropa leg (part of the Zoo TV tour taking place in Europe and dubbed 'Zooropa'), the big screens were filled with images of a boy playing a drum (it was an extract from a nazi propaganda film by Leni Riefenstahl for the 1936 Berlin Olympic Games), slogans ('what do you want?,' *warum, que veux-tu?,*' 'It's very simple'), images from sports personalities, dicta-tors (Nicolae Ceausescu), famous weddings (Prince Charles and Diana Spencer), a nun, a fœtus. On the left, on another screen, the twelve stars which symbol-ised the European Union in 1993 were falling off one after the other. Suddenly, Bono's silhouette appeared, superimposed on the screen, one of his arms making the Nazi salute while the other was pulling it down. All the symbols of a dicta-torial past or present (Nazism, communism, religion) crystallised the end-of-cen-tury general confusion that people experienced at times and the first song, 'Zoo Station', was a good choice, illustrated by words and slogans such as 'war, nigger, Japan, boom, baby, fish, psycho, paranoia, bomb, racist, job'; 'It's your world, you can change it, it's your world, you can charge it; all that is not forbidden is com-pulsory; celebrity is a job, contradiction is balance; watch more TV; believe in everything; cry more often; remember what you dream; call your mother; future is fantasy; enjoy the surface; death is a career move; watch more TV.' Remote control in hand, Bono would hop relentlessly from channel to channel and would stop for a while on a particular programme. The link between television channels, remote control, slogans, songs, attitudes and appearance was blurred. Anyone, anywhere could watch the same thing provided they owned a TV and a satellite dish. This was postmodernism – a philosophical and intellectual movement which goes against the certainties of modernism, against rational thought and tries to create instead a world where boundaries between cultures are erased, and where everything gets confused – at its best, or at its worst.

Later during the show, and in a public display of deconstruction, Bono called out to his old self during 'Where the Streets Have No Name', saying 'Hey, you', while a film of U2 in the American desert in 1987 was being shown in the background. It could be interpreted as comical, even ironic. But it was more than that. It symbolised the fact that the old U2 was dead and buried and that the new U2 was on stage in Sydney. The burial of the myth was a public occurrence, as if the band wanted to prove that they had done what was expected of them, that they had finally entered the world of cool and humour. The Zoo TV tour was also a place where strange events happened like Bono trying to phone George Bush in the White House, or ordering 10,000 pizzas, or phoning home (during one of the Dublin concerts in 1993), getting the answering machine and hearing his young daughter Jordan ordering him to take his horns off before he got back home.

During the break in the tour, U2 recorded *Zooropa*, which belongs to the same musical and visual phase. The sleeve looks like a child's drawing, a circle with two big dots for eyes, one for the nose and a line for the mouth. The same circle is surrounded by another divided in two parts on the upper and on the lower parts, with two antennae at the two extremes of the division, at the top. Twelve yellow stars surround the drawing. The purple background gives the impression of a torn veil. Behind that veil are photographs which become clearer when you turn the CD. Amongst the photographs, we see part of a woman's face, a woman's mouth, a photograph of Lenin, a blurred photograph of Mussolini and one of the Romanian dictator, Nicolae Ceausescu. None of those photographs are clear. But they are all symbolic of the European leg of the Zoo TV tour because the politicians on the sleeve are all part of Europe's history and are very much present through the use of nazi footage for instance. Nicolae Ceausescu symbolised the recent European past, with the fall of the Berlin wall in 1989 and the subsequent disintegration of the USSR. In fact, one could say it was U2's most political and intellectual tour, despite the fact that they wanted people to forget that aspect. Mr MacPhisto was created during the Zooropa leg. Bono's three alter egos were actually the same. MacPhisto was the Fly some years down the road. They shared similar features: for instance, the mirror. The Fly watched himself on television, the Mirrorball man watched himself in a mirror and MacPhisto watched himself in a mirror and in the audience. The postmodern model of a mirror in a mirror in a mirror and so on is 'an interplay between multiple looking glasses which reflect each other interminably'[30]; what you see is not the reality since it is deformed so many times through the use of mirrors. It is a labyrinth of mirrors where, as Richard Kearney said: 'the image of the self (as a presence to itself) dissolves into self-parody.'[31] The MacPhisto character and the others can be seen as parody, a parody of the devil, a parody of the decadent rock star, a parody of the rock world and of the importance of appearance. The Fly's discourse is ironic, he is self-confident, loves his image and pretends to have knowledge. MacPhisto is the fallen rock star in the skin of the Fallen Angel. However, far from the MacPhisto character stagnating, he is evolving and his evolution also tells a story, maybe the story of rock 'n' roll, the story of the first rock star, Elvis Presley, from his humble beginnings, to his apotheosis, to his downfall. From here, we can hypothesise and say that the U2 started reinventing themselves without the myth around the time of the Zoo TV tour, but succeeded to completely dismantle it with the following album, Pop. How did U2 do it? They had to trample underfoot the myth and its representation by parodying U2. But the paradox is that they are also fascinated by Elvis Presley and by the singer's fall from grace, which in fact did not change anything to Elvis' myth. One cannot help wondering if U2 did not destroy their own myth because they also feared a fall from grace. But they were clever and decided to use irony against themselves. Irony, parody, the image and its power over others, television, Dada, the Cabaret Voltaire are confusing. The first four elements are today seen as postmodern and are in contrast with the last two, which are anchored in modernism, although already on the postmodern trail. Despite Dada and the Cabaret Voltaire, the story told takes place at the end of the twentieth century and is therefore postmodern. But it was also a performance. Bono said to Michka Assayas:

> Never trust a performer, performers are the best liars. They lie for a living. You're an actor in a certain sense. But a writer is not a liar. (…) I am able to write, always, because as a writer, I am always unable not to be true. As a performer, it's not always so. You know the thing that keeps me honest as a performer? The fucking high notes I have to sing. Because unless I am totally in that character, I actually can't sing – it's out of my range. That's what keeps me honest on a stage.[32]

During Zoo TV, Bono was in character and the performance was brilliantly staged. The truth was in the songs.

The last concert of the Zoo TV tour took place on 10 December 1993 in Japan. But the Zoo TV concept was not quite over yet. In 1995, U2 wrote the theme song for the film *Batman Forever* called 'Hold Me Thrill Me Kiss Me Kill Me'. The clip shows images of the movie, but also snippets from the Zoo TV tour and images of the band, as characters in a cartoon. As such, they are shown as superheroes. The story goes that the members of U2 did not have time to shoot a video and this was a way of getting around the problem. In a way, the video crystallises and concludes the Zoo TV period and the changes that occurred. It contains some essential elements of the band's career: the U2 singer of the 1980s seen by the press as a megalomaniac, journalists chasing him, Bono's transformation into the Fly and then MacPhisto, the band fighting against Batman, wanting to break the image of them as the good samaritan. Bono is both characters and no one knows who is whom. Batman could indeed have been another of Bono's alter egos. But Batman is a comic strip hero and plays the good guy, whereas MacPhisto can be good at times but can also be bad. In pages of a comic strip, it reads: 'This man is a so-called rock star! So righteous! So honest! So what?' It is underneath a drawing of Bono holding a halo over his head. He then brings the halo down and it turns into the fly shades. He is reading the Gotham newspaper and three words are in the headlines: 'Bono, Bono, Bono.' The band and Bono are here laughing at themselves and at the singer. At the end of the video, Bono no longer knows who he is. The band are walking in the street and Bono is reading *The Screwtape Letters*, by C. S. Lewis, letters from a trainee demon to his uncle. He does not see the car coming towards him and while the others move away, Bono is knocked down by none other than Elvis Presley! He is taken to the hospital, wakes up in restraints and, because of a short circuit, is electrocuted and becomes (again) MacPhisto. This video is the height of irony but is also the end of an era.

The reason Bono felt the transformation was necessary was because the press had previously been referring to him as a saint. Bono wanted to reverse the trend by becoming, at least symbolically and in costume, a little demon. It was probably to demonstrate that each of us has two sides and we cannot be totally good or evil.

Although 'Hold Me Thrill Me Kiss Me Kill Me' marked the end of the Zoo TV concept, technology and colour were not left behind and continued to inspire U2 with the album *Pop*.

What is striking about that album at first is the sleeve. It is very interesting, colourful, psychedelic, just like the songs in the album. The video for the single 'Discothèque' shows the image the band wanted to promote, as well as the dance music they were influenced by: the disco surroundings, the band members being themselves and playing other characters, dancing, posing, adjusting their clothes and their hair. Finally, U2 turn into the 1970s band, the Village People. Bono plays the policeman, Larry is the cow-boy, Adam Clayton is the sailor, and The Edge is the biker. The clip is representative of the feeling of the album, its sounds and ideas. But not all the songs are as light as 'Discothèque.' If *Pop* sounds like a fun 'pop' album, U2's social consciousness is never far away as a song like 'Please' illustrates. Although the lyrics may be confusing and are more subtle than 'Sunday Bloody Sunday', the video is very explicit, using images of the conflict in Northern Ireland: religion (the nuns and the bishop), violence (the young man throwing a stone through a window). It also uses images of hope, with the little girl in white and the doves. The clip is symbolic of the sectarian divide.

U2 wanted the PopMart tour to be even bigger than the Zoo TV tour. It was first announced in the United States in a supermarket in February 1997. It was undoubtedly the most innovative. Many people will have heard about or even seen the giant lemon and the toothpick with the olive on top which U2 used during the tour. At one stage during the show, they emerged from the lemon. The arch towering over the lemon was 30 metres high, as well as the toothpick. The lemon was only 12 metres high! The band were dressed as different characters, but still themselves. Bono was a boxer, Adam was a factory worker, The Edge was a cowboy and Larry was a soldier. It seemed the members of U2 were not ready to slip back into their own skin yet. Pop was in everything, including the opening song that played when U2 came on stage; 'Pop Muzik' by M, a 1979 hit, remixed for the tour. All this was done to try and outdo the Zoo TV tour, with not as much success. Some shows were not sold out, which may have been a sign that U2 fans were getting tired of the band's massive shows. A downsizing was necessary.

U2 in the 2000s

Pop is really the end of what I would call U2's 'technological trilogy'. Bono called Zoo TV 'a strategy'. He said: 'The strategy was judo: to use the force of the attacker to defend yourself. And we were being attacked from all corners, because we were open [...]. We could feel the media about to close in on us.'[33] That was after the *Rattle and Hum* 'debacle'. *Zooropa* and *Pop* were the logical steps during or after Zoo TV. A new decade and a new century dawned and a new U2 was born (again). Irony was left behind, masks were again taken off, the music recovered some of its straightforwardness, the image was purified and returned to what the members of U2 really are: four friends making music that touches millions.

All That You Can't Leave Behind was as much a rebirth as *Achtung Baby*. It was back to basics, back to the spirit of rock 'n' roll. It was a return to black and white photography for the record sleeve. The members of U2 were now, on average, 40 years old and knew that it was time to change again. The sleeve picture was taken in an airport (Roissy-Charles-de-Gaulle, a few kilometres outside Paris). It gives the impression of a new start, a reconstructed image. There are pieces of luggage and people surrounding U2. But the most interesting aspect is the message seen on the left-hand side of the picture and which is normally a sign showing the gates to the departure lounges. 'J 33-3' may be a spiritual message, referring to the Bible's Old Testament and the Book of Jeremiah, which says: 'Call unto me, and I will answer thee, and shew thee great and mighty things, which thou knowest not.' This may be an allusion to the beginnings of U2, to their faith in the band, and their belief at the time in their future success. But what is clear is that spirituality has never left the band. What was the real reason for this message? Was it a way of showing that the members of U2 have always trusted God and had faith that they would succeed in their chosen career, and that their constant reinvention was just a part of what they are? Bono singing 'Hallelujah' at the end of the song 'Walk On', to close the concerts of the Elevation tour was a way of giving thanks to God and to the crowd and of expressing the band's faith in themselves and in God.

The video for 'Beautiful Day' takes the sleeve's iconography and brings it further. It was filmed in Terminal 2 of Charles-de-Gaulle airport and it is again a performance video. The song is uplifting and is a return to an image closer to U2's origins. However, despite entering their forties, U2 were still as enthusiastic about their music as before and that is important. They were confident and if they didn't have anything to prove any more, they still wanted to be relevant to a new generation.

That impression became even more clear during the Elevation concerts. The show was simple and unsophisticated. It was a 'back to basics' concept and the only element that was striking was the heart-shaped area at the front of the stage into which about 300 people could be admitted. During the Elevation tour concert in Boston, Bono talked about U2 as being a family business, where everyone has their place and takes part in it to make it successful.

The Importance of Image and U2's Identity

What can we now conclude about U2's image? It has evolved positively, albeit in an oblique manner. And it seems to have come full circle. The latest release, *How to Dismantle an Atomic Bomb*, is more proof that U2 have returned to basics, to big tunes, and to black and white. The latest videos ('Vertigo', 'Sometimes

You Can't Make It On Your Own', 'City of Blinding Lights', 'All Because of You') and the Vertigo tour are all positive signs of U2's will to show the band's intrinsic character, in other words what they are deep down.

The only drawback are the videos, which are not as interesting as the music. Even at the height of the Zoo TV period, the videos were not very imaginative and showed the band in performance, with the community as its focal point. That approach has its merits but maybe some of the songs deserved different treatment visually. However, the videos are in line with the image of the band, as a live act and most were constructed bearing that in mind.

There are three phases in U2's career, each belonging to a decade, the third having started in 2000 and the release of *All That You Can't Leave Behind*. This could be a coincidence. But having started in 1980 and by the end of the decade, being called the band of the eighties, it seemed logical that a new decade would bring new challenges and changes.

Their star identity (or star-text, as Andrew Goodwin calls it) is built upon their reputation as the best live act in the world. The star-text identifies the representation and identity of a star. The persona of the star is built upon interviews to the media, image (video-clips, the live aspect, direct contact with the fans) and critical commentary. This concept gives us access to U2's image but also helps us explain the myth. It is evidence of an authenticity that is rarely felt to such an extent by fans and other people. U2 were and are still seen as a true rock act, in the romantic sense of the word. They represent the rock aesthetic, coupled with high standards of ethical authenticity. The U2 community, U2's social consciousness, their spirituality, their refusal of an image are all part of their star identity. And U2 were not liked by some because of that. Paradoxically, and as we have seen, they were not accepted in the world of rock because they were not cool. Bono says that they wanted to be hot, in other words, they wanted to be like no one else in the music business at the time.[34]

The bands that developed alongside U2 had little in common with them with many using synthesisers, and not touring, therefore lacking that vital communication with their audience.

The release of *The Unforgettable Fire* triggered the myth which had been latent since *War* and which would emerge during Live Aid. One more element which makes up U2's star identity is their fascination with America. The album *The Joshua Tree* made them into superstars. As we have seen, they changed their image to fit the American myth (a certain idea of America, as a country capable of allowing people to make their dreams come true) that they were so fascinated with. They then discovered their ignorance of real rock conventions. They had to collaborate with classical rock musicians as well as black musicians in order to understand rock conventions, something which gave them a new level of authenticity. These encounters rooted their authenticity in a very classical model, as seen in chapter 3. But U2 wanted for a while to root their music in America, the cradle of rock 'n' roll. However, U2's star identity was put off balance when people did not understand what the band were trying to do. Bono remembers:

> We had a big record [The *Joshua Tree*], and the natural thing to do would be to just make a live album at that point of the tour, cash in and go on holidays. But we decided: 'Oh no, we can't do that.' So we wrote songs to put on this. We'd have new songs. We'd make a film about our journey through America. (...) We'd make a double album (...), and rather than being a band who thought they were the centre of the world, we would put these musicians that we were fans of at the centre of our world, and in the artwork, with pictures of Johnny Cash. We wrote songs – not all great songs – but we would sort of declare ourselves as the fans that we are. And this *Rattle and Hum* thing came out. But the opposite came back at us. It was like, 'Oh, this is egomania, they think they are now one of the pantheon of these great artists, and they feel they can quote our music.' I remember thinking, 'This is exactly exactly the opposite of what we are trying to do.' But we actually couldn't undo that. It was just a given that these so-called fans had now lost the run of themselves.[35]

I have always loved that album and film. It is always a pleasure to watch it because it captures that particular moment when U2 had become huge but still retained their identity. The band is the antithesis of 1980s rock, yet achieved superstardom in that very decade. And U2 were the voice of a generation. It did not fit in a certain image of rock, which says that a band must first imitate their idols and then find an identity for themselves and not the other way around, something which U2 didn't do, but which also says that a rock band must be cool, something U2 weren't in those days. It was therefore if not acceptable, then at least understandable that Rattle and Hum should have been decried. U2's identity was reinvented (just like everything else) in the 1990s. Authenticity became irony, seriousness became humour, uncool became cool. The media were seduced (and tricked!). They accepted U2 and their new identity as it finally fitted in with what was expected of them. However, the band's live performance remained intact. U2 put on two of the biggest rock shows ever, in seven years. Bono, Larry, The Edge and Adam behaved like rock stars.

Whereas singers like Madonna wanted to be recognised as true artists, U2 had been there and had done that and were now doing the reverse. They were putting forward the superficial. They attracted crowds, gained new fans, proved they could do even more than the media thought. The strategy was a runaway success and U2 were again the best and the biggest.

But the question is where did the real band fit in. For some, they had denied their heritage, their true identity. In other words, they had sold out. Despite the fact that some people believe that U2 have gone more commercial than ever (endorsing the i-Pod could indeed have been construed as a commercial move – but it was more than that; it was a statement that said that music hardware had evolved and songs could now be downloaded legally from the Internet, so it was better to buy them for a small price than listening to them illegally), many more are still enthralled about U2's ability to create free music.

Another point I want to talk about is the narrative in U2 videos, in other words, the process of telling a story and the sequence of events in which the story happens. I want to link it to U2's star identity and see to what extent the latter dominated the narrative, in other words what is more important in U2's videos: the narrative or the star identity. The images shown in the clips have helped construct the band's identity. The videos most often show the band in performance, and leave the story of the song in the background. I suggest therefore that U2's star identity dominates the narrative in the videos.

There are two distinct streams in time: that of the 1980s and that of the 1990s. In the first stream, almost all clips are performance clips, with or without an audience. They are very homogeneous. In the second stream, it is very much the same, but the clips are more sophisticated and more heterogeneous. The attention is drawn to the band and the music each time, and not to the clip as visual entertainment. It is quite clear in videos such as 'Pride (In the Name of Love)', which could have shown pictures of Martin Luther King for instance.

The Star Identity and the Myth
Constructing an identity for rock musicians is an essential step to success. And the myth can only emerge from that identity and its representation, both of which constitute identification and anchorage points for the audience, which means that the U2 audience will identify with what U2 are and do and will see U2's identity as a stable point in which to root part of their own identity. In other words, the elements that make up the myth come from that star identity. In U2's case, their roots can be found in the early 1980s. The myth was firstly created by the band themselves, whether intentionally or not. They are part of its creation

because the musical values carried by the band are classically anchored in 1960s rock an era when rock gave birth to most of its mythical heroes such as the Beatles, the Stones, Jimi Hendrix or Jim Morrison. From that point of view, U2 are closer to the 1960s than they might themselves realise. Secondly, the myth was created by the media which praised the band, promoting their sense of respect, their integrity, even their spirituality, which is something odd since, spirituality is generally frowned upon by the music media. And thirdly, the myth was created by the audience, who wanted to believe in it. The U2 audience was going to a sacred celebration when going to a concert. An audience needs heroes and U2 fans definitely crystallised that aspect in their favourite band. U2 fans saw the band as their heroes. They still do.

Conclusion

From authentic authenticity to authentic inauthenticity, U2's image changed drastically over the years. But the colourful phase was fabricated whereas the earlier phase also may have been fabricated but not acknowledged as such.

U2's survival could only happen with reinvention, with listening to the present, with being relevant. And it could only happen with the seduction of the audience. That was most apparent in the 1990s. Suddenly U2 were seen as sexual beings. In the 1980s, they were almost asexual, ascetic, trying to hide behind their music. They tried to keep their sexuality in the background. Historically, sexuality is an important aspect of rock 'n' roll. Elvis Presley, Jim Morrison, Jimi Hendrix were all sexy and played with that aspect of their personas. It is therefore peculiar that U2's myth was not founded on the sexual aspect, on the sexiness of the band. The myth developed from U2's social consciousness. U2 took on almost every social cause going in the 1980s, starting from Live Aid and before. However, Live Aid anchored the myth and gave it power. Despite its humanitarian character, Live Aid was for U2 a springboard from arena to stadium band. And with it was born a huge phenomenon. When Bono climbed down from the stage, and hugged those girls, it was communication with the audience at its smallest and at its biggest. Music transcended the band and the fans put them on a pedestal. U2's actions are to be emulated and the fans can start telling the band's story intertwined with their own.

The story is also told by the media and the biographies though. The first official biography, *The Unforgettable Fire*, by Irish sports journalist Eamon Dunphy, was published in 1987. Choosing a sports journalist with no connection to music was a surprising choice and, the band distanced themselves from the book. It was indeed full of inaccuracies but was very complimentary of the band. It helped the myth develop, particularly regarding U2's musical roots, which Dunphy said are almost non-existent. In fact, what the book says about that is very close to what the band say. The sociologist Barbara Bradby says of the choice of Dunphy as the writer of the biography: 'Dunphy's ignorance of rock music, as well as his particular viewpoint on sport in Ireland make him well suited for this contribution to U2 mythology.'[36] Dunphy's ignorance of music may have indeed contributed to give the myth a lot more substance. His ignorance allowed U2 to gain for a while a position as a group without an origin, an ex-nihilo creation. In other words, U2 would have been the creators of Irish rock, would have been the first band to appear on the Irish rock scene. Since this is completely untrue, the myth became ambiguous, stuck between its classical definition as an invented story and that of the myth as a true and exemplary story. However, there were other bands in Ireland before U2. But U2 are definitely partly responsible for the opening of Ireland to the international music industry and acted as a catalyst for the local industry to flourish. U2 were also an example for other bands. The Irish four-some carry in themselves an ideal when it comes to success, an ideal which is healthy and straightforward.

The members of U2 have offered their audience an ideal image. The positive aspects are brought forward while the problems are dealt behind closed doors. Although Bono, The Edge, Adam Clayton and Larry Mullen have often denied some of the accepted characteristics of U2(seriousness, lack of humour, righteousness), they have used those moral aspects that were their trademark in the 1980s to their advantage. Their integrity, their sincerity, their authenticity are all characteristics which contributed to the myth and have brought the band to the height of fame. People like to have heroes and U2 fulfil that role well for their fans.

There are, of course, other Irish rock bands that have become successful since the 1990s. It is difficult to compare them to U2 though, especially in terms of success. The everlasting question torturing the Irish press is: who will be the next U2? The answer to that question lies in the elements that constitute the U2 myth but also in other factors. No Irish (or other) band has reached U2's level of success and it seems difficult to follow in their footsteps. Their success is indeed a combination of factors, some tangible and others that are caused by luck. I doubt that this combination of factors can occur often. It may well be that U2 are too big for a country like Ireland, in that the phenomenon has been integrated within Ireland with some difficulty, and that another such phenomenon may only occur after their demise.

But U2's Irish audience is also responsible to a certain extent for this unique phenomenon which is U2, for what John Waters suggested might even be an aberration in people's minds, in other words, something that could have occurred in Ireland only by chance and that was really a 'freak', that didn't fit in with Ireland. He suggests that the Irish lack self-confidence, therefore Ireland could not be responsible for the phenomenon of U2: 'It is part of our national inferiority complex to believe that we can only be invaded, we cannot invade. Therefore, a band as popular, creative and successful as U2 could only have originated here by accident.'[37] Other Irish bands have conquered the world. But their success and impact remain small compared to that of U2.

For the myth to take complete shape in all of its complexity, the band must reach immortality, something that can only happen after the demise of U2.

For that reason, U2 may have been able to dismantle their myth in the 1990s. Roland Barthes said that 'if we penetrate the myth, we free it, but we destroy it. If we leave it as it is, we respect it, but we still give it back as it is'.[38] U2 penetrated their myth. They trampled it underfoot, hiding behind technology, and playing roles. They were then able to discard their myth, as well as the place where it was held, a world that many fans liked but that prevented U2 from finding another way to create. By doing so, U2 could enter a new phase in their career, by rejecting that baggage. They didn't want to be burned at the stake of their own myth by their fans or the media. They refused to still be thought of as righteous, humourless. They had to trick the media (by becoming what the media wanted them to be) and to surprise the fans, in a bid to transcend the myth.

But U2 were also able to deconstruct their myth because they were partly responsible for it. They were responsible for their image (or non-image), for their actions and for the fact that they promoted their Irish origins as an essential factor. I am not saying here that they were wrong. On the contrary, being proud of one's origins and integrating those origins is essential to one's identity. But the fact that they came from Ireland made the myth even more powerful because of a collective unconscious abroad perceiving Ireland as being a country full of ghosts and mysterious stories. They are Irish and want the world to know about it. They turned that aspect of their identity into one of the prime characteristics of the band. They write rock songs but they write them in Ireland. And the motherland is inspirational. It has its own myths and legends. They then export those songs. And the reaction abroad is in accordance with what is expected. In America, they are a symbol of success in Ireland. They never had to emigrate to succeed in their career.

The deconstruction of the myth did not go without its difficulties. Fans who weren't happy with the deconstruction of the myth and the U2 of the early

1990s wanted to keep that image of U2 as described above. They wanted U2 to continue their self-sacrifice and turned their backs on them when they didn't. Bono put it wryly in an article he wrote about Elvis Presley: 'Why is it that we want our idols to die on a cross of their own making, and if they don't, we want our money back?'[39] Therefore, the mythical image is replaced with the image without myth, or at least an image with a shrunken myth.

So, is the emergence of another U2 a possibility? Probably not. A set of circumstances made the band come to life. Another set of circumstances might yield a different result. There was only one band called the Beatles and there is only one band called the Rolling Stones. There can only be one band called U2. But there may some day in Ireland be one band that will transcend what U2 have done, in a different way, and that will be unique in its own right. Only time will tell.

Conclusion

GENERATIONS

To conclude this book, I want to look at the different generations who have been touched by U2's music. I have discovered throughout my research and throughout the years of being a U2 fan that we share many of the same thoughts and ideas when it comes to what U2 mean to us.

I have asked myself what U2 represent for my generation, but also for younger ones. It is essential to examine that representation to understand what U2 stand for and to understand why they have stayed on top for so long.

The roots of the U2 phenomenon, an occurrence which is striking and exceptional because of its qualities and which we can also observe as it is growing and evolving – where the band are now, through the labyrinth of time and place, of chance encounters or fateful encounters, of luck versus faith as Bono would put it, of modernism versus postmodernism – are all ways of finding out why U2 were seen in many ways as the voice of a generation, and how the band have continued supporting other generations, and how they has shaped people's identities, as well as giving rock a new lease of life.

Time and Place

U2 were born in Ireland. That they are Irish is an accident of birth or a parental choice. That they met in Mount Temple school was a complete accident. Or maybe some would contradict me and say that it was fate. Possibly. However, that Larry, Bono, Edge and Adam were a product of their environment is completely true. They were in search of meaning, like all their generation. They were looking for something that couldn't be found in a school book or in parental advice; and ended up playing music together. They grew up together and when their first album, *Boy*, was released, Adam Clayton remembers:

> We were tremendously green, but mixed with a kind of self-assuredness. I remember feeling what we were doing wasn't in isolation. It was part of what Echo and The Bunnymen were doing, what The Teardrop Explodes were doing, The Comsat Angels, Associates, The Sound. It was about a generation getting a voice.[1]

U2 were definitely part of that generation. But they were also part of a music generation that wanted something different. From the punk music that inspired them, they took the best:

> The ephemeral side of punk laid waste to dozens and dozens of smash-and-grab groups who, after packing everything into a few short years, just disappeared (…) U2 were different because from the outset they didn't just take the superficial safety-pins of punk style dress, dress them up into the uniform of a band and push it down people's throats, but like English contemporaries Wire, Joy Division and The Durutti Column used the space afforded by punk to forge a new identity for rock.[2]

Their songs already had melodic qualities and the band tried to play music that would make the listener listen. They played according to Mark Prendergast, an 'emotionally connecting music'.[3] U2 were looking for a new identity for rock but also an identity for themselves and, by extension, for their fans.

What has always made U2 songs great are the tunes coupled with clever, poetic lyrics. U2 are able to produce great songs because of that combination. Those songs make sense musically and lyrically, and the use of the latest technology is most of the time in the background, considering that on stage, U2 are still four guys playing a gig. They are still a punk rock band producing raw music, yet they were like a progressive rock band during the Zoo TV tour, or even for some, an alternative band. They are everything at the same time and they are always relevant to the present.

But they also found a new identity for (Irish) rock. Indeed, in the past (and in the present in many ways), rock musicians had to deviate from conventional behaviour to become part of that world. They couldn't be ordinary, like everyone else. But they could come from a place where things were ordinary. People are not necessarily aware of this and who could blame them, as many famous rock musicians have kept alive the myth that they came from ordinary working-class backgrounds. In fact, the contrary would be true. Some came from well-to-do families and attended or even came across each other at British art schools in the 1950s and 1960s. For instance, Ron Wood, Pete Townsend and Freddy Mercury went to Ealing, while Brian Eno went to Ipswich/Winchester. Musicians and bands could rehearse in colleges and play in front of their first audiences (the other students) there. Sociologists Simon Frith and Howard Horne, in their study of art schools and their relation to pop, identified three main waves of musicians: the rock bohemians, whose progressive rock was tinted with their bohemian attitude; the pop art bands 'who applied art theories to pop music making';[4] and the pop situationists whose involvement in the creation and development of punk rock in the late 1970s is central. Brian Longhurst says about the rock bohemians: 'it was possible at this moment to sell lots of records (as albums) and still not be seen to be "selling out" to the marketplace', while

> the later situationists were more aware of the intertwining of pop, commerce and art. They were not so concerned to remain authentic artists, and there-fore to be above commerce, as to subvert both terms, suggesting that art and commerce were inextricably linked and that art could not be defined outside of commercial relationships, which were not necessarily criticised. The art industry could be exploited from within, there was no need to attempt to create a "pure" space outside of it.[5]

U2 rejected the idea that a rock band must be deviant in more than one way. They were polite, well-behaved Christians in stable relationships, and all of this was common knowledge. They became commercially successful while making original music, following the situationists' philosophy of mixing art and com-merce. But contrary to them, U2 have embraced authenticity because for them, it is essential to their art. U2 have also been making music for over 25 years. They broke the longevity record. Even the longest running rock band in the world, the Rolling Stones, have long forgotten their original line-up. U2 are artists and want to be considered as such, yet they have always refused to be part of the independent ghetto and they have always rejected the notion that being commercially successful equals selling out. U2's place in rock is quite unique in that they have been able to integrate art and commerce on a massive scale and continue doing so for years. By doing that, they have been able to touch a large audience, selling millions of records in the process, while still keeping as an objective music as art. But it is more than that. Not only is it music as art, it is rock as mass art, a music capable of touching many people, most of those young and, nowadays, less young. U2's music was able to touch different generations over the years but at first, it touched my generation, the one that was twenty in the mid-1980s. That U2 left a deep mark is undoubtedly true.

My Generation

Who are the people of my generation? What was it like being a teenager or young adult in the 1980s? What did U2 do for us? Why are they still important to some people of my age?

Quite a lot of U2 fans are over 35. They still love U2 and still believe that that particular encounter changed their lives.

Were we a generation in search of meaning? Undoubtedly. We were born in the 1960s, raised in different corners of the earth, we didn't know each other, yet one thing, amongst others, bound us together: U2.

I am only able to talk about my own experience in France. But we were witness to a phenomenon, which I consequently discovered, was given the name of postmodernism by French philosophers in the 1960s. We weren't really aware of it but knew something was going on, a loss of belief in values that people didn't share any more. U2 gave us back that sense of values, that everything matters, that cynicism is not a trait that is to be valued; that you can dream while being realistic; that you can rage against the world because it's not what you would like it to be. 'I am not in any way at peace. I still think that the world is a really unfair and often wicked place and beauty is a consolation prize. And it's not enough for me. It just isn't. There's always been a kind of rage in me and it does still bubble up,' Bono says. You could see that even on television, in U2's videos. As I explained before, the band was promoted as having something to say.

Television is supposed to represent postmodernism, to be its most potent symbol and so MTV must have been crowned king of postmodernism. Other programmes on French TV were probably better than MTV. Les Enfants du Rock was a brilliant attempt at bringing mostly English-speaking rock to a wider audience. The programme would have been as important as The Old Grey Whistle Test or Top of the Pops in Britain. It showed videos. In that regard it was closer to MTV. We would see clips of Dire Straits or Simple Minds or The Cure or indeed U2. A lot of us knew in an instinctive way that U2 were head and shoulders above everyone else because they played raw music, they spilled their guts, they weren't pretending to be something they weren't. We liked their naivity, their spontaneity, their way of touching people. They made us feel alive and part of something special. Journalist Sean O'Hagan said in 1987: 'U2 are a group very much aware of their place in the scheme of things, in the rock 'n' roll tradition. It's an old-fashioned viewpoint while all around them music scatters into fragments and disparate reflections of a truly atrophied post-modern culture.'[6]

What I only realised recently, is that U2 is the soundtrack of our lives, yet carries a heavier meaning than just that. We remember growing up with U2, falling in love with U2 in the background, getting a job, getting married, having children. But we also remember the importance of the songs, what we thought they said or meant (rightly or wrongly), the underlying message, the courage that they gave us, the hope that this world could really be a better place.

We had missed out on the sixties, being but babies. U2 brought us that energy, that power, from another time. They were our Beatles. It was the four Beatles who made that music. U2 have that. They have that chemistry. But they have something more. They have lasted. Circumstances were different for The Beatles. They were pioneers. The rock music industry was rather new as well. All this made The Beatles and The Rolling Stones make mistakes, not least of the business kind. The Beatles were symbols of freedom, music and fun. They meant emancipation from everything that could make a young person feel trapped or inadequate. They helped a generation find a place of its own. Rock had the power of creating the possibility of an ideal world. And it helped in the struggle towards that ideal world.

My generation, however, had not had a sexual or social revolution. Aids was hardly looming on the horizon. We were already free. Others had fought for us. Our world, of course, was not without its problems; some struggles still needed to be fought, but we took for granted what our elders had gained: human rights in the western world, social rights, women's rights, the legacy of the French May 1968 movement. That was before Band Aid and Live Aid. That the band should have a strong interest in these causes made me even more interested. I wasn't the only one to react in that way. Many U2 fans over the years got interested in various organisations like Amnesty and Greenpeace. That U2 played a part in that interest is doubtless.[7] Their influence was and is strong, and the ideas they defend and promote are part of what the band are in essence. A band concerned with the world around them and conscious that they may be able to play a more important role in society than just play music.

Generations in Search of Meaning and Identity
U2 embracing humanitarian causes was also a way of forging an identity and

finding meaning in the 1980s and added to their impact on the musical level. U2 gave their generation music that not only rocked their world but that also created a framework for raising people's consciousness when it came to society.

Through the band's music, U2 fans have found an identity that differentiates them from other types of fans. One could, of course, argue that all rock fans feel the same, or different, that they feel a particular identity when it comes to their band. In that case, how are U2 fans different? The fans have an emotional relationship with the band but they also have an intellectual relationship. They are not blind and not ready to play sycophants to the members of U2. They are, 'serious' fans, serious about U2's music, which is something they hold dear, which is part of them and of a youth identity that many have kept, despite now being U2's age.

The creation of a U2 identity is linked to the branding of the band. Branding is 'the unique quality of an act [which] would become instantly recognisable and condensed into a specific image which could become a trademark.'[8] The branding of U2 is linked to their image but it is also a marketing tool. The senior executive of a record company told sociologist Keith Negus:

> You try and brand the artist, in the way that U2 are branded. The most brilliant corporate branding I have ever seen, without anyone ever thinking that they were being corporately got. Brilliant. You never saw a picture of U2 if it wasn't in front of the joshua tree. Bono was out there [clenching his fist]. He was an OK kind of guy because he was saying the right things. I say this as a huge U2 fan. Brilliant piece of marketing.[9]

U2 may not have wanted to become a trademark, but their image in the 1980s was as much branded as anybody else, whether intentionally or not. Although there have been major changes since then, I believe that that particular image of U2 in the 1980s is forever etched in the fans' collective unconsciousness. U2 are therefore a unique brand, and as such have also shaped the fans' identity. If U2 have been branded as unique, it could be assumed that another band could not be branded in the same way and could not have the same characteristics. Therefore, and by extension, the fans' identity is also unique.

On another level, identity in this case is not connected to nationality. It may be different in Ireland where the fact that U2 are Irish is indeed important and a matter of pride, but it obviously goes beyond that in other countries, and maybe even in Ireland. People who love U2 recognise each other as belonging to the same group despite their different origins and upbringings. When people meet and discover that they have U2 as a common ground, that U2 are their common heritage, they already have something to discuss.

There is also the idea that identity can be seen as ideological, in other words that people of the same group share a set of ideas and beliefs, or are influenced by a set of ideas and beliefs and decide to follow them. The U2 identity can be seen as such because most fans were attracted to the band not only for their music but for what their music and U2 mean. There is a sort of tribal feeling within the U2 community of fans. Bono said of the Irish fans at Slane Castle in 2001 that: 'this is our tribe.' I believe that the tribe is far bigger than just the Irish fans and encompasses every fan from all corners of the earth. What are the common aspects of the 'U2 tribe'? Common love of the 'leadership' (U2), common political and social beliefs, common musical ancestry (one discovers that many members of the tribe like the same bands outside of U2).

U2 have been the answer to something fans have been looking for: meaning in music, meaning in social construct and development of a social consciousness. U2 are therefore not only musically but also culturally and socially important in the fans' lives. They have a wider meaning than some other bands.

The early fans and the newer fans found the same thing in U2, albeit at different times. 'Alternately stark and spectacular, their music, lyrics and imagery reflect the alienation and striving of a generation', says an Irish journalist.[10] He goes on to say of Irish-Americans: 'For Irish-American kids, still struggling for their place in American society, U2 have been a beacon.'[11] It is well-known of course, that U2 are an example of success in Ireland and in America. Even with the Irish economic boom and success stories in the country itself, U2 are still a successful example to follow because of the length of their career.

On a more concrete level, the appropriation of U2 songs by fans has been a way of shaping the fans' identities. Those songs may have been used in different circumstances, but they have in common the fact that the fans' identities were partly built upon the songs.

Let's take some examples. 'One' must be a favourite U2 song. However, the lyrics are often misunderstood. It's a love song but it's a bitter love song. At the 27 June 2005 concert in Dublin, there was a group of people sitting in front of us and when U2 started playing 'One', one of the people broke down in tears. And I thought, 'that's exactly what that song should elicit, great sadness.' Whatever the reason was for that young man's broken heart, I was finally seeing the real meaning of the song in front of me. But most reactions to that song are positive. The reason is that U2 songs lift people up, even the saddest ones. 'U2 are a celebration to all of us, to the world and especially to Ireland', says one Irish fan, who chose 'A Celebration' as one of his favourite U2 tracks.[12]

Every fan has a story connected to a U2 song, whether it's the birth of a child, the death of a loved one, encountering love, being somewhere special, being sick, being depressed, or simply being happy. People tell of how a U2 song helped them through a tough time. 'Their songs of innocence and of experience seem to have become enmeshed in all of our lives. They've become part of our shared memories of good times and bad. But apart from their global success, U2 have written the soundtrack for generations of Irish people', said Gerry Ryan during the U2 special on Irish television on 25 June 2005. But it is also true that fans from around the world feel connected to U2 in a very special way.

U2's music has always refused to be elitist, letting only the initiated in. It is both complex and simple, yet it can be understood by everybody, despite the fact that it has an intellectual element to it. What makes it universal is that U2 have learned how to craft a song over the years and even their early work had freshness and energy. Therefore, they touch people at a deeper level than many other bands and their rejection of elitism is possibly one of the reasons for the band's refusal of 'indie' culture, a musical culture which by its very rejection of commercial values and focus on authenticity forms an elite group which completely rejects the mainstream, and whose members try to avoid the big record companies, running the risk of not selling many records. The struggles that U2 have been going through for the past 30 years add an element of humanity to the band and their music. That struggle is ongoing and, during the 27 June 2005 concert in Dublin, Bono said: 'We do a job as a band. We don't feel it's done. We have some unfinished business ...'

The identities of U2 and their fans have been largely based on the connection between the two and on the human aspect of the U2 phenomenon. However, things don't always go smoothly. Every time U2 reinvent themselves, a threat from their fans comes from the inside. There is a risk involved in reinvention. The fans can become discontented because they don't like the band's new image or the band's new sound or songs. In this case the identity they built is threatened by that 'new' U2, that new identity that U2 themselves have created and that the fans must integrate. On another level, every time they don't conform to certain standards, the threat comes from the inside and from the outside. For a short while for example, at the end of August 2005, U2.com only allowed paying members of the site to visit the discussion forum, whereas it is normally open to anybody who is registered. That created an angry response from the fans. The official reason was that it was done to prevent troublemakers from using the forum. Subsequently, everything returned to normal and a letter of apology was issued on the forum. The fan identity is not only based on songs but also on the moral standards of the band that they must uphold. It is a difficult position to be in but one that U2 can't really deviate from if they want to keep their fans happy.

Even when U2 changed their image and music drastically in the early 1990s, the band were still showing signs of following the same principles, despite the Fly shades, the cross-dressing and the overtly seductive attitude.

Fighting Postmodernism

U2 have never been postmodern despite the fact that they used some postmodernist ideas in the 1990s. They only played with it and it helped them in the reinvention process so familiar to the band. Postmodernism is an idea, it's a philosophical concept that fights the modern. According to the philosophers who have developed the concept, we live in an era of postmodernism.

Postmodernism is a concept which defies clear definition. Although it is primarily an intellectual movement which originally fought the values of modernism, the certainties of a rational scientific explanation for everything, it is difficult nowadays to say exactly what it is. In postmodernism, boundaries between high culture (the culture of the elite, the classical culture) and low culture (popular culture, mass culture) are blurred. Postmodernism is ambiguous. It denies the idea of origin or end. It blends everything together. Postmodernism celebrates the surface, the superficial and parodies itself. No wonder U2 used it to their advantage during the Zoo TV tour. 'Enjoy the surface' was one of the slogans of the tour.

Postmodernism is best represented by television, as I said before. Video, according to postmodernist theorist E. Ann Kaplan, are the best examples of the era. Videos are evolving rapidly, however, and I don't know to what extent some of Kaplan's points are still relevant today. She talks of MTV as the definitive version of postmodernist music. She takes MTV music as commodified, in other words something which is bought and sold, something which is consumed. The problem lies with interpretation, as postmodernism lends itself to many kinds of different visions. I could interpret a video in one way and someone else in another. We are surrounded by meaningless and endless images, with no narrative or chain of events that would make them comprehensible to the viewer. We are therefore detached from the present or the past, we don't know where it all begins or ends. While we all witness these types of events at one stage or another, I believe that some artists like U2 have fought that trend and have tried to make sense of it all, to retain a sense of history and make language an essential tool in communicating with their audience. Contrary to the postmodern idea of the world being meaningless and of playing with nonsense, even at the height of Zoo TV, U2 wanted to inject meaning to their art. If text has lost its meaning in the world as seen by postmodernists, in U2's world, text still holds a meaning that generations of fans have understood.

In music, modernism was symbolised by bands like The Beatles or The Rolling Stones. Other bands like The Velvet Underground, Negativland, or musicians like Patti Smith or Laurie Anderson are considered by some as part of the postmodernist music trend. They are (were) avant-garde artists, making music, inventing sounds, trying to make people to listen to them. They were the good side of postmodernist music. People like The Velvet Underground were innovators. Their shows were 'a cacophony of avant-garde noise, light, and humans interacting with images and sounds'.[13] They were consciously trying to break down barriers, to abolish the conventions of rock to suit their goal. They were helped in that by Andy Warhol and their performances became multi-media events that 'mixed musical styles and messages in a way ideally suited for expressing the multiple, contradictory textures of postindustrial urban life'. Was it pure coincidence that a re-formed Velvet Underground played support to U2 during the *Zooropa* leg of the Zoo TV tour? By giving this example, I want to show that those of U2's generation and later have always lived in this so-called postmodern society. Postmodern it may be, but some of us didn't quite agree to it and tried to make sense of it all through arts, notably music.

So, in the case of U2, how did they fight this very unsuitable postmodern society?

U2 wanted a voice, they needed to be heard, and they found an audience to listen. We, as fans, needed something to hold on to and it is obvious that nowadays younger generations need that as well. Bands of substance have been back in vogue for a while now, and it is reassuring to see that young people still want to say something through their choice of music. Although it is worrying that programmes like Big Brother should still be watched by so many (the lack of substance here is dismal), there is hope that newer generations are also in search of meaning in a world even more so devoid of the same than it was back in the 1980s. Indeed, the consumerist trend seems to be intensifying, the cinemas are full of films that resemble each other to the point of nausea, and popular music is definitely in need of another U2.

U2 fought postmodernism firstly by working from the outside and, in the process, being swallowed up in their own myth, in other words, their myth became so big that they were unable to control it, and secondly by working on the inside from the early 1990s onwards.

If we take into account the influence that Dadaism had on U2, for instance, at the beginning of their career and then later on, if we examine the influences that bands like the Velvet Underground or musicians like Patti Smith had, if we look at the sound exploration that U2 embarked upon, if we look at the Zoo TV and PopMart tours, we could then say that U2 themselves became a postmodern band in the 1990s on the surface, in that they had for instance themselves crossed the boundary between low and high culture (inviting Salman Rushdie on stage for instance), or used the symbol of postmodernism, the television, in their concerts. Although we know it is not true.

U2 could never be such a band. The music they played and the type of rock 'n' roll they created was influenced by the earliest examples of the genre, as well as by later examples. Their form of rock 'n' roll was classical in spirit, privileging the live aspect. U2 took their primary inspiration from modernist bands and they followed in their footsteps, indirectly borrowing from other later bands.

Only when they reached the 1990s did they allow a postmodern trend to seep through their music and performance. What they didn't do, however, was lose faith, sincerity or integrity. Although their authenticity was ironic, it was a form of authenticity and most fans weren't fooled. But U2 also wanted to shield themselves from the pain that came from exposing too much of themselves. Bono admitted: 'Every decade needs a band that will stand up and reflect the spirit of its time without any shield. U2 did that in the 1980s and they are not going to do it any more, it's too painful.'[14]

That's why U2 could never be postmodern; because there is hope and beauty in their music and they offer an experience that is not devoid of meaning. On the contrary, this experience makes sense to every U2 fan.

U2, therefore, fought postmodernism on its own ground, turning it around in the 1990s to their own advantage, making it into a spectacle of gigantic proportions and denouncing it as empty.

People of different generations who love U2 have refused to surrender to a culture of cynicism. At the end of the 1980s, it was already obvious:

Ten years later, ten years down the road from two tone, the funny haircuts, the miserabilists, the postmodern ironists and the pop schemers, who would have thought that the dreamers would hold the balance? Who would have thought that with thousands moving on a new psychedelic groove thang or finding themselves moving in a new orbit of future funk, that in 1989 the most potent rock 'n' roll show on the planet would be one based on a rigorous assertion of those old unfashionable concepts 'love' and 'peace'?[15]

The fact that, up until now, U2 have refused to be associated with commercial products has played a big role in sealing their image as a band with ethics, refusing consumerist society for its own sake. That may be why people didn't understand what U2 were advocating in the 1990s, thinking they had become schizophrenic.

When U2 were offered $23 million for permission to use 'Where the Streets Have No Name' for a car advertisement and declined the offer, Bono remembers why and explains the reasoning:

If a U2 show is going askew, as it can, the one song you can rely on to get the room back is 'Where the Streets Have No Name'. We didn't want some sixteen-year-olds turning to each other at a U2 gig and saying 'Oh, great! They're playing the song from the car ad'. Now, had it been a different song from the U2 canon ... We don't want to embarrass our fans, we don't want to change the mood in which this song is perceived. In another life (as a lobbyist), I will be asking for $223 million![16]

U2 must obviously think hard about commercial moves because they are too well known for not endorsing products that wouldn't be suitable. I personally don't have a problem with the iPod endorsement, since it's a music product and U2 are musicians. Promoting music is what they're supposed to do after all and the iPod goes hand in hand with the downloading possibilities offered by the Internet. U2 fighting postmodernism doesn't mean that they shouldn't live in today's world and avail of the latest technological developments.

An Active Identity

Just like any type of identity, U2 fans' identities are constructed; in other words the fans will have built their identities overtime, evolving with the band's own growth. These identities are therefore ever-evolving and open to change. They are open to outside factors and variations. In the aftermath of the 11 September 2001 terrorist attack in the United-States, U2 were one of the first bands to play in Madison Square Garden, on 24 October. Bono says:

After 9/11, our audience was very porous, very vulnerable, very open. They really didn't know what was going to happen next. It's worth remembering, those of us who came out against the war, that in the United States they really thought it was a matter of weeks or months till the next hit happened, and what's it going to be – some suitcase bomb taking out a corner of Chicago? They were on tenterhooks. The fists were up but they were very vulnerable.[17]

Four years later, the audience in America is different:

Now, I think America has taken a position and they are less easy, in one sense, to reach … Their convictions are tougher and they feel they were right, most of them, in the war in Iraq. And, of course, as a band who's taken a position against that … You know the bit in the show where I put a headband over my eyes, I take on this kind of hostage thing and then we put the declaration of human rights? People are clapping nervously, because they don't know if we're getting at them.

Outside factors can therefore influence an audience tremendously and can even make them wonder what some symbols mean, whereas, in this particular case, they undoubtedly know why U2 are saying what they're saying.

The truth of it is we totally respect the US military and US navy – even if you don't agree with the war, anyone who would put their lives in harm's way, you have to respect them, and lots of them are kids who have no hope, no jobs. I mean, for me the bravery of people who would fight for what they believe in, or take a job fighting for what they might not believe in but think it's the right thing to do – you have to give respect to that. It's not my position, I don't know where they're coming from, particularly, but you must give respect to that. So there's been an uneasiness in America about that part of the show – 'Are they getting at us?' – and then we say, 'No, we're just making a point'.[18]

Identity in U2 fans can therefore take on new directions and faces. It is also active in that, although not always, it often leads to concrete action, as we have seen, in various domains, notably that of humanitarian work. 'Songs and musical styles do not simply "reflect", "speak to" or "express" the lives of audience members or musicians. A sense of identity is created out of and across the processes whereby people are connected together through and with music.'[19]

U2 and their audience, as well as U2's audience amongst themselves, are connected through the band's music, not only because of music but also because of ideas. That is one way for them to expand what is called their musical and otherwise cultural capital,[20] a concept developed by French sociologist Pierre Bourdieu where social classes in capitalist societies are defined not only by their economic status or capital but also by the access they have to culture, which is as unequal as the economic capital. Lower classes, for instance, will not have as much access to culture as upper classes and they will not be able to build their cultural capital as much as the upper classes. They will also be more exposed to low than to high culture. In consumption terms, it is 'the preference of individuals and social groups for particular texts – for example, European movies or Hollywood action movies – and the role such tastes play as both means of self-identification and as social indicators to others'.[21] People will indeed have a preference for a certain type of movie or a certain style of music (rock, heavy metal or rap for instance). They will identify with a particular type of music for instance, build part of their identity on that music, and show others that they belong to a particular group because of their musical tastes. As for U2 fans, by listening to and liking U2 and other 'progressive' bands, fans will be able to discuss the band, will join fan clubs on Internet websites, will have ideas on such and such a song, or on such and such an aspect of U2, but they will also buy records, concert tickets, will download concerts from the Internet, will collect memorabilia, etc. It is this pleasurable dimension of being a fan that is turned into a cultural activity.[22]

But I will go further and say that a band like U2 can expand people's cultural capital or even social capital by opening their eyes to problems that go beyond music. Fans are not disempowered. As the examples of how U2 fans can go against the band prove, fans are very active in their fandom. Lisa Lewis, editor of *The Adoring Audience: Fan Culture and the Popular Media*, summarising Lawrence Grossberg's contribution to the book, says:

> By participating in fandom, fans construct coherent identities for themselves. In the process, they enter a domain of cultural activity of their own making which is, potentially, a source of empowerment in struggles against oppressive ideologies and the unsatisfactory circumstances of everyday life.[23]

And in a way, U2 have nurtured that aspect in their fans, have pushed them to take a position, to basically do something to help make a positive change in the world. U2 fans consider themselves as serious fans or aficionados. Roy Shuker says: 'These are fans in terms of the word's origins in "fanatic", but their fanaticism is usually at a more intellectual level and focused on the music per se rather than on the persona of the performer(s).'[24] Indeed, although U2 fans do love Bono or The Edge and talk about them with real passion, their primary concern lies in the music and what emotions it provokes in them. It must be original and distinct, not resemble anything they've done before, yet still be recognisable. There is a 'sensibility' in being a fan, as described by cultural theorist Lawrence Grossberg, who believes that fans work in conjunction with 'affect or mood' when it comes to their relation to the cultural domain.[25] Grossberg developed the concept of affect and says that popular music creates an affective space amongst the audience. 'Affect is not purely emotional/physical but also functions in a social sense, as a form of cultural capital, contributing to the formation of taste cultures,' says Roy Shuker. That dimension is essential, of course, to understand U2's relationship to their fans and the influence the band have on them. People will often think of them as friends or brothers. It is undoubtedly true that people's musical tastes and styles are affected by social factors such as gender, age, class or ethnicity.[26] Depending on whether you were born male or female, whether you are black or white, whether your father was a factory worker or a doctor, your musical tastes will be influenced by all those factors. But equally, taste is not something that can be totally explained by social factors. I, for instance, love U2's music at a different level than just because of my age/class/upbringing/ethnicity. I love their sense of melody, the structure of the lyrics, the way Bono sings and that is quite difficult to explain, in the end. Why do I love U2? That's where, I believe, affect comes in. Lawrence Grossberg observes:

> The most obvious and perhaps the most frightening thing about contemporary popular culture is that it matters so much to so many different people. The source of its power, whatever it may seem to say, or whatever pleasures it may offer, can be identified with its place in people's affective lives, and its ability to place other practices affectively (...) Affect operates across all our senses and experiences, across all the domains of effects which construct daily lives. Affect is what gives 'colour', 'tone' or 'texture' to the lived.[27]

Therefore, U2's influence is found not only in their music but in the affective power they have over their audience. While it is true of other bands or performers, U2's power in this field is quite astounding. That particular aspect is most obvious during live performance, of course. The unity of the crowd, the fusion between the band and the crowd (although not always true for every concert) show the level of commitment and emotional investment on both sides. I say on both sides because the members of U2 invest themselves emotionally with their fans too. If that aspect wasn't reciprocal, it would not be possible for U2 to exist and to elicit such a response from their audience. But on the other hand, U2's affective power over their fans is also an explanation as to why fans react with anger to any action undertaken by the band that is considered wrong. It's simply because it matters so much to them that the band should follow certain rules that were created by U2 themselves that, if they don't and change course, then it causes mayhem amongst the band's followers. There is definitely an affective investment in the band. Lawrence Grossberg points to the fact that:

> Popular culture, operating with an affective sensibility, is a crucial ground where people give others, whether cultural practices or social groups, the authority to shape their identity and locate them within various circles of authority (...). By making certain things matter, people authorise them to speak for them, not only as a spokesperson but also as a surrogate voice (e.g., when we sing along to popular songs). People give authority to that which they invest in; they let the objects of such investments speak for and in their stead. They let them organise their emotional and narrative life and identity.[28]

What is obviously important is that by investing themselves emotionally in U2, fans let them shape their identity (to a certain extent, I would add), because they are bound by affect. Although they do fight that aspect sometimes, they 'come crawling back', as one fan told me, even if the band does something that is unsuitable in their eyes. Affect is therefore stronger than many other aspects.

Conclusion

Today's young generation, like previous generations, is undoubtedly in search of an ideal, especially in places like America, where certainties have been shattered, only to be replaced by doubt and fear about the future. U2 are trying to make sense of it all through song and action and that is one of the reasons why they are still as successful.

U2 are quite a unique phenomenon. No band in the history of rock has lasted this long without changing its line-up, with such consistent success and with changes that were a challenge to themselves and to their fans.

What I have discussed in the previous chapters, U2's permanent features, are all elements of this uniqueness. If one of those had been missing, I doubt that the band would have had such an impact on rock, on their fans and on society. Take away the spirit of community, and the edifice crumbles under rows and disagreements. Take away their 'Irishness' and independence, and they would have been just another rock band. Take away their creative endeavours and talent for reinvention and they would have churned out the same tune over again. Take away their spirituality, and they would not have had the same inspiration and faith. Take away their social consciousness, and the myth would not have taken such gigantic proportions, while Bono would not have invested himself in his fight for Africa. Take away their ambition, and none of this would have been possible.

This book is not, however, complete yet. Since I have talked about the fans' identity and generations of them following U2, I wanted to give them the last word, because in the end, take away the fans and U2 simply wouldn't have existed or wouldn't be the phenomenon that they still are.

Epilogue

WHAT THE FANS HAVE TO SAY

Finding out what the fans have to say about the band is one more way to understand the phenomenon, as they are essential to U2's success.

This epilogue is based on a random panel of 70 interviews/questionnaires that I conducted in September/October 2004 and March/June 2005. Some people were interviewed while others were sent a questionnaire by e-mail. 36 of the fans are males aged between seventeen and 42, and 34 are females aged between sixteen and 44. Many different nationalities are represented: American, Argentinian, Belarusian, Belgian, Belizean, Brazilian, British, Canadian, Czech, Croatian, French, Irish, Italian, Russian, Scottish, Serbian, Slovak and Spanish. This panel is, I believe, representative of the U2 fan base of today, and it is interesting to notice that the ratio of male to female fans is balanced, as well as the ages covered. This leads to a first tentative conclusion that U2 have indeed touched both sexes as well as successive generations. There is also strong evidence that cultural differences are erased and that people's opinions seem to converge despite that.

However, fans do not agree with everything U2 say or do. 'The rock audience, the U2 audience, does tend to be smarter than your average bear. They're not like a bunch of arty-farty types, they're not intellectuals, but they're thinking people,' says Bono.[1] When, on 9 July 2005 in Paris, Bono talked to the Stade de France audience about Jacques Chirac and his contribution to helping Africa, the reaction to the French president was less than enthusiastic, which proves his point. But Bono also adds: 'Fans of U2 are kind of easygoing. Generally we have a very good relationship with our fans, but sometimes they go too far. I know the fringe people who deny you your privacy and are sort of rooting through your dustbins (...) are not our audience. I do not judge our audience by them.'[2] He also related a story about U2 fans to Dave Fanning:

[It was during the] Elevation tour. We're filming the tour for the DVD in Boston, we have a row with our fans, right, because there's people on the road who are in the first row every night. There's like a caravan of them. We're saying, can we just play to the people of the town we're in, instead of one that's following us? They organise a sitdown in the heart of the stage front. You wouldn't do that while we're filming! I mean, we understand you make a protest but not while we're filming. So even our audience are rough. Go to U2 internet sites, they're murder.

One of the reasons, perhaps the only reason why the U2 audience is tough on the band is because the fans have high expectations. They expect U2 to be the best all the time and to deliver on their promise to be the best. If anything goes wrong, they are not very forgiving. However, the fans are soft-hearted all the same when it comes to their favourite foursome.

But before I move on to the heart of U2 fans, I need to define a fan. The word itself is loaded. People generally accept the term because there is no other way to describe fans. As Cyril, a French fan and former singer with the now defunct French U2 tribute band, Apolo-j, says: 'I don't like the word too much. You can call followers of Céline Dion fans, but there's a bit of a contradiction between what U2 represent and the word fan. U2's music is rather adult and mature, whereas the word fan is a bit derogatory and can be applied to teenagers rather than adults.' People might indeed say that they are 'into' such and such a band rather than fans, or that they are aficionados, but it is the same thing. People who love U2 may be fans but they are not fanatics. Most lead normal lives, and have other things to worry about outside of U2.

I attended a U2 evening before the 9 July 2005 concert in Paris. There were television cameras present and the journalist wanted to talk to fans who go overboard when it comes to the band. I found it was unwarranted as the vast majority of U2 fans are not like that. The U2 fan is a singular species. Many of them are now in their thirties and even forties and have matured along with the members of the band. There is therefore a connection that goes beyond mere fandom.

The questionnaire that the fans responded to was devised so that anyone could answer it. It is based on seventeen questions about U2. They all have a connection with the themes of this book.

Discovery

Whether people discovered U2 in 1981, as was the case for American accountant Julie who is 44, or fell in love with their music in 2002, like nineteen year-old Scottish student Jillian, the reaction is always one of enthusiasm when asked what they felt when they heard a U2 song for the first time. 29-year-old French engineer David, former bass player with Apolo-j, said that he was 'stuck to his seat' when he heard 'With or Without You' and saw the video of the song, and that 'it had a great impact [on him]', while 35-year-old Belgian head of personnel Tina remembers:

> I went to the Rock Torhout/Rock Werchter festival in 1983 for the first time [with my two older brothers]. I lost my brother (the youngest one joined me) after five minutes of our arrival, so there I was, thirteen, amidst a crowd of 25,000 people, alone. I found nothing better to do than go to the very front, close to the stage, to watch all the bands come and go. And that was my first 'official' contact with U2. Their performance just blew me away.

The adjectives that come back most often are 'incredible', 'great', mind-blowing', 'powerful', exciting', 'amazing'. Some also talk about a life-changing experience, like 28-year-old American company director Mary-Kathleen, who says:

> I was in our high school freshman locker room after school. I found a copy of October on the ground and was bored so I played it. The cassette was set to play 'I Threw a Brick Through a Window'. I was thirteen years old and my life changed in an instant. That song completely stopped me cold. I listened to it over and over and over again. I didn't even know there were other songs on the album until two weeks later! I immediately threw myself into a now fifteen-year obsession with the band. I saved my allowance and begged my parents to take me to the music store where I immediately purchased Boy. When I heard 'A Day Without Me', I knew this was it for me. This was to be my band. I am a different fan from most because I did not know their music before I listened to their first two albums. I had not heard the hits (The Joshua Tree, namely). I fell in love with early U2. I had memorised Boy, October, and War before I even heard The Joshua Tree.

Others don't actually remember the first time they heard a U2 song, but do remember the first time a U2 song made an impression on them. 21 year-old Italian Valentina says:

> I don't remember when I first heard a U2 song. I mean, I have vague memories of having seen the 'One' video (and I was impressed because the singer was very charming …) and loved the song. I also have vague memories of the hate I had for 'Discothèque' when it came out: I used to change the TV channel and things like that …
>
> I can remember the moment I fell in love with this band. I was in my kitchen and I was waiting for the coffee to be ready. The TV was on because I used to watch MTV while having breakfast. All of a sudden, a sky with clouds, followed by a close-up of a man with black sunglasses and a fabulous chin who came on the screen. The music filled my kitchen and was so great that I was kind of hypnotised.

Valentina is talking about the 'Beautiful Day' video, while 24 year-old American student Rebekah has a sweet personal story to tell: 'The first time I ever heard U2 was when, as a baby, my mother put a pair of headphones on me while playing a U2 album. That was the first time I'd ever heard any music. I wish I could remember! I do have that picture framed and I look at it often and smile – it's almost like U2 is my heritage.'

What is obvious here is that at one moment or another in the lives of U2 fans, one song changed what they may have previously thought of the band, or for early fans, the first impression was a lasting one.

Meaning

On another level, I was interested to know what U2 represents for their fans. The answers are always passionate and meaningful. U2 obviously stand for a lot in the lives of their fans, whether in a musical or a more spiritual way. Software consultant Vidhya, a 33-year-old Canadian, says:

> Today, the band represents for me: a) the best of humanity, because of their commitment to world issues; b) the best of creativity, because I love that they push themselves and find new creative directions with each album they produce; c) the best of energy and spirit, because their music can trigger in me the inspiration to dance, cry, laugh, meditate or simply feel joy, depending on the day and depending on the song I'm listening to.

Again, the words that come back often are: passion, integrity, sincerity, hope, energy, inspiration, happiness, freedom, life possibilities, escapism, awakenings, life soundtrack.

Some fans are more explicit about what U2 stand for. For instance, Tomislav, who is a nineteen-year-old Croatian student living in the USA, says: 'U2 has lots of meanings for me. Although they represent a sort of a mixture of raw passion, deep depression and pure joy in each and every song, they still seem to remain modest and peaceful, just trying to do what they believe they can do – turn poetry into music.' 24-year-old British student Thomas is adamant that: 'For me the band represents integrity, passion, caring and the ability to dream it all up again. U2 also represents an awareness of art and philosophy which is incorporated into their work.' Jennifer, a 32-year-old British woman who works in the paralegal profession and is also an activist, feels that: 'U2 represents the power music has to bring about true change in the world', while 29-year-old independent contractor Andy says that: 'The band represents to me the last of the true rock stars.' American student Brendan, who is 25, says that: 'In the end it's about soul, not virtuosity.' Fabrice, who is the 22-year-old former drummer with Apolo-j and a commercial engineer, believes that: 'U2 represents a model ... a band that started 25 years ago, it's very inspiring to me.' 31-year-old British manager Mark R. says: 'To me the band represent a guilty pleasure: they will never be cool or hip, and Bono is often an annoying fundamentalist preacher, but I can see beyond that to see that their music connects thoroughly to the central themes of what it is to be alive in our society.' But to temper some more extreme opinions, American Dan, who is 42 and self-employed, believes that: 'That question is a loaded one. As much as I love them and as much as I am devoted to them, they are still just a band.'

Sharing

Very often, the fans will share their passion with other people who are or have become fans of the band, some of them with close friends, siblings or spouses. Rebekah's mother is a fan, for instance. Lindsey, a 26-year-old graphic designer from the USA, also has U2 fans in her family:

My older sister went to a couple of shows on the Popmart Tour with me, and she pulls out their records and listens to them occasionally. My mother (whom my friends have affectionately dubbed 'Bonomama') is a much bigger fan. She makes me take her with me to at least two or three shows every time that they tour, and she's always been the strongest supporter of my U2 obsession.

Indeed, during the concerts, we are seeing more and more children or teenagers with their parents, some of them undoubtedly early U2 fans.

Sometimes, family and friends are forced to listen to U2, as in the case of 24-year-old medical student Géraldine, who is French: 'I don't share this passion with any member of my family. I would rather say that my family are obliged to share this passion with me. I talk about it a lot and that's the reason why. When I lived with my mother, everybody had to listen to U2's music!'

A lot of fans, who subsequently became friends, met through websites, another way of sharing their passion.

As to whether fans talk about their passion, the answer is a resounding yes. They say that people in general react positively, although some are surprised at the passion U2 provoke. Tara, a 26-year-old Canadian graduate student, says: 'I talk all the time, so U2 comes up a lot. When people realise how serious I am they are surprised because I am well educated, married and supposedly rational. They think that this devotion is immature and irrational. It is irrational, but I don't see there being a problem with that', while Valentina observes: 'I can't avoid it, especially when I'm in my car. People tend to react with admiration. Except one girl: she really hates them. Or better, she just can't stand Bono and she considers him a cretin. I tried to explain to her the job that Bono does, but she still goes on with her opinion…' 34 year-old Brennan, who is an American working in film/TV production, confesses:

I find it quite hard to conceal my passion for U2, so yes I do talk about it whenever they [U2] come up. I try not to be one of those fanatics who can't talk about anything but one subject matter, but if they come up (I try not to raise them as a subject myself), my passion inevitably comes out and I can go on and on … People react to that passion in a variety of ways: if they've heard my 'rap' before they might roll their eyes with a detachment, if this is the first time they are hearing me talk about U2, they normally claim to be impressed, wowed or, even, 'scared' at the focus and passion I hold for U2 and their music.

Some people are indeed quite over the top when it comes to talking about the band. Rebekah is one of them:

I talk about U2 a lot! Everyone at my job knows about it, all my friends do … I have U2 vanity plates that say BONO GRL, so I get asked about it often. Some people have really gotten into very articulate discussions with me about U2's music, spirituality and purpose. Some people still don't seem to understand that Zoo TV was really all about parody and still think Bono is actually The Fly – I love to set that record straight!

Flavia, a 24-year-old interpreter/translator from Argentina, is also very talkative:

[I talk about U2] all the time. And whenever I open my mouth and say U2/Bono/Larry/Adam/Edge, they just roll their eyes and say 'Oh no! Not again.' But they just say that to tease me. They know how much I love and respect the guys. When I finally got to meet Bono in Dublin, they were thrilled for me. They knew how much I wanted it to happen, especially after my 'incident' during a PopMart concert (one of the nights they played in Buenos Aires, Bono picked me to dance with him during 'With or Without You', but as the security guys were pulling me out of the crowd, this girl came from nowhere, jumped the rail, grabbed Bono and got onstage. There's no need to tell you I was shocked and mad and upset).

I think deep inside everybody likes the band, whether it is for the powerful songs, for their political commitment or just for Bono's charisma.

Although some fans do temper their passion for U2. Sean, who is a 24-year-old American student, says very wittily:

I tend not too [talk] very much [about U2] just so I don't freak people out. That and I could end up talking for hours, I try to keep myself in denial. I have with girlfriends, close friends, family from time to time. Or when I am drunk, God help whoever is there to hear this drunkard preparing a dissertation on the spiritual themes of the *Pop* album. People usually will just eventually try and be polite and change the subject.

As for Irishman Stephen, who is a 32-year-old lecturer:

If U2 comes up in conversation I will always jump in with plenty of comments, though I don't go around trying to speak about U2 all the time – having a passion is fine but over exposing it just sends people running for the door. I am prone to over-doing it a little when it's a matter of defending U2 (something I try to be objective about – some criticisms may be valid). How do people react? As an Irish language lecturer people rarely expect you to be a serious U2 fan (for some reason) so when this does come to light they're often a little surprised.

Who's the Favourite?

Another question that elicited a passionate answer is a crucial one: who is your favourite band member and why? Not unlike the John/Paul match within The Beatles fan community, there is clear evidence that Bono and The Edge are the ones whose names come out most often in the survey with, unsurprisingly, Bono as the clear winner.

However, a lot of fans tend to say that they like the band as a unit and they choose one of the members almost reluctantly. Laura, who is a 39-year-old American sales manager, says: 'All four members are unique to me, but if I must choose a favourite, it's Bono.' Brennan has the same reaction: 'That's tough because I love each one of them for very distinct reasons, i.e., what they actually bring to the band. But I suppose if push came to shove, I'd go with the obvious and say Bono.' Some definitely have no favourite, like Dzmitry, who is a 22-year-old computer expert from Belarus: 'U2 is a four-legged table for me. I like their music, their causes and ideals, personal achievements. Each of them is unique in his own way. But I like them much more together.' Boomer, a 33-year-old American programmer/analyst, agrees: '[I have] no real favourite. I find all four members extremely interesting; they all have their quirks, pros/cons, etc. I probably know more about Bono for he is the one making the news everyday.' Then he adds surprisingly: 'But I must say that the fifth member is my favourite and that is Paul McGuinness. If it wasn't for him, I may never have had the chance to answer these questions. Plus his last name has a ring to it: McGUINNESS! Brilliant!' And Leandro, an Italian bank employee who is 28, turns poet and says: '[I love] all four: Bono is the heart, Edge is the brain, Adam is the lungs, Larry is the blood.'

Sometimes, people find it difficult to decide and there are ties, for instance between Bono and The Edge or between Bono and Adam, and more surprisingly, between Larry and The Edge or between Larry and Bono. Valentina is torn: 'The match is between Bono and Adam. I mean, Bono is such an incredible human being according to me ... But Adam is so charming! I love his slow way of moving, the poses he has when he's playing his bass. And his low, deep voice thrills me!' And twenty-year-old American student Katie can't decide either:

> I like them all for different reasons, but probably Larry and Bono most of all (and I can't pick between them) for very different reasons. Bono's a very

eloquent and entertaining speaker, and I continue to marvel at how he can continue to craft his messages to suit and appeal to so many different audiences. That ability, coupled with the talent to continue to create some of the most gorgeous lyrics I have ever laid eyes and ears on, is astounding to me. The favouritism towards Larry though, is a bit more simplified. I am also a drummer (amongst other things), which triggered the onset of the favouritism, but especially in reading some of the more recent interviews of him, I like the heart he seems to be expressing. Bluntness with heart is a hard thing to express.

Larry is also a favourite with Tomislav: 'My favourite member is the actual founder of U2, Larry Mullen Jr, because of his unique drumming style. He contributed a lot to their musical expression, and after all, I believe he is the main reason why I started playing drums.' He is also loved by sixteen-year-old Liesbeth, who is Belgian:

My favourite band member's always been Larry. I recognise his background working in my own life ... not minding to take a step back if it means you can have your privacy. I've always had the feeling he's always looking a bit grumpy, because he feels uncomfortable in the range of cameras or fans, but in familiar company, he's a very nice, funny, warm-hearted man and I'm a bit the same ... I'm mostly in the background, because I don't like a lot of attention from strangers, but when I feel at ease, I think I'm a very open, gentle person too, also with a lot of sarcasm, which I recognise in all four of them. So that's why I prefer Larry.

Adam, on the other hand is a favourite with Sébastien and Anna, who are both French. Sébastien is a 22-year-old student who says: 'Adam is my favourite because he lives in his own world', while Anna, who is a 35-year-old communication consultant and moderator with the French web-based fan-club u2achtung.com, confesses that: 'The teenager in me would say that Larry is my favourite and let's face it, he is so cute! But as an adult, I would like to meet Adam. I think that I would have more things in common with him and I've always liked people who are in the background.'

The Edge is the second most well-liked member of the band and a favourite with people like Stéphanie, a 35-year-old French secretary: 'I have a great passion for The Edge. He's my darling. He has a very ordinary side, very natural and cool. He is humble and on top of everything, he is a brilliant guitar player.' Mark

R. also says of the guitarist: 'My favourite member is The Edge. Even if he does have a silly name! A dogmatic refusal to tolerate bullshit, and a geek's tolerance for detail and science. And a cool goatee', while Devlin, a 27-year-old American editor and moderator of the U2 website, interference.com, reveals:

> I definitely have a crush on him but I also admire his intelligence, humour and talent. He has a great way of saying things. He has a beautiful singing voice. He's an inventive guitarist. He's a fantastic performer. He's also a completely unique person who doesn't mind being different, being a little nerdy or odd, and that comfort and confidence is very admirable.

Last but not least, Bono is quoted 44 times, out of the 70 people asked, as being the favourite (nineteen males and 25 females). Words like hero, role model, charisma, passion and cool come back regularly when fans talk about the singer. Girls often describe themselves as 'Bonogirls', while many say that they love all members of the band but eventually choose Bono. It also appears that the singer's work outside U2 has touched the fans' unconsciousness, and many state that particular side as one of the reasons why they like him. Let's give the fans the opportunity to say what they really think of Bono:

> Bono has truly been a hero of mine for years. His actions have informed a lot of my opinions, socially, politically and otherwise over the years. And let's face it ... he's fucking cool. By the time I got to high school I had grown my hair long *à la* his *Joshua Tree* phase and incorporated elements of his style into my own. When he cut his hair, I cut mine. I had the leather jacket from the 'One' video. I had the shades. When I think of 'cool', I think of Bono. And I know he'd strongly disagree ... (Aaron, 31, American actor)

> Bono is my favourite. Why? Where do I begin? It's Bono! Isn't that enough? He is amazing! He's smart beyond his years ... It's not even necessary to talk about his musical talent and the lyrics he writes because that is self explanatory. But Bono is about so much more than just his music – he is passionate about people and the world. I love him and respect him for everything he is trying to do in Africa ... More people need to be like him. Bono is my idol ... I have great respect and admiration for the man. (Nina, 30, graphic designer from Serbia and living in Canada)

> There are many, many reasons why I love Bono. But I think the main reason is because Bono's lyrics resonate deep within me. They touch my soul

(…) They are like poetry. He writes songs that are meaningful and that people can relate to on a soul or deeper level. He knows how to grab your heart and touch you and connect with you through his lyrics and his passion. His voice is so unique and his heart and soul and passion come out in the way he sings. (…) When I hear his voice, I feel closer to God. I feel a spiritual connection. I cannot explain it, I can only feel it. (…) The times I am the most happy is within a U2 song. I also love Bono because he is someone I admire and strive to be like not only as a singer, songwriter and performer but also as a human being. He has used his celebrity power and status to help the world be a better place. He has the courage to speak up and fight for his convictions. He has the courage to help those less fortunate. And I love that he is friends first with all the band mates. His love for his band mates, his family and friends and his utmost respect for women make him stand out in his profession. He is certainly one of a kind. (…) His belief in God and himself makes him what he is … an outstanding human and frontman. He is the Elvis of our time and Bono and the Edge are my John Lennon and Paul McCartney … respectively. (Delphine, 34, American aesthetician)

I love his voice and his style. I feel we are similar people and I guess he is my hero, even though I'm a little too old for hero's … role model then. I think it's healthy to have a role model, someone to look up to … as long as they are worthy and I cannot think of many better role models than Bono. He also makes me laugh a lot. He is an amusing little man and even though I am a man and don't know him personally … I love him in a non-sexual way! (Thomas)

However, all is not praise when it comes to Bono and twice he comes out as the 'loser' amongst the fans. Michal, a seventeen-year-old Slovakian student, says: 'I'm sure my favourite is not Bono', while Christophe, a 35-year-old French civil servant, says:

It's strange to say that, but the one I like the least is Bono. When it comes to what he does outside of the band, I already had my own opinions on the matter and I worked for charities, and he didn't bring anything new as far as I'm concerned when he started doing that. I don't do more or I don't do less because of that. I would almost be tempted to do less because Bono is a bit annoying when it comes to that, and some fans may have felt that he was putting the band in jeopardy in 2001. I love U2 for their music and not for the outside shell, even though what Bono is doing is good, but it is something different.

So much for Bono! He is, however, definitely the fans' darling, something understandable in view of his place in the band. But the other three members of U2 don't lose out either, as U2 are definitely perceived as a unit, a whole, a real band, and that is rare.

Reinvention

When it comes to the fans opinion on U2's music and image and how they evolved over the years, there is an unusual consensus. Most of the people interviewed say that the musical changes and the evolution of their image are positive, like Flavia:

> Change is necessary in all aspects of life. You need to change in order to grow up and develop your personality. Change is good as long as you keep the good things you have learnt in the past. And I think that's what U2 did. I believe they have always changed for good, exploring new areas and checking out how far they can go. Some people can criticise some of Bono's political/social endeavours, but they are a minority. Most people know the band has been committed to certain causes since the beginning of their career and they are using their celebrity status to raise awareness of what's going on in the world.

Delphine agrees and adds:

> Well, I think that their image has come full circle. Back in the '80s, they were sort of known as a Christian band that spoke out against injustice in their country of Ireland and the world ... People respected them because they had strong convictions and were not afraid to use their music to relay them to the world. Nowadays, their image is the same in the sense that they are a God-believing band; however, they do not belong to any denomination. They still use their fame and music to reach out to their fans and the world to help those in need. They let people know that they can make a difference in the world. I think their image is more realistic than the messianic image they had back in the '80s. They show that they can balance having fun and not going over board. Their image is a sensible one in the sense that they are not goodie-goodies any more. Moreover, they are still good, soft-hearted people who try to help those less fortunate than themselves, and now they use their songs and performances as a platform to speak of world peace and to help those in need.

Nina also loved the change:

> I actually welcomed the change. I know there are people who were not too

231

impressed with the '90s music the band made ... But I didn't have a problem with it. It was a departure from the typical U2 music, but I respected them for not being afraid to try something new. However, they quickly went back to 'their' music, and their real fans I think welcomed them with open arms. U2 is in my opinion getting better and better. To me, their music is continuously evolving.

Devlin observes that: 'I think any changes the band has made over the years to its music and image are positive because they happened organically.' And Rebekah is adamant that: 'U2 has always been relevant and even cutting edge for all their albums.'

What transpires is that fans feel U2 had to evolve to remain relevant and of their time. But they also defend them fiercely when people don't understand what U2 are doing, like Katie:

I know the predominant attitude is that U2 has not changed for the better, but I'll absolutely disagree. Maybe it's because I was able to absorb U2's back catalogue in a short amount of time, but their evolution has made them vital today when a lot of bands close to their age and fan scope are pure crap. I see them more as trying new things than 'changing'. When U2 fans talk about a lot of the 'problems' with the band, they seem to cite *Pop* a lot, but I think that's just because it was such a drastic evolution. I LOVE *Pop*; in some ways I love it more than *All That You Can't Leave Behind*. *Pop* reminds me of the party that was life before September 11th, while *All That You Can't Leave Behind* was the comfort afterwards that everyone needed for a little while. Now, *How to Dismantle an Atomic Bomb* almost echoes that feeling of frenzy that people (including myself) seem to feel. Everything's a little less certain and a jumble that ranges in tone, tempo, and volume. With every album, U2 seems to almost tell their audience that the band's not only listening to them, but to the aura of the times.

When it comes to *Pop*, people tend to say that this is the album they found the hardest to get into, although Aaron says that: 'To this day, *Pop* is the most interesting album I've ever heard. I think you can only be relevant to other people if you're relevant to yourself.' Julie says: 'I had a hard time getting into *Pop*, but love the album now. I think being the age of the band makes it easier to understand the flow they've always expressed and written about their lives. They make some of the most personal music in the business.'

Tina believes that: 'They have no image. They are just four guys making music and having a lot of fun doing so.'

However, some people are conscious that not everybody shares the same consensus when it comes to U2's career. Mark thinks that:

Evolution is essential to being a successful artist creatively. Without it, one stagnates. Like the shark that does not move water through its gills, any band that does not move drowns in its own inertia. I think their evolution is positive, even if I do not always agree with the direction they went in. Recently they have confused 'Best' and 'Biggest' as being interchangeable. I would prefer less of the Bon Jovi-esque big stadium gestures of the last two albums mind you, as they now appear to have found a successful formula and are mining it for commercial gain. Also, I think the fact that U2 is a business has become blatantly obvious recently and is now affecting their perception as artists following the iPod/Tour Presale/u2.com fiasco.

But Vidhya says:

I do make an effort to really think about their efforts, musically and socially, and I try to be critical of it. I am still slightly wary about their affiliation with Apple's iPod and the band's appearance in the iPod commercial. I find myself having to defend U2 to my friends by declaring that they 'haven't sold out commercially.' I have to keep reminding myself, however, that the quantity of money which they receive from record sales or sponsorships or touring should not matter – it's what they do with that money that counts. And they do direct a fair share of their earnings to help the world's needy, so should I really be upset about one little iPod commercial?

On another negative note, Mary-Kathleen observes:

I think that the image has definitely changed. Most casual 'Top 40' fans are not aware of *Pop* or *Zooropa* which was, obviously, a huge image change for the band. I think Bono's political stances have absolutely affected the band's image, sometimes for the good but many times for the bad. People get annoyed with Bono's preaching and I definitely believe this affects the other members. For the last eight years or so, more people see Bono in pictures with a government official than with Adam Clayton.

Indeed, many people may know Bono more through his activism than his singing and it may upset fans that he is more famous amongst the general public for his activism than for his music. What most fans see though is that artistically, U2 are strong and still have things to say. Delphine C., who is a 25-year-old French customer representative, explains it this way: 'Some say that now they just think about money with their new tour and the Apple iPod for instance. But they need sponsors for this big show! They don't want to risk bankruptcy, as they did after the Zoo TV tour!'

Politics

Bono's activism and U2's political songs are another topic that I wanted to ask the fans about. I was interested to know if U2 songs or their activism had had an impact on the fans, had strengthened or changed their political opinions, had got the fans involved in humanitarian work and if Bono's actions are to be emulated.

53 fans answered that U2 had an impact or at least an indirect influence on how they see the political world and that the band had, if not changed, then strengthened their opinions, although not many actually got involved in humanitarian action. Seventeen rejected the notion of impact, but all of the 70 interviewees said they admired Bono for being so active on the social front. They believe that his actions should be emulated by the rich and famous and that, on their scale, community work seems to be the answer.

The band's influence is obvious in Stephen's words: 'I think my willingness to support organisations such as Amnesty International certainly has its roots in listening to U2. They have strengthened my opinions, yes, especially in the past few years where Bono now speaks much more astutely on matters of politics. He is now very well informed, though I don't necessarily agree with every single approach he takes.' 34-year-old Jessica, who is Canadian and a charity fundraiser, feels the same: 'U2 were probably the reason I joined Amnesty way back in the late '80s. They probably influenced me to become a charity fundraiser and do good things for the world too. They also brought awareness of issues of which I had been pretty clueless. But my opinions have always coincided with theirs, so if anything it was just reinforcement.'

But U2 also have sometimes a greater influence, as testified by Mark K., an American teacher of 33: 'I came from a conservative, church-going family. I used to think of many things as black and white. For example, when I was young, I felt homosexuality was an abomination. As I have grown older, I have become much more liberal. The negative image portrayed in my country of sex, homosexuality, contraception, etc., makes me sick to my stomach', while 22-year-old student Tomas, from Argentina, says: 'I think about U2's performance of "Sunday Bloody Sunday" in *Rattle and Hum* or the satellite links with Sarajevo during the Zoo TV Tour, and I can´t understand people ignoring those things. I have completely changed my mind on so many aspects because of U2's politics.' Jennifer agrees:

> There are so many issues I had not been informed of until Bono and/or U2 brought them to my attention. I don't believe in everything Bono believes in, but his opinion does count big time with me. Have his actions made me act in turn? Yes. I have been a member of Greenpeace and Amnesty International since '87. I am extremely active with Amnesty. U2 and Bono have impacted how I see the world and what I am willing to consider doing in order to bring about change … or at least do my part.

But not everyone is impressed. Some, like David or Régis (27-year-old former guitarist with Apolo-j) say that music is more important than U2's so-called message. Nationalities differ in their opinion. The French tend to refute the idea of U2 having a great impact on their political choices, although some say that there may be a slight influence, while Americans are more willing to admit to that influence. It doesn't mean, however, that they are naive. The French sense of independence and difficulty accepting any outside influence on their culture or opinions may explain their attitude.

Laura says: 'I'm moved by the motivation behind many U2 songs ("New Year's Day", "Mothers of the Disappeared", "Bullet the Blue Sky") and respect their collective activism (although Bono seems to get the lion's share of publicity), but I can't say I've changed politically as a result.' Lee also has his own opinions:

> [U2 have had an impact] only to the point that they have made me aware about certain situations. My job revolves around current affairs, so I feel I have a pretty broad understanding of world events anyway. I don't think that the band's actions or songs have necessarily impacted on my beliefs. U2's point of view is not necessarily the only point of view, however honourable their intentions are. I am capable of forming my own opinions without blindly following theirs. I haven't acted in turn, but I personally believe that Bono is genuine in his campaigning. I think it's unfair for so much criticism to be levelled at him, after all, he doesn't have to do what he does at all if he didn't want to.

Finally, on Bono's actions, Brendan says: 'Yes, [his] actions are absolutely to be emulated – in the sense of believing that you can "dream out loud". But Bono himself is a difficult role model to follow. You can't try to be Bono. You can only try to believe as much as he does', while Mark R. is rather annoyed at certain aspects of Bono's behaviour:

> Bono's passion is to be admired. But he should try to establish a clear divide between his music and his activism, as his activism often affects his performance in the Day Job. (The first night of the tour in San Diego sounds awful because Bono is plainly under-rehearsed, and can't remember the words or the songs, which at upwards of $100 a ticket, is criminal and insulting).

Origins

I was interested also in U2's Irish origins and wondered if the fans find them important when it comes to the music. Those origins are obviously very important as 55 fans answered 'yes' to the first part of the following question: Do you think that the fact U2 originated in Ireland was a decisive factor in the creative process and in the success of the band? The second part triggered a less unanimous answer, however. Vidhya says: 'I think that their spirituality and their concern about social issues arise from the fact that they grew up in Ireland and were surrounded by the topics of religion and civil strife on a constant basis. I think their success, however, has mainly to do with the fact that they are determined and soulful musicians who can appeal to humanity on a large scale.' Tara agrees:

> I think that [U2's origins are] part of the creative process definitely in that all products are affected by every factor in creation – so nation is definitely a factor. I think that Dublin is in fact a factor that turns out a different sound rather than Cork, or even Belfast. I don't think it is a factor in their success. I think that they became popular DESPITE being Irish, not because of it.
>
> As a Canadian, I see Ireland operating as we do in relation to England. And so it was harder for them to break out of there. Especially since they stayed in Dublin and did not relocate to London.

Fabrice, on the other hand, says that their origins did influence their success and puts it this way:

> They are different from others. Rock bands are generally British or American. I don't know any other four Irishmen like U2. It has definitely influenced their success. Ireland is known for some names in general

musical terms and the fact that they exported their music to the US was important. It may have been difficult for U2 at the beginning to break America, but
their Irish origins undoubtedly helped because of the ties with the US.

Mary-Kathleen concurs:

Yes, absolutely. In America, anything even remotely perceived as 'Irish'
immediately becomes cool. See University of Notre Dame for a perfect
example. They sell more merchandise than any other university in North
America. This is simply because they are known as The Fighting Irish. Irish
bars are everywhere … they are run and filled with people that will never go
to Ireland and know nothing about the country. This was a huge plus for the
band. Secondly, I don't think this band would have made it this far had they
been from America. We are much too cynical and too willing to brush a
band off after five years, not to mention 25 years!

As for whether fans see the band as an Irish rock band or solely as a rock
band, twenty people answered the former, while most others answered the latter,
or they see U2 as a rock band from Ireland. This goes to show that the band has
colonised people's unconsciousness with a music that now definitely transcends
nationality, although their Irish roots are still present, but maybe less visible. But
Anna says: 'U2 have largely done everything for people to see them as a great
Irish rock band. They've always positioned themselves as such, and as much as we
don't necessarily know where some bands come from (US or Great-Britain), with
U2, it's always been very clear that they are from Ireland. We know it clearly
because they've always flown the Irish flag.' And it is true. Many fans say that the
Irish element is present all the same. As Nina puts it: 'I see them as a rock band
… a very unique band with LOTS of Irish flare …' I strongly believe that people
want to claim U2 as their own because they feel that the band has no frontiers
and can appeal to anybody, as they do. Lee is adamant that: 'Because of Ireland's
close relationship with Britain, many people in Britain have claimed them as
their own. I guess I have in a way, so I'd have to say I see them as rock band alone,
rather than an Irish rock band (and I guess, half the band are technically English
anyway.)' Lee is undoubtedly right, as the 'Outstanding Contribution to British
Music' award at the 2001 Brit Awards testifies. Irishman Stephen agrees: 'U2
doesn't belong to the Irish. I like the fact they are Irish, I have a feeling of pride
but I think the music transcends all that. Also, they have never played up to this
"stage-Irish" mentality and have avoided narrow nationalism.'

U2 also brought awareness of the conflict in Northern Ireland to the minds of people who are not Irish. Samuel, a 23-year-old Brazilian journalist, says: 'Because of U2 I studied the history of Ireland, I saw lots of movies because of U2's influence, like *Michael Collins*, *In the Name of The Father*, etc. Ireland has a great history, and U2 is part of it.' Erica, who is a 22-year-old American working as a studio operator for an environmental artist, is of the same mind:

> After I became a fan, I did pay close attention to the fact that they were from Ireland. Just as when we become interested in anyone or anything, we like to find out more about them. Without some background information, we're not able to make a clear assessment or judgement of what they're all about. So, when I became a U2 fan, I wanted to know more about where they came from. If I didn't know where it was they came from, I don't think I'd be able to fully understand them or their music.

Finally, when asked if they had been to Ireland and if it was primarily because of U2, 1/3 of the foreign fans visited Ireland at least once, either because their families originated from there, or because they simply wanted to see the country. U2 were, of course, a big factor in their decision to visit, although not always the main reason. Vidhya puts it this way:

> I visited Ireland in 1994 and spent a number of weeks touring the country, and roaming around various spots in Dublin of historical relevance to U2. I think that I would have eventually found myself visiting Ireland, even if I had never discovered U2. My background is Sri Lankan, and so I find myself naturally interested in Ireland because both Sri Lanka and Ireland are island nations that have endured violence and civil strife over a significant period of time. I find it interesting to learn about how the Irish deal with the problems in their land.
>
> Having explained this, however, I do feel that being such an ardent fan of U2 is what precipitated my visit to Ireland. I would say that I spent the majority of my time in Ireland visiting buildings and places that, I felt, had some sort of relevance to U2. So although my initial interest in Ireland was because of its political history, my visit to Ireland was actually driven by my love for U2.

As for those who haven't been there yet, most of them want to go because they are attracted to the place and mainly because of U2. As Jillian says: 'I have never been to Ireland, but I am sure to go soon – I have to complete my pilgrimage!'

Spirituality

If U2 fans are attracted to Ireland partly because of the band, they also admit that the country had an influence on the band members' religious beliefs. I asked the fans whether the fact that Bono, Larry and The Edge were religious bothers them, or if they think that it gives them another dimension. There is complete consensus on U2's faith and spirituality. U2's religious beliefs appear as something personal, which fans respect and see as an essential part of the band's identity. Lisa, a 33-year-old American communications consultant, says:

> I am not into religion at all, but I respect that they have their beliefs. Their religious beliefs drive a lot of their music – which is something I love to listen to. Songs can have different meanings to different people. They might have produced a song due to a spiritual thought or feeling – but that doesn't bother me at all because the end product is beautiful. Everyone has a right to believe whatever they want. I think that there are many other things they believe in (love, humanity, equality, etc.) that are very powerful – and that is what touches me more than anything.

Flavia believes that 'they have achieved the right balance between spirituality and rock 'n' roll', while Carrie thinks that:

> I think it humanises them a bit because it reminds you that these are not men who are out doing drugs and womanising on the weekends. They have moral standards that seem to be important to them. As an agnostic myself, however, it doesn't sway me one way or the other, because I don't feel that the presence or absence of religious beliefs makes you better or worse than any other person.

There is definitely a moral dimension for fans that is evident through U2's spiritual side. Even non-believers are touched by the latter. Firas, for instance, who is a 27-year-old graduate student from America said: 'I am an atheist, but I think some religious U2 songs even speak to me: "Wake Up Dead Man" is the prime example. When Bono questions God, that is when I get very interested, and when he questions those who use religion as a tool to oppress, like in "Please"', while Julie admits: 'I take many of their songs on the secular level, except for straightforward praise songs, though I've always felt the spirituality of the band. My first concert was better than church. I think it just adds another dimension to the band. I love that they believe in something other than money.' Dave, 24, an American production associate, sees it the following way:

I myself subscribe to the same beliefs of those three members. I think it gives their music a completely different dimension. To know that U2, even without setting out to do so, or without having a religious agenda, can reach so many people with lyrics and songs about God when a good portion of the audience doesn't even know it, is a very powerful thing. It just goes to show that Christians can be cool. They can be in a cool rock band, and they can make some of the most relevant music since the Beatles.

Finally, Brendan sees the darker side of U2: 'It absolutely gives another dimension to the band. In fact, it very nearly defines the band. U2's unique combination of faith and doubt – the fact that they can be at once so dark, so angry, and so hopeful – is inseparable from what makes them great', and Stephen adds:

U2's interest in spiritual matters is behind their ability to celebrate, to raise people above the mundane. But their spiritual side is also what lies behind the darker songs, making U2 more interesting than mere witnesses for God. You know the way some true believers are overbearingly certain about their salvation and God's love, etc. Bono has never been like that, he has always expressed his weaker, darker self, even surrenders to it – making his spiritual side all the more interesting.

Longevity

The final question I asked the panel of fans was: what is the secret of U2's longevity? Brendan follows the God idea and says:

Several things – mainly, their desire always to be great. Art is motivated by discontent with the way the world is; U2, in part because of their belief in God, have never become content with the way the world is.

Their patience is also important. If they released an album every year instead of every three or four years, there'd be a lot more crap floating around out there. Let me return to the God issue. If you enter the music world as a young person with a muddled, half-formed, self-centred world view, all your songs are going to be motivated by things like romance and sex and the righteous indignation of youth. Art is motivated by discontent, and your discontent is going to concern not getting what you want. Then, when you get older, you'll either settle down or burn out. You will either satisfy yourself – get married, clean up, etc. – or you'll shout yourself hoarse. Either way, your inspiration will go. You'll be condemned to mediocrity. If, on the other hand, your world view in youth is big enough to incorporate things beyond yourself – if your sights are ultimately directed at God, however imperfectly – the passion of your youth will remain all your life.

If spirituality is indeed very important for some in U2's longevity, others cite friendship as the basis for it; 30 of them actually do so, seeing friendship as the cement that allowed U2 to continue on their path for years. Mark K. says: 'The secret to U2's longevity is brotherhood. They were mates before musicians. They grew together as a band and each member is necessary for the sum of U2. Without just one of the four members, then U2 would not exist. It couldn't exist.' Dan observes:

Their ability to get along personally has to be considered a major factor. They seem to have common goals and that makes it a lot easier to reach them. They have been able to consistently put out strong work for many years and that is a testament to their ability to judge their own work objectively, which is something every artist struggles with and for whatever reason they are able to do.

Fans also say that reinvention, relevance, honesty and, above all, great music are other qualities that make U2 a long-lasting phenomenon. Erica says:

I think the band's love and commitment for each other and what they do is a big part of their longevity. If they didn't have a deep commitment and love for one another, I don't think they would have made it very far. Because they've been through ups and downs and experienced so much together, I think their bond is pretty tightly sealed [...] When one of them was weak, they'd hold him up. They're strongly grounded.

I also think what attracts people to U2 is that they're relatable. The members of U2 are real people who have stuff they deal with everyday and they talk about it through their music. That's what people identify with and what keeps people interested in what U2's doing. If U2 were the typical rock band and sang mostly about sex and drugs, it would get old pretty quick. I think people like music with substance. They want music that's politically aware, examines spiritual matters, and deals with real life issues.

Lisa thinks that:

> They have stuck together through ups and downs. They value this special thing called U2. They know it is special and they love music, which is why they stick together in my opinion. It is pretty amazing to hear stories about how they make music – how they count on each other ... give in to each other ... and work together. They have great chemistry – and they all know their roles. I also think that their desire to be the best in the world – even after all these years – is probably the most important factor in their longevity. They are never satisfied, which is why they keep creating incredible albums. Without that desire – who knows when they would have called it quits.

Creative drive is an element that fans see as absolutely essential to U2 and is sometimes akin to magic, as in Brennan's case, who sees U2's music almost as sacred:

> It's definitely something unspoken. Something that can't quite be defined in verbal terms. It is simply, magic. What they have, I have never seen before. You could throw out terms like craftsmanship, 'Irishness', a never-ending willingness to push themselves forward, always learning and yearning, but what it boils down to is magic ... The magic of U2, the four of them in a room and playing music together and that is best left unexplored – enjoy and celebrate their music, but don't deconstruct it.

Finally, let's give the last word to Anna, whose opinion is rather different, and who says, tongue in cheek:

> The reason for U2's longevity is that the only one who has an over-inflated ego is Bono. Thankfully, the others haven't, otherwise U2 would have disappeared a long time ago!

I'm sure Bono would love it.

Appendix

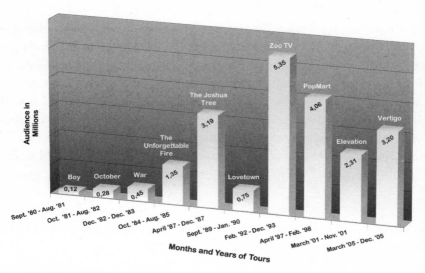

Table 1: Number of U2 concerts per year.
Table compiled from: Mark Chatterton, *U2: The Complete Encyclopedia* (London, Firefly, 2001), pp. 241-251, and from u2.com for the year 2005 (accessed on 12 June 2005).

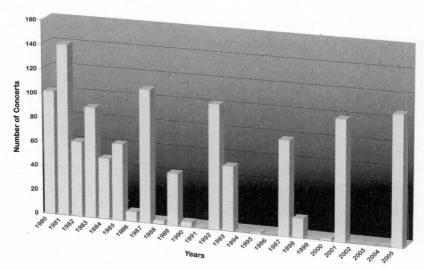

Table 2: Attendance numbers at U2 concerts per tour.
Table compiled from Pimm Jal de la Parra, *U2 Live!: A Concert Documentary* (London, Omnibus Press, 2003), and from *Mojo* 140, July 2005, p. 85.

ENDNOTES

Introduction
1. Simon Frith, *Performing Rites: Evaluating Popular Music* (Oxford, Oxford University Press, 1998), p. 273.
2. Ibid., pp. 249-250.
3. Roland Barthes, 'The Grain of the Voice', in Simon Frith, Andrew Goodwin (eds), *On Record: Rock, Pop and the Written Word* (London, Routledge, 1990), p. 293.
6. Ibid., p. 299.
7. Keith Cameron, 'Faith', *Mojo*, 140, July 2005, pp. 85-86.
8. Gérard Côté, *Processus de création et musique populaire* (Paris, L'Harmattan, 1998), p. 73.
9. Michka Assayas, *Bono on Bono* (London, Hodder and Stoughton, 2005), p. 65.
10. Ibid., p. 118.
11. Bill Flanagan, *U2: At the End of the World* (London, Bantam Press, 1995), p. 264.

Chapter 1
1. Mícheál Ó Súilleabháin, 'Around the House and Mind the Cosmos': Music, Dance and Identity in Contemporary Ireland', in Richard Pine (ed.), *Music and Ireland 1848-1998* (Cork, Mercier Press, RTE, 1998), p. 86.
2. Ibid.
3. *Raising the Volume: Policies To Expand the Irish Music Industry*, Music Industry Group, IBEC, 1998, p. 10.
4. *Shaping the Future: A Strategic Plan for the Development of the Music Industry in Ireland*, Music Board of Ireland, p. 29.
5. Chrissy Iley, 'Group Therapy', *Sunday Times Magazine*, 7 November 2004.
6. Bertrand Ricard, *Rites, code et culture rock, Un art de vivre communautaire* (Paris, L'Harmattan, 2000), p. 7.

7. Niall Stokes, *Into the Heart: The Stories Behind Every U2 Song* (London, Carlton Books, 2001), p. 14.

8. John Waters, *Race of Angels: The Genesis of U2* (London, Fourth Estate, 1994), p. 60.

9. Ibid., p. 59.

10. *Achtung Baby: The Videos, The Cameos and a Whole Lot of Interference From Zoo TV*, directed by Maurice Linnane, 1992.

11. Chrissy Iley, op. cit.

12. Steve Averill was at the time a member of the punk band The Radiators From Space and a designer for the advertising agency Arrow. He was contacted by Adam Clayton who asked him about a name for the band but also asked him to become U2's manager, an offer he refused. He has since become a close associate of the band and takes care of the design of the album covers, amongst other things.

13. Mark Chatterton, *U2: The Complete Encyclopedia* (London, Fire Fly, 2001), p. 19.

14. Simon Frith, *The Sociology of Rock* (London, Constable, 1978), p. 9.

15. Paul McGuinness is also often thought of as the fifth member of U2. According to many newspaper articles and industry sources, he gets twenty per cent of the money that U2 make, as much as any member of the band. It is difficult not to compare him to Brian Epstein, The Beatles' manager, who was also considered as the fifth member of the British band.

16. Hugo Ball became disillusioned with Dada in 1917, believing that the principle of destruction followed by creation had given way to a very messy sort of movement that was an assault on the human condition and that had given way to chaos, something he could never agree with. He decided to leave and become a writer.

17. John Waters, op. cit., p. 58.

18. Ibid., p. 62.

19. Liam Mackey, 'Articulate speech of the heart', *Hot Press*, vol 7, n° 15, 5 August 1983.

20. Neil McCormick, 'Autumn fire', *Hot Press*, vol. 5, n° 20, 16 October 1981, in: Niall Stokes (ed.), *The U2 File: A Hot Press U2 History* (Dublin, Hot Press, 1985), p. 73.

21. Jann S. Wenner, 'Bono: The Rolling Stone Interview', *Rolling Stone* 986, 3 November 2005

22. Ibid, p.100.

23. Niall Stokes, op. cit., p.109.

24. Bill Flanagan, op. cit., p. 410.

25. Niall Stokes, op. cit., p. 99.

26. Ibid, 1995, p. 414.

27. Chrissy Iley, op. cit.

28. Andrew Goodwin, *Dancing in the Distraction Factory: Music Television and Popular Culture* (Minneapolis, University of Minnesota Press, 1992), p. 107.

29. Ibid., p. 108.

30. Niall Stokes, op. cit., p. 99.

31. *U2: The Best of 1990-2000*, 2002.

32. Mark J. Prendergast, *Irish Rock: Roots, Personalities, Directions* (Dublin: The O'Brien Press, 1987), p. 172.

33. *U2 Go Home*, DVD, 2003.

34. *Hot Press Yearbook and Irish Music Directory 2002* (Dublin, Hot Press, 2001), p. 53.

35. Mark J. Prendergast, op. cit., p. 177.

36. Liam Mackey, 'The Gospel according to Paul', *Hot Press Yearbook*, 1986, p. 20.

37. Mark J. Prendergast, op. cit., p. 177.

38. Bill Graham, 'U2: The band of the decade', *Hot Press*, Christmas / New Year 1989-1990 Special.

39. Ibid.

40. Neil McCormick, 'Foul Play!', *Hot Press*, vol. 11, n° 23, 3 December 1987, p 11.

41. Andrew Goodwin, op. cit., p. 102.

42. David Fricke, 'U2: Serious Fun', *Rolling Stone*, 640, 1 October 1992.

43. *U2, Zoo TV: Live From Sydney*, directed by David Mallet, 1994.

44. John Waters, op. cit., pp. 58-59.

45. Greil Marcus, *Lipstick Traces: A Secret History of the Twentieth Century* (London, Faber and Faber, 2001), p.19.

46. John Waters, op. cit., p. 59.

47. Dave Thompson, *Bono In His Own Words* (London, Omnibus Press, 1989), p. 64.

Chapter 2

1. Paul Hewson, 'The White Nigger', in Richard Kearney (ed.), *Across the Frontiers: Ireland in the 1990s* (Dublin, Wolfhound Press, 1988), p. 189.

2. John Waters, op. cit., p. 38.

3. Ibid., p. 39.

4. John Waters, op. cit., p. 103.

5. Michka Assayas, op. cit., p. 169.

6. Richard Kearney, op. cit., p. 187.

7. Although Horslips is an earlier example of an attempt at staying in Ireland. But their success was short lived.

8. 'Cherishing the Irish Diaspora', Address to the Houses of the Oireachtas, by President Mary Robinson on a matter of public importance, 2 February 1995.

9. Michka Assayas, op. cit., p. 35.

10. Ibid., p. 34.

11. Dennis Kennedy, in Paddy Logue (ed.), *Being Irish* (Dublin, Four Courts Press, 2000).

12. John Waters, op. cit., p. 133.

13. Caroline Legrand, 'Nation, Migration and Identities in Late Twentieth-Century Ireland', *Narodna Umjetnost*, Vol. 42, no.1, 2005,

14. Robin Denselow, op. cit., p. 170.

15. Michka Assayas, op. cit., p. 171.

16. Richard Kearney, op. cit.

17. Caroline Legrand, op. cit.

18. Richard Kearney, op. cit., p. 190.

19. John Waters, 'Bono TV', *The Irish Times*, 30 May 1992

20. Dennis Kennedy, op. cit.

21. John Waters, op. cit., p. 121.

22. Ann Scanlon, 'Conquistador', *Sounds*, 1 August 1987.

23. John Waters, op. cit., p. 37.

24. Kathy Donaghy, 'U2 frontman hits right note in speech as he gives politicians a lesson in reality', the *Irish Independent*, 9 July 2003.

25. Ibid., p. 190

26. This is a tax exemption scheme originally set up by the then Minister for finance, Charles Haughey, in 1969, to allow artists (musicians,painters, sculptors, writers) not to pay tax on some of their earnings, provided that they are resident in Ireland and that their work is original.

27. Paul McGuinness, U2 Night, RTE 2, 25 June 2005.

28. John Waters, op. cit., p. 125.

29. Ibid.

30. Michka Assayas, op. cit., p. 40.

31. Robin Denselow, 'Playing With Mr Big', *The Guardian*, 13 October 1995.

32. Michka Assayas, op. cit., p. 43.

33. B.P. Fallon, Zoo TV Tour Programme 1992.

34. Mark Prendergast, op. cit., p. 79.

35. Ibid.

36. Ibid., p. 81.

37. John Waters, op. cit., p. 97.

38. Ibid., p. 98.

39. Mark Prendergast, op. cit., p. 86.

40. June Skinner Sawyers, *The Complete Guide to Celtic Music* (London, Aurum Press, 2000), p. 240.

41. *Uncut Legends 3: U2*, 'What makes U2 tick? N° 2: Irishness'?, p. 60.

42. Michka Assayas, op. cit., p. 35-36.

Chapter 3

1. Bertrand Ricard, op. cit., p. 146.

2. Michka Assayas, op. cit., p. 17.

3. Bono's comment in John Waters, op. cit., p. 118.

4. Robert Hilburn, 'Where craft ends and spirit begins', *Los Angeles Times*, August 2004.

5. *U2 The Joshua Tree*, directed by Philip King/Nuala O'Connor, 1999.

6. Dave Fanning, 'You can't make it on your own', *Irish Independent*, 19 June 2005; 'Bono, Edge ... and Dave', Music Express, 25 June 2005, RTE2, produced and directed by David Blake Knox.

7. *The Making of the Unforgettable Fire*, directed by Barry Devlin, 1985.

8. Bill Flanagan, op. cit., p. 214.

9. Robert Hilburn, op. cit.

10. Niall Stokes, op. cit., p. 55.

11. Ibid., p. 7.

12. Jean-Marie Reusser, 'Collection de printemps', *Best*, n°225, April 1987.

13. Niall Stokes, op. cit., p. 107.

14. Simon Frith, op. cit., p. 169.

15. Ibid., p. 180.

16. Ibid., p. 170.

17. Robert Hilburn, op. cit.

18. Ibid.

19. Antoine Hennion, *La Passion musicale: Une sociologie de la médiation* (Paris, Métailié, 1993).

20. Keith Negus, *Producing Pop: Culture and Conflict in the Popular Music Industry* (London, Edward Arnold, 1992), pp. 87-88.

21. *The Making of the Unforgettable Fire*, op. cit.

22. Michael Ross, 'No band in the history of music has been as assiduously designed as U2', *The Sunday Times*, 13 July 2003.

23. Gilles Renault, 'En attendant Bono', *Libération*, 9 October 2000.

24. The Frankfurt School was founded in 1923, at the University of Frankfurt, a school of thought on critical theory that was developed 'as an attempt to further social change from within a broadly Marxist understanding of the structure of society.' (Brian Longhurst, *Popular Music and Society* (Cambridge, Polity Press), 1995, p. 4.)

25. A small area in New York, where music publishers were located and where composers were paid to write formatted songs by the minute. The expression 'Tin Pan Alley' was coined by Monroe Rosenfeld, who was a writer and composer of sad love songs. The noise made by all the composers actually resembled that of tin pans, thus the nickname.

26. Brian Longhurst, op. cit., pp. 3-14.

27. Stuart Bailie, 'Rock 'n' roll should be this big', *New Musical Express*, 13 June 1992.

28. Ed Power, 'Why U2 don't rock my world', *Irish Independent*, 17 February 2005.

29. Michael Ross, op. cit.

30. Jerome Reilly, 'U2 fans let fly at expensive online ticket sale fiasco', *Irish Independent*, 30 January 2005

31. Jean-Marie Reusser, 'U2 : Eux 5', *Best*, October 1984.

32. Michael Coyle, Jon Dolan, 'Modelling Authenticity, Authenticating Commercial Models', in Kevin J.H. Dettmar, William Richey (Eds), *Reading Rock 'n' roll: Authenticity, Appropriation, Aesthetics* (New York, Columbia University Press, 1999), p. 20.

33. Niall Stokes, op. cit., p. 133.

34. Brian Boyd, U2 interview, *Cara*, June 2005, p. 41

35. U2 *PopMart*, directed by Maurice Linnane, September 1997.

36. R.J. Warren Zane, 'Too Much Mead', in Kevin J.H. Dettmar, William Richey op. cit., p. 39.

37. In the words of Lawrence Grossberg who is Professor of Communications. In: A. Curthoys, T. Fry, L. Grossberg, P. Patton (eds.), *It's a Sin: Postmodernism, Politics and Culture*, (Sydney: Power, 1988); cited in R.J. Warren Zane, ibid.

38. Bill Flanagan, op. cit., p. 27.

39. Gilles Renault, op. cit.

40. Bill Flanagan, op. cit., p. 27.

41. Gilles Renault, op. cit.

42. Jean-Marie Reusser, op. cit.

43. Steve Stockman, *Walk On: the Spiritual Journey of U2* (Lake Mary, Relevant Books, 2001), p. 15.

44. John Waters, op. cit., p. 148.

45. Niall Stokes, op. cit., p. 32.

46. John Waters, op. cit., p. 1.

47. Paul Rees, 'Riders on the Storm', Q 220, Nov. 2004

48. Niall Stokes, op. cit., p. 100.

49. Ibid., p. 104.

50. John Moore, '"The Hieroglyphics of Love": The Torch Singers and Interpretation', in Richard Middleton (ed.), *Reading Pop: Approaches To Textual Analysis In Popular Music* (Oxford, Oxford University Press, 2000), p. 264.

51. Robert Hilburn, op. cit.

52. Joe Jackson, 'Bono's Burning Rage Within', *Irish Independent*, 29 October 2000.

53. Niall Stokes, op. cit., p. 37.

54. Ibid., p. 39.

55. Ibid., p. 156.

56. Ibid.

57. Ibid., p. 137.

58. Ibid., p. 70.

59. Donal Lunny was a member of traditional folk bands Planxty and Moving Hearts, amongst others.

60. Ibid., p. 41.

61. Michka Assayas, op. cit., p. 247.

62. Bertrand Ricard, op. cit., p. 165.

63. Richard Kearney, *The Wake of Imagination*, 2nd ed., (London, Routledge, 2001), p. 387.

64. Ibid., p.361

65. Ibid., p.366

66. Bertrand Ricard, op. cit., p. 146.

67. Ibid., p. 176.

68. Dave Fanning, op. cit.

Chapter 4

1. Niall Stokes, op. cit., p. 139.

2. Jean-Marie Reusser, op. cit.

3. Roy Shuker, *Key Concepts in Popular Music* (London, Routledge, 1998), p. 51.

4. Ibid.

5. Steve Stockman, op. cit., p. 3.

6. See the following web pages on this topic for instance: 'Bono's thin ecclesiology', http://www.christianitytoday.com/ct/2003/003/29.37.html 21 February 2003 (accessed on 25 June 2005); Tim Stafford, 'The Church: Why bother – The Bono effect' http://www.christianitytoday.com/ct/2005/001/26.42.html (accessed on 17 September 2005).

7. Jann S. Wenner, op. cit.

8. 'Bono's thin ecclesiology', op. cit.

9. Ibid. It actually elicited a fierce reaction from readers who defended Bono's position.

10. Dave Thompson, op. cit., p. 93.

11. Bill Flanagan, op. cit. p. 447-448.

12. Susan Fast, 'Music, Contexts, and Meaning in U2', in Walter Everett (ed.), *Expression in Pop-Rock Music: A Collection of Critical and Analytical Essays* (New York and London, Garland Publishing Inc., 2000), p. 35.

13. David Hatch and Stephen Hilliard, *From Blues to Rock* (Manchester Manchester University Press, 1987), p. 58

14. Michka Assayas, op. cit., p. 25.

15. Jann S. Wenner, op. cit.

16. Ibid.

17. B.P. Fallon interview, Zoo TV Tour Programme 1992.

18. Bill Flanagan, op. cit., p. 440.

19. Steve Stockman, op. cit., p. 5.

20. Henry VanderSpek, 'Faith, Hope and U2', http://individual.utoronto.ca/john-bowen/dare/u2.html (accessed on 15 September 2005)

21. Michka Assayas, op. cit., p. 24.

22. Ibid., p. 25.

23. Dave Thompson, op. cit., p. 90.

24. Ibid., p. 26.

25. Keith Cameron, op. cit., p. 82.

26. Ibid.

27. Niall Stokes, op. cit., p. 27.

28. Keith Cameron, op. cit.

29. Ibid.

30. Michka Assayas, op. cit., p. 33.

31. Jann S. Wenner, op. cit.

32. David Fricke, 'U2 finds what it's looking for', *Rolling Stone*, 640, 1 October 1992.

33. Niall Stokes, op. cit., p. 138.

34. Ibid., p. 139.

35. Niall Stokes, 'Matters of life and death', *The Hot Press Annual* 2002, p. 82.

36. Robert Hilburn, op. cit.

37. Sean O'Hagan, 'The gospel of Heaven and Hell', *New Musical Express*, 19 December 1987.

38. Ibid.

39. Ibid.

40. Bill Flanagan, op. cit.,

41. Angela Pancella, 'Drawing Their Fish in the Sand', http://www.atu2.com/lyrics/biblerefs.html (accessed 30/09/2005)

42. Ibid.

43. Niall Stokes, op. cit., p. 33.

44. Robert Hilburn, op. cit.

45. Raewynne J. Whiteley, Beth Maynard (eds), *Get Up Off Your Knees: Preaching the U2 Catalog*, (Cowley, 2003), p. 133-134.

46. Michka Assayas, op. cit.

47. Michka Assayas, op. cit., p. 167.

48. Ibid., pp. 167-168.

49. Dave Thompson, op. cit., p. 95.

50. He even confessed that his wife Ali had a copy made for him when the original ones were falling apart from wear and tear.

51. Michka Assays, op. cit., pp. 201-202.

52. http://www.nme.com/news/111907.html (accessed on 18 June 2005)

53. Ibid., p. 148.

54. Robert Hilburn, 'Music and mission are one', *Los Angeles Times*, 4 April 2005.

Chapter 5

1. Roy Shuker, op. cit., p. 223.

2. Lawrence Grossberg, *We Gotta Get Out of This Place: Popular Conservatism and Postmodern Culture* (London, New York, Routledge, 1992), p. 168.

3. Robin Denselow, *When the Music's Over: The Story of Political Pop* (London, Faber and Faber, 1989), p. 158.

4. Ibid, p. 164.

5. Robin Denselow, op. cit., p.170

6. Eamon McCann , 'Bullet the Blue Sky', U2 Christmas Special '89, *The Evening Press*, 24 December 1989.

7. In 2004, the song was re-recorded for its twentieth anniversary with the line-up completely changed, as the likes of Robbie Williams sang on it. Bono, however, was again asked to take part.

8. Ibid.

9. Robin Denselow, op. cit., p.171.

10. Ibid, p. 170.

11. John Waters, op. cit., p. 187.

12. Ibid.

13. Dave Bowler, Brian Dray, *U2: A Conspiracy of Hope* (London, Sidgwick and Jackson, 1993), p. 105.

14. The term was coined by Roy Shuker to designate the 'mega-events', such as Live Aid and the Mandela Tribute, which took place in the 1980s.

15. Bill Flanagan, op. cit., p. 272.

16. Ibid, p. 279.

17. Dave Bowler, Brian Dray, op. cit., p. 99.

18. Ibid.

19. Josh Tyrangiel, 'Can Bono save the world?', *Time Magazine*, 4 March 2002.

20. Declan Walsh, 'Bono and O'Neill's African odyssey may help to open wallets', *The Irish Times*, 3 June 2002.

21. James Foster, 'Bono hopes tour of Africa will prove point to "sceptical O'Neill"', *Irish Independent*, 22 May 2002.

22. Niall Stokes, 'Matters of life and death', op. cit.

23. Deaglán de Bréadún, 'Bono threatens to take to the streets in defence of world's poorest people', *The Irish Times*, 9 July 2003

24. Kathy Donaghy, 'U2 frontman hits right note as he gives politicians a lesson in reality', *Irish Independent*, 9 July 2003.

25. Ann Scanlon, op.cit.

26. *Irish Independent*, 3 May 2004.

27. Michael Ross, 'Born Again Bono', *The Sunday Times*, 21 February 1999.

28. Ibid.

29. Vincent Browne, 'Geldof and Bono out of tune on G8', *The Irish Times*, 25 July 2001.

30. Sam Smyth, 'Bono: Why I was laughing with Putin and Blair as Genoa was flowing with blood', *Irish Independent*, 28 July 2001.

31. Vincent Browne, op. cit.

32. Brendan O'Connor, 'Dr Bono shows himself to be a genuine healer', *Irish Independent*, 13 July 2003.

33. Derek O'Connor, 'Pro-Bono', *Dubliner*, 45, June 2005, p. 22.

34. Larissa Nolan, 'Bono feared being sacked', *Irish Independent*, 1 January 2005.

35. Ibid.

36. Chrissy Iley, op. cit.

Chapter 6

1. 'Absolutely McGuinness', *Propaganda*, 1987.

2. Liam Mackey, op. cit., p. 18.

3. 'Absolutely McGuinness', op. cit.

4. Ibid.

5. Compiled from Mark J. Prendergast, op. cit., p. 297.

6. Mark Goodier 'When U2 comes to town', *Vox*, April 1992 (Highlights of BBC Radio One interview).

7. Michka Assayas, op. cit., p. 99.

8. Ibid.

9. 'Absolutely McGuinness', op. cit.

10. Ibid.

11. Michael Ross, op. cit.

12. Vincent Power, *Send 'Em Home Sweatin': The Showbands' Story*, (Dublin, Kildamore Press, 1990).

13. Mark Prendergast, op. cit., p. 12.

14. Ibid., p. 14.

15. Source: International Federation of Phonographic Industries.

16. Liam Mackey, op. cit., p. 18.

17. James Henke, 'U2: Here comes the next big thing', *Rolling Stone*, 337, 19 February 1981.

18. Graham Walsh, 'U2 – Doing the Business', *Business & Finance*, 15 September 1995, p. 16.

19. Paul T. Colgan, 'U2's tangled financial web', *Sunday Business Post*, 19 June 2005.

20. Quoted in: Des Crowley, 'The money just rattles and hums', *Magill*, March 2001, p. 15.

21. Paul T. Colgan, op. cit.

22. Ibid.

23. Ibid.

24. Michka Assayas, op. cit., p. 289.

25. JoJo Gould, 'Regional Music Industry Overview of the Republic of Ireland', http://www.MusicJournal.com, http://www.irishunsigned.com/fullarticle.php?id=1 (accessed 16 September 2005.)

26. 'Raising the Volume: Policies To Expand the Irish Music Industry, A Submission To Government', op. cit., p. 11.

27. Ibid.

28. Ibid., p. 10.

29. Brian P. Kennedy, *Dreams and Responsibilities: The State and the Arts in Independent Ireland*, (Dublin, Criterion Press, 1992), p. 211.

30. According to keith Donald, they received 4,500 requests for information and in 1995, the number increased to 5,500, which could be termed a success.

31. 'U2 wins "outstanding" accolade at Brit Awards', *The Irish Times*, 27 February 2001

32. Bord Fáilte.

33. This is a tax exemption scheme originally set up by the then Minister for Finance, Charles Haughey, in 1969, to allow artists (musicians, painters, sculptors, writers) not to pay tax on some of their earnings, provided that they are resident in Ireland and that

their work is original.

34. Christina Saraceno, 'U2 2001's top touring Act', *Rolling Stone*, 28 December 2001.

35. Robert Lafranco, Mark Binelli, Fred Goodman, 'U2, Dre Highest earning stars', *Rolling Stone*, 13 June 2002.

36. *Generation Hit*, 27 July 2003.

37. *Irish Independent*, 19 December 2005

38. Michka Assayas, op. cit., p. 297.

39. Ibid., p. 298.

Chapter 7

1. Mircea Eliade, *Aspects du mythe* (Paris, Gallimard, 1963), p.17.

2. Gabriel Segré, PhD thesis, 'Elvis Presley: Héros mythique et objet de culte', 2000, p.26

3. Ibid.

4. Roland Barthes, *Myhologies* (Paris, Le Seuil, 1957), p. 193.

5. Micea Eliade, *Mythes, rêves et mysteres* (Paris, Gallimard, 1957), p. 31.

6. Edgar Morin, *Les Stars*, (Paris, Le Seuil, 1972), p. 8

7. Gabriel Segré, op. cit., p. 65.

8. Enrico Fulchignoni, *La Civilisation de l'image*, (Paris, Payot, 1972).

9. Daniel J. Boorstin, *The Image: A Guide to Pseudo-Events in America*, (New-York, Atheneum, 1987), p. 185.

10. Ibid., p. 193

11. Ibid.

12. Ibid.

13. John Waters, op. cit., p. 111.

14. Michka Assayas, op. cit., p. 152.

15. *Achtung Baby: The Videos, The Cameos and a Whole Lot of Interference From Zoo TV*, op. cit.

16. *U2 PopMart*, op. cit.

17. Ibid.

18. Lawrence Grossberg, 'The Media Economy of Rock Culture: Cinema, Postmodernity and Authenticity', in Simon Frith, Andrew Goodwin, Lawrence Grossberg (Eds), *Sound and Vision: The Music Video Reader* (London, Routledge, 1993), p. 185.

19. Gabriel Segré, op. cit., p. 266

20. Mark Chatterton, op. cit., p. 177. He was also on the cover of the 'U2-3' and 'I Will Follow' singles.

21. At least two sociologists, Andrew Goodwin and E. Ann Kaplan, have worked on the concept of the video and have come up with different categories for it. The categories mentioned in the text are very similar and are part of those found by Goodwin and Kaplan.

22. *U2: Wide Awake in Dublin*, RTE, 1985.

23. *Live Aid (13 July 1985) 10th anniversary*: Produced by the BBC. 1995.

24. In Richard Kearney, op. cit., p. 234; In D. Hounam on the *Paris, Texas* Movie, *In Dublin*, 214, 1984, pp. 10-11.

25. *Rattle and Hum*. Directed by Phil Joanou. 1988.

26. Gavin Martin, 'Rockin' in the not so free world' (Part 1), *New Musical Express*, 16 December 1989

27. For instance, the video of 'Red Hill Mining Town', directed by Neil Jordan in 1987.

28. Alan Light, 'Behind The Fly', *Rolling Stone*, 651, 4 March 1993.

29. Stuart Bailie, 'Rock 'n' Roll should be this big', *New Musical Express*, 13 June 1992.

30. Richard Kearney, op. cit., p. 253

31. Ibid.

32. Michka Assayas, op. cit., p. 36-37.

33. Ibid.

34. Michka Assayas, op. cit.

35. Ibid. p. 139.

36. Barbara Bradby, 'God's Gift to the Suburbs?', *Popular Music*, 8, 1 (January 1989), p. 109.

37. John Waters, 'Finding the hidden truth as U2 goes 'Pop', *The Irish Times*, 4 March 1997.

38. Roland Barthes, op. cit, p. 247.

39. Bono, 'Elvis Presley', *Rolling Stone*, 946, 15 April 2004.

Conclusion

1. Keith Cameron, op. cit.

2. Mark Prendergast, op. cit., p. 172.

3. Ibid.

4. S. Frith and H. Horne, *Art Into Pop* (London, Routledge, 1987), p. 100.

5. Brian Longhurst, *Popular Music and Society* (Cambridge, Polity Press, 1995), pp. 61-62.

6. Sean O'Hagan, 'The Gospel of Heaven and Hell', op. cit.

7. See the Epilogue.

8. Ibid.

9. Keith Negus, *op. cit. p.71-2*

10. Arthur, 'Lemon Lady', *Dubliner*, 45, June 2005, p. 61.

11. Ibid.

12. U2 Night, RTE 2.

13. Larry McCaffery, 'White Noise, White Heat: The Postmodern Turn in Punk Rock', *American Book Review*, March/April 1990, p. 4.

14. Bill Flanagan, op. cit., p. 64.

15. Gavin Martin, op. cit.

16. Brian Boyd, op. cit., p. 44.

17. Dave Fanning, *Music Express*, op. cit.

18. Ibid.

19. Simon Frith and Charlie Gillett (eds), *The Beat Goes On: The Rock File Reader* (London, Pluto Press, 1996), p. 133.

20. The concept originates in the work of French sociologist Pierre Bourdieu.

21. Roy Shuker, op. cit., p. 78.

22. Roy Shuker, *Understanding Popular Music*, 2nd edition (London, Routledge, 2001), p. 215.

23. Lisa Lewis (ed.), *The Adoring Audience: Fan Culture and the Popular Media* (London, Routledge, 1992), p. 3., cited in Roy Shuker, ibid.

24. Roy Shuker, ibid., p. 213.

25. Lawrence Grossberg, op. cit., p. 56.

26. Roy Shuker, *Key Concepts in Popular Music*, op. cit.

27. Lawrence Grossberg, op. cit., pp. 80-81.

28. Ibid., p. 84.

Epilogue
1. Michka Assays, op. cit., p. 277.

2. Ibid., p. 310.

BIBLIOGRAPHY

Books and chapters in books:
This non-exhaustive section contains the books that I have used as references in this work, as well as others that I would recommend for anyone interested. I have divided it into two parts, the first about U2 itself, and the second about music and other more general topics (sociology, philosophy), although most of the works cited centre on rock music.

U2:
Allen, Carter, *U2: The Road To Pop*, (London, Faber and Faber, 1997)
Assayas, Michka, *Bono on Bono* (London, Hodder and Stoughton, 2005)
Bordowitz, Hank (ed.), John Swenson, *The U2 Reader: A Quarter Century of Commentary, Criticism, and Review* (Milwaukee, Hal Leonard, 2003)
Bowler, Dave and Dray, Brian, *U2: A Conspiracy of Hope* (London, Sidgwick and Jackson, 1993)
Brothers, Robyn, 'Time to Heal, "Desire" Time: The Cyberprophesy of U2's "Zoo World Order"', in Dettmar, Kevin J.H. and Richey, William (eds), *Reading Rock 'n' roll: Authenticity, Appropriation, Aesthetics* (New York, Columbia University Press, 1999)
Chatterton, Mark, *U2: The Complete Encyclopedia* (London, Fire Fly, 2001)
De La Parra, Pimm Jal, *U2 Live: A Concert Documentary* (London, The Omnibus Press, 2nd ed., 2003)
Dunphy, Eamon, *The Unforgettable Fire: The Story Of U2* (London, Viking, 1987)
Fast, Susan, 'Music, Contexts, and Meaning in U2', in Everett, Walter (Ed.), *Expression in Pop-Rock Music: A Collection of Critical and Analytical Essays* (New York and London, Garland Publishing Inc., 2000)

Flanagan, Bill, *U2: At the End of the World* (London, Bantam Press, 1995)

Graham, Bill, *Another Time, Another Place: U2 The Early Days* (London, Mandarin, 1989)

Graham, Bill (Caroline van Oosten de Boer), *The Complete Guide to the Music of U2* (London, Omnibus Press, 2nd ed., 2004)

Jackson, Laura, *Bono: The Biography* (New York, Citadel, 2002)

Stein, Atara, '"Even Better Than the Real Thing": U2's (love) songs of the self', in Dettmar, Kevin J.H. and Richey, William (eds), *Reading Rock 'n' roll: Authenticity, Appropriation, Aesthetics* (New York, Columbia University Press, 1999)

Stockman, Steve, *Walk On: The Spiritual Journey of U2* (Lake Mary, Relevant Books, 2001)

Stokes, Niall (ed), *The U2 File: A Hot Press U2 History* (Dublin, Hot Press, 1985)

Stokes, Niall (ed), *U2: Three Chords and the Truth* (Dublin, Hot Press, 1989)

Stokes, Niall, *Into the Heart: The Stories Behind Every U2 Song* (London, Carlton Books, 2001)

Thompson, Dave, *Bono In His Own Words* (London, Omnibus Press, 1989)

Waters, John, *Race of Angels: The Genesis of U2* (London, Fourth Estate, 1994)

Whiteley, Raewynne J. and Maynard, Beth (eds), *Get Up Off Your Knees: Preaching the U2 Catalog*, (Cowley, 2003),

General

Barthes, Roland, 'The Grain of the Voice', in Frith, Simon and Goodwin, Andrew (eds), *On Record: Rock, Pop and the Written Word* (London, Routledge, 1990)

Boorstin, Daniel J., *The Image: A Guide to Pseudo-Events in America, Twenty-fifth Anniversary Edition* (New-York, Atheneum, 1987)

Denselow, Robin, *When the Music's Over: The Story of Political Pop* (London, Faber and Faber,   1989)

Dettmar, Kevin J.H. and Richey William (eds), *Reading Rock 'n' roll: Authenticity, Appropriation, Aesthetics* (New York, Columbia University Press, 1999)

Eliade, Micea, *Mythes, rêves et mystères* (Paris, Gallimard, 1957)

Farrell, Anthony, Guinness, Vivienne and Loyd, Julian (eds), *My Generation: Rock 'n' Roll Remembered* (Dublin, The Lilliput Press, 1996)

Frith, Simon, *The Sociology of Rock* (London, Constable, 1978)

Frith, Simon and Goodwin Andrew (eds), *On Record: Rock, Pop and the Written Word* (London, Routledge, 1990)

Frith, Simon, Goodwin, Andrew and Grossberg, Lawrence (eds), *Sound and Vision: The Music Video Reader* (London & New York, Routledge, 1993)

Frith, Simon, *Performing Rites: Evaluating Popular Music* (Oxford, Oxford University Press, 1998)

Gillett, Charlie and Frith Simon, *The Beat Goes On: The Rock File Reader* (London,

Pluto Press, 1996)

Goodwin, Andrew, *Dancing in the Distraction Factory: Music Television and Popular Culture* (Minneapolis: University of Minnesota Press, 1992)

Grossberg, Lawrence, *We Gotta Get Out of This Place: Popular Conservatism and Postmodern Culture* (London, New York, Routledge, 1992)

Harper, Colin and Hodgett, Trevor, *Irish Folk, Trad & Blues: A Secret History*, (Cork, The Collins Press, 2004)

Hatch, David and Millward, Stephen, *From Blues to Rock: An Analytical History of Pop Music* (Manchester, Manchester University Press, 1987)

Hennion, Antoine, *La Passion musicale: Une sociologie de la médiation* (Paris, Métailié, 1993)

Jameson, Fredric, *Postmodernism or, the Cultural Logic of Late Capitalism* (Durham, Duke University Press, 1991)

Kaplan, E. Ann, *Rocking Around the Clock: Music Television, Postmodernism and Consumer Culture* (London, Routledge, 1987)

Kearney, Richard (ed), *Across the Frontiers: Ireland in the 1990s* (Dublin, Wolfhound Press, 1988)

Kearney, Richard, *The Wake of Imagination* (London, Routledge, 2nd ed., 2001)

Kennedy, Dennis, in Paddy Logue (ed), *Being Irish: Personal Reflections on Irish Identity Today* (Cork, Oak Tree Press, 2001)

Longhurst, Brian, *Popular Music and Society* (Cambridge, Polity Press, 1995)

Lull, James (ed), *Popular Music and Communication* (Newbury Park, Sage, 1992)

Marcus, Greil, *Lipstick Traces: A Secret History of the Twentieth Century* (London, Faber and Faber, 2001)

McRobbie, Angela, *Postmodernism and Popular Culture* (London, Routledge, 5th ed., 1998)

Middleton Richard (ed), *Reading Pop: Approaches To Textual Analysis In Popular Music* (Oxford, Oxford University Press, 2000)

Morin, Edgar, *Les stars* (Paris, Seuil Points Essais, 1972)

Negus, Keith, *Producing Pop: Culture and Conflict in the Popular Music Industry* (London, Edward Arnold, 1992)

O'Connor, Nuala, *Bringing It All Back Home: The Influence of Irish Music* (London, BBC Books, 1991)

Ó Súilleabháin, Mícheál, '"Around the House and Mind the Cosmos": Music, Dance and Identity in Contemporary Ireland', in Pine, Richard (ed), *Music and Ireland 1848-1998* (Dublin, Cork, Mercier Press, RTE, 1998)

Power, Vincent, *Send 'Em Home Sweatin': The Showbands' Story* (Dublin, Kildamore Press, 1990)

Prendergast, Mark J., *Irish Rock: Roots, Personalities, Directions* (Dublin, The O'Brien Press, 1987)

Savage, Jon, *England's Dreaming: Sex Pistols and Punk Rock* (London, Faber and Faber, 1991)

Segré, Gabriel, University of Nanterre Paris X, PhD thesis 'Elvis Presley : Héros mythique et objet de culte', 2000
Shuker, Roy, *Key Concepts in Popular Music* (London, Routledge,1998)
Shuker, Roy, *Understanding Popular Music* (London, Routledge, 2001)
Skinner Sawyers, June, *The Complete Guide to Celtic Music* (London, Aurum Press, 2000)

NEWSPAPER ARTICLES, JOURNALS AND MAGAZINES
Arthur, 'Lemon Lady', *The Dubliner*, 45, June 2005.
Bailie Stuart, 'Rock 'n' roll should be this big', *New Musical Express*, 13 June 1992
Bono, 'Elvis Presley', *Rolling Stone*, 946, 15 April 2004
Bono, 'This Generation's Moon Shot', *Time Magazine*, 1 November 2005
Boyd, Brian, U2 interview, *Cara*, June 2005
Bradby, Barbara, 'God's Gift to the Suburbs?', *Popular Music*, 8, 1 (January 1989)
Browne, Vincent, 'Geldof and Bono out of tune on G8', *The Irish Times*, 25 July 2001
Cameron, Keith, 'Faith', *Mojo*, 140, July 2005
Colgan, Paul T., 'U2's tangled financial web', *Sunday Business Post*, 19 June 2005
Crowley, Des, 'The money just rattles and hums', *Magill*, March 2001
De Bréadún, Deaglán, 'Bono threatens to take to the streets in defence of world's poorest people', *The Irish Times*, 9 July 2003
Denselow, Robin, 'Playing With Mr Big', *Guardian*, 13 October 1995
Donaghy, Kathy, 'U2 frontman hits right note in speech as he gives politicians a lesson in reality', *Irish Independent*, 9 July 2003
Fanning, Dave, 'You can't make it on your own', *Irish Independent*, 19 June 2005
Foster, James, 'Bono hopes tour of Africa will prove point to "sceptical O'Neill"', *Irish Independent*, 22 May 2002
Fricke, David, 'U2: Serious Fun', *Rolling Stone*, 640, 1 October 1992
Fricke, David, 'U2 finds what it's looking for', *Rolling Stone*, 640, 1 October 1992
Goodier, Mark, 'When U2 comes to town', *Vox*, April 1992
Gould, JoJo, 'Regional Music Industry Overview of the Republic of Ireland', http://www.MusicJournal.com, http://www.irishunsigned.com/fullarticle.php?id=1
Henke, James, 'U2: Here comes the next big thing', *Rolling Stone*, 337, 19 February 1981
Hilburn, Robert, 'Where craft ends and spirit begins', *Los Angeles Times*, 8 August 2004
Hilburn, Robert, 'Music and mission are one', *Los Angeles Times*, 4 April 2005
Hot Press Yearbook and *Irish Music Directory 2002* (Dublin, Hot Press, 2001)
Iley, Chrissy, 'Group Therapy', *Sunday Times Magazine*, 7 November 2004
Jackson, Joe, 'Bono's Burning Rage Within', *Irish Independent*, 29 October 2000
Lafranco, Robert, Binelli, Mark and Goodman, Fred, 'U2, Dre Highest Earning Stars', *Rolling Stone*, 13 June 2002
Legrand, Caroline, 'Nation, Migration and Identities in Late Twentieth-Century Ireland', Narodna Umjetnost, *Croatian Journal of Ethnology and Folklore*

Research, vol. 42, n° 1, (2005), pp.47-63

Light, Alan, 'Behind The Fly', *Rolling Stone*, 651, 4 March 1993

Mackey, Liam, 'Articulate speech of the heart', *Hot Press*, vol 7, n° 15, 5 August 1983

Mackey, Liam, 'The Gospel according to Paul', *Hot Press Yearbook*, 1986

Martin, Gavin, 'Rockin' in the not so free world' (Part 1), *New Musical Express*, 16 December 1989

McCaffery, Larry, 'White Noise, White Heat: The Postmodern Turn in Punk Rock', *American Book Review*, March/April 1990

McCann, Eamon , 'Bullet the Blue Sky', U2 Christmas Special '89, *The Evening Press*, 24 December 1989

McCormick, Neil, 'Foul Play!', *Hot Press*, vol. 11, n° 23, 3 December 1987

McKenna, Gene, 'Bono threatens a disobedience campaign over aid backsliders', *Irish Independent*, 9 July 2003

O'Connor, Brendan, 'Dr Bono shows himself to be a genuine healer', *Irish Independent*, 13 July 2003

O'Connor, Derek, 'Pro-Bono', *The Dubliner*, 45, June 2005

O'Hagan, Sean, 'The Gospel of Heaven and Hell', *New Musical Express*, 19 December 1987

Power, Ed, 'Why U2 don't rock my world', *Irish Independent*, 17 February 2005

Raising the Volume: Policies to Expand The Irish Music Industry, report prepared by the Music Industry Group (Irish Business and Employers Confederation, 1998)

Reilly, Jerome, 'U2 fans let fly at expensive online ticket sale fiasco', *Irish Independent*, 30 January 2005

Renault, Gilles, 'En attendant Bono', *Libération*, 9 October 2000

Reusser, Jean-Marie, 'U2: Eux 5', *Best*, 197, October 1984

Reusser, Jean-Marie, 'Collection de printemps', *Best*, 225, April 1987

Ross, Michael, 'Born Again Bono', *The Sunday Times*, 21 February 1999

Ross, Michael, 'No band in the history of music has been as assiduously designed as U2', *The Sunday Times*, 13 July 2003

Saraceno, Christina, 'U2 2001's top touring Act', *Rolling Stone*, 28 December 2001

Scanlon, Ann, 'Conquistador', *Sounds*, 1 August 1987

Shaping the Future: A Strategic Plan for the Development of the Music Industry in Ireland, presented by the Music Board of Ireland to the Minister for Arts, Sports and Tourism, (November 2002)

Smyth, Sam, 'Bono: Why I was laughing with Putin and Blair as Genoa was flowing with blood', *Irish Independent*, 28 July 2001

Stokes, Niall, 'Matters of life and death', *The Hot Press Annual 2002*

Tyrangiel, Josh, 'Can Bono save the world?', *Time Magazine*, 4 March 2002

'U2 wins "outstanding" accolade at Brit Awards', *The Irish Times*, 27 February 2001

VanderSpek, Henry, 'Faith, Hope and U2',
    http://individual.utoronto.ca/johnbowen/dare/u2.html

Walsh, Declan, 'Bono and O'Neill's African odyssey may help to open wallets', *The Irish Times*, 3 June 2002

Walsh, Graham, 'U2: Doing the Business', *Business & Finance*, 15 September 1995

Waters, John, 'Finding the hidden truth as U2 goes 'Pop', *The Irish Times*, 4 March 1997

Waters, John, 'Bono TV', *The Irish Times*, 30 May 1992

Wenner, Jann S., 'Bono: The Rolling Stone Interview', *Rolling Stone*, 986, 3 November 2005

VIDEOS
Television appearances by U2 or its members.

The following television appearances are cited in the book, as are some of their quotes. There are, of course, many more but you can find them in other publications, notably in Mark Chatterton's book, *The Ultimate U2 Encyclopedia*.

From a Whisper to a Scream, produced by RTE, 2000.

Live Aid (13 July 1985) 10th anniversary, produced by the BBC, 1995

Outside It's America – The Old Grey Whistle Test, produced by the BBC, 1 January 1988

The Late Late Show, produced by RTE, 16 December 1988

U2 Night, produced by RTE, 25 June 2005

U2 PopMart, directed by Maurice Linnane, produced by Not Us Limited, September 1997

U2: Wide Awake in Dublin, produced by RTE, 1985

Commercially Available Videos about U2

Some of the quotes in the book come from the following commercially available videos and DVDs:

Achtung Baby: The Videos, The Cameos and a Whole Lot of Interference From Zoo TV, directed by Maurice Linnane, produced by Island/Polygram, 1992

The Best of 1990-2000, produced by Ned O'Hanlon, produced by Dreamchaser for U2 Ltd, 2002

The Making of the Unforgettable Fire, directed by Barry Devlin, produced by Island/Polygram, 1985

U2 Go Home, directed by Hamish Hamilton & Enda Hughes, produced by Ned O'Hanlon. 2002

U2 The Joshua Tree, directed by Philip King/Nuala O'Connor, produced by Island/Polygram. Classic Albums Series, 1999

Zoo TV: Live From Sydney, directed by David Mallet, produced by Island/Polygram, 1994

DISCOGRAPHY

ALBUMS

Boy, October 1980 (Island, ILPS 9646, CID 110)

October, October 1981 (Island, ILPS 9680, CID 111)

War, March 1983 (Island, ILPS 9733, CID 112)

Under a Blood Red Sky (Live), November 1983 (Island, IMA 3, CID 113)

The Unforgettable Fire, October 1984 (Island, U25, CID 102)

Wide Awake in America (Live), July 1985 (Island, CID U2 2)

The Joshua Tree, March 1987 (Island, CID U2 6)

Rattle and Hum, October 1988 (Island, CID U2 7)

Achtung Baby, November 1991 (Island, CID U2 8)

Zooropa, July 1993 (Island, CID U2 9)

Pop, March 1997 (Island/Polygram, CID U2 10)

The Best of 1980-1990, November 1998 (Island, CID U2 11)

All That You Can't Leave Behind, October 2000 (Island, CID U2 12)

The Best of 1990-2000, November 2002 (Island/Universal, CID U2 13)

How to Dismantle an Atomic Bomb, November 2004 (Island/Universal, CID U2 14)

SINGLES

Singles released in only one country are not included here except for Ireland. The albums they are excerpted from are between brackets.

'U2-3: Out of control/Stories for Boys/Boy Girl' (*Boy*, except for 'Boy Girl'), September 1979 (CBS, CBS 7951)

'Another Day/Twilight' (*Boy*, except for 'Another Day'), February 1980 (CBS, CBS 8306, Ireland only)

'11 O'clock Tick Tock/Touch', May 1980 (Island, WIP 6601)

'A Day Without Me/Things to Make And Do' (*Boy*, except for 'Things to Make and Do'), August 1980 (Island, WIP 6630)

'Fire/J. Swallow' (free EP live with '11 O'clock Tick Tock', 'The Ocean', 'Cry', 'The Electric Co.' included) (*October*), July 1981 (Island, WIP 6679)

'Gloria/I Will Follow (live)' (*October*), October 1981 (Island, WIP 6733)

'A Celebration/Trash Trampoline and the Party Girl', March 1982 (Island, WIP 6770)

'New Year's Day'/'Treasure' (Whatever Happened To Pete the Chop, (*War*, except for 'Treasure'), January 1983 (Island, WIP 6848)

'Two Hearts Beat As One/Endless Deep' (with free remixed versions of 'New Year's Day' and 'Two Hearts Beat As One') (*War* except for Endless Deep), March 1983 (Island, IS 109)

'Pride (In the Name of Love)/Boomerang 2' (*The Unforgettable Fire*, except for 'Boomerang 2'), September 1984 (Island, IS 202)

'The Unforgettable Fire /A Sort of Homecoming (live)' (*The Unforgettable Fire*), April 1985 (Island, IS 220)

'With or Without you/Luminous Times (Hold On To Love)/Walk To the Water', (*The Joshua Tree*, except for 'Luminous Times', 'Wak To the Water'), March 1987 (Island, IS 319)

'I Still Haven't Found What I'm Looking for/Spanish Eyes/Deep In the Heart' (*The Joshua Tree*, except for 'Spanish Eyes/ Deep In the Heart'), May 1987 (Island, IS 328)

'Where The Streets Have No Name/Race Against Time/Silver and Gold/The Sweetest Thing' (*The Joshua Tree*, except for 'Race Against Time', 'Silver and Gold', 'The Sweetest Thing'), August 1987 (Island, IS 340)

'In God's Country/Bullet the Blue Sky/Running to Stand Still' (*The Joshua Tree*), November 1987 (Island, IL7-99385)

'Desire/Hallelujah (Here She Comes)', (*Rattle and Hum*, except for 'Hallelujah [Here She Comes]'), September 1988 (Island, IS 400)

'Angel of Harlem/A Room at the Heartbreak Hotel' (*Rattle and Hum*, except for 'A Room at the Heartbreak Hotel'), December 1988 (Island, IS 402)

'When Love Comes to Town/Dancing Barefoot' (*Rattle and Hum*, except for 'Dancing Barefoot'), April 1989 (Island, IS 411)

'All I Want Is You/Unchained Melody' (*Rattle and Hum*, except for 'Unchained Melody'), June 1989 (Island, IS 422)

'The Fly/Alex Descends into Hell for a Bottle of Milk' (*Achtung Baby*, except for 'Alex Descends into Hell for a Bottle of Milk'), October 1991 (Island, IS 500)

'Mysterious Ways/Mysterious Ways (Solar Plexus Magic Hour Remix)' (*Achtung Baby*), December 1991 (Island, IS 509)

'One/Lady With the Spinning Head' (*Achtung Baby*, except for 'Lady With the Spinning Head'), February 1992 (Island, IS 515)

'Even Better Than the Real Thing/Salomé' (*Achtung Baby*, except for Salomé), June 1992 (Island, IS 525)

'Who's Gonna Ride Your Wild Horses/Paint It Black' (*Achtung Baby*, except for 'Paint It Black'), November 1992 (Island, IS 550)

'Numb' (*Zooropa*, only as a video single), August 1993 (Island, 088 162 3)

'Lemon' (*Zooropa*, only as a promotional single), October 1993 (Island, 12LEMDJ1)

'Stay (Faraway, So Close)/I've Got You Under My Skin' (*Zooropa*, except for 'I've Got You Under My Skin' with Frank Sinatra), November 1993 (Island, IS 578)

'Hold Me Thrill Me Kiss Me Kill Me' (Theme from *Batman Forever* by Eliot Goldenthal), June 1995 (Island, A 7131 CD)

'Discothèque/Holy Joe' (*Pop*, except for 'Holy Joe'), February 1997 (Island, CID 649-854775-2)

'Staring at the Sun/North and South of the River/Your Blue Room' (*Pop*, except for 'North and South of the River', 'Your Blue Room'), April 1997 (Island, CID 658/854975-2)

'Last Night On Earth/Pop Muzik/Happiness Is a Warm Gun' (*Zooropa*, except for 'Pop Muzik', 'Happiness Is a Warm Gun'), July 1997 (Island, CID 664/572051-2)

'Please/Dirty Day/I'm Not Your Baby' (*Pop* for the first song, *Zooropa* for the second song, except for 'I'm Not Your Baby'), September 1997 (Island, CID 673/572129-2) (CD1)

'Please (Live from Rotterdam)/Where the Streets Have No Name (Live from Rotterdam)/ With or Without You (Live from Edmonton)/Staring at the Sun (Live from Rotterdam)' (*Zooropa*, except for 'Where the Streets Have No Name' and 'With or Without You'), September 1997 (Island, CID 673/572129-2 (CD2)

'If God Will Send His Angels/Slow Dancing/Two Shots of Happy One Shot of Sad/Sunday Bloody Sunday (live From Sarajevo)' (*Zooropa*, except for 'Slow Dancing/Two Shots of Happy one Shot of Sad/Sunday Bloody Sunday, December 1997) (Island, CID 684/572189-2) (CD1)

'MoFo (Phunk Phorce Mix)/MoFo (Mother's Mix)/If God Will Send His Angels' (*Zooropa*), December 1997 (Island, CID 684/572189-2) (CD2)

'The Sweetest Thing/Twilight (*Live from Red Rocks 1983*)/An Cat Dubh (*Live from Red Rocks 1983*), November 1998 (Island, CID 727/572466-2) (CD1)

'The Sweetest Thing/Stories For Boys (*Live from Boston 1981*)'/Out of Control (*Live from Boston 1981*)' November 1998 (Island, CID 727/572466-2) (CD2).

'Beautiful Day/Summer Rain/Always' (*All That You Can't Leave Behind*, except for

'Summer Rain', 'Always'), October 2000 (Island, CID 766/562945-2) (CD 1)

'Beautiful Day/Discothèque (Live from Mexico City)/If You Wear That Velvet Dress
(Live from Mexico City)' (*All That You Can't Leave Behind*, except for
'Discothèque', 'If You Wear That Velvet Dress' October 2000) (Island, CID
766/562945-2) (CD 2)

'Stuck In a Moment You Can't Get Out of/Beautiful Day' (Live at Farmclub)/New York
(Live at Farmclub) (*All That You Can't Leave Behind*), January 2001
(Island, CIDX 770/572779-2) (CD1).

'Stuck In a Moment You Can't Get Out of/Big Girls Are Best/Beautiful Day (remix by
Quincy & Sonance) (*All That You Can't Leave Behind*, except for 'Big Girls Are
Best')', January 2001 (Island, CIDX 770/572779-2) (CD2)

'Elevation' (Tomb Raider Mix)/Last Night On Earth (Live from Mexico City)/ Don't
Take Your Guns to Town' (*All That You Can't Leave Behind*, except for 'Last
Night On Earth', 'Don't Take Your Guns to Town'), July 2001 (Island,
CIDX780/588673-) (CD1)

'Elevation (Tomb Raider Mix) / Elevation (Escalation Mix) / Elevation (The Vandit
Club Mix)' (*All That You Can't Leave Behind*), July 2001 (Island, CID
780/588685-2) (CD2)

'Walk On/Beautiful Day (Live from Farmclub.com)/New York (Live from
Farmclub.com)' (*All That You Can't Leave Behind*), November 2001 (Island,
CD1 - 314572819-2) (CD1)

'Walk On (radio edit)/Big Girls Are Best/Beautiful Day (Quincey and
Sonance Remix)' (*All That You Can't Leave Behind*, except for 'Big Girls Are
Best'), November 2001 (Island, CD2 – 314572820-2) (CD2)

'Electrical Storm / New York (Nice Mix) / New York (Nasty Mix)' (*The Best of 1990-
2000*), October 2002 (Island, CIDX 808/063 909-2) (CD1)

'Electrical Storm/Live medley of Bad, 40, Where The Streets Have No Name (Recorded
live at the Elevation tour in Boston)' (*The Best of 1990-2000*, except for 'Bad',
'40', 'Where The Streets Have No Name'), October 2002 (Island, CIDX
808/063 910-2) (CD2)

'Vertigo/Are You Gonna Wait Forever?' (*How to Dimantle an Atomic Bomb* except for
'Are You Gonna Wait Forever?'), November 2004 (Island, UN 901)

'Sometimes You Can't Make It On Your Own (Radio Edit)/Fast Cars (Jacknife Lee Mix)'
(*How to Dimantle an Atomic Bomb*), February 2005 (Island, UN9870373)

'City of Blinding Lights (Radio Edit)/All Because Of You (Killahurtz Fly Mix)' (*How to
Dimantle an Atomic Bomb*), June 2005 (Island, UN987193)

INDEX